GEORGE S. KAUFMAN
AND
HIS COLLABORATORS

THE AMERICAN DRAMA LIBRARY

The American Drama Library is an ongoing series of American plays in anthology format, in which we plan to emphasize nineteenth and early twentieth century plays. Each volume will be edited by a specialist in the field, with the purpose of revisioning a particular genre, historical perspective, or individual playwright. The greater portion of the plays will be those which are previously unpublished, out-of-print, or difficult to find.

Much of our dramatic past has been ignored, belittled, or misunderstood, with the result that dramatic literature as a genre has not taken its rightful place in American letters. A serious loss in the study of American drama is the unavailability of published plays, and the commentary on them by which an art form and its audience interrogates itself and its responses to social and artistic change, from an historical point of view. This is the all-important process by which a field of study matures in relationship to the new ideas of any age. It is also the basis from which a dramatic repertoire grows.

The American Drama Library will, we believe, bring many more plays, new interpretations of dramatic form and cultural history, and reconsideration of literary reputations to our readers. Perhaps in the reflection of American experience this new material gives back to us, we may see in greater detail how, as a society, we give form to our feelings in the art of drama.

The Publishers

George S. Kaufman and His Collaborators

June Moon
[with Ring Lardner]

Bravo!
[with Edna Ferber]

The Late George Apley
[with John P. Marquand]

Preface by Anne Kaufman Schneider

Performing Arts Journal Publications
New York

© *June Moon* Copyright 1929 by Ring Lardner and George S. Kaufman; Copyright 1930 by Charles Scribner's Sons; renewed 1957 by Ellis A. Lardner and George S. Kaufman; renewed 1958 by George S. Kaufman.
© *Bravo!* Copyright 1948 (unpublished) by Edna Ferber and George S. Kaufman; 1949 (published); renewed 1976.
© *The Late George Apley* Copyright 1944, 1946 by John P. Marquand and George S. Kaufman; renewed 1971, 1973.

First Edition
All rights reserved
No part of this publication may be reproduced or transmitted in any form or by any means, electronic or mechanical, including photocopy, recording, or any information storage or retrieval system now known or to be invented, without permission in writing from the publishers, except by a reviewer who wishes to quote brief passages in connection with a review written for inclusion in a magazine, newspaper, or broadcast.

All rights reserved under the International and Pan-American Copyright Conventions. For information, write to Performing Arts Journal Publications, 325 Spring Street, Room 318, New York, N.Y. 10013.

Library of Congress Cataloging in Publication Data
George S. Kaufman and His Collaborators
CONTENTS: *June Moon, Bravo!, The Late George Apley.*
Library of Congress Catalog Card No.: 84-61070
ISBN: 0-933826-65-6 (cloth)
ISBN: 0-933826-66-4 (paper)

CAUTION: Professionals and amateurs are hereby warned that *June Moon, Bravo!*, and *The Late George Apley* are fully protected under the Copyright Laws of the United States, Great Britain, Canada and all other countries of the Copyright Union, and are subject to royalty. All rights including professional, amateur, motion picture, recitation, lecturing, public reading, radio, television and foreign translations are strictly reserved.

Inquiries on productions of *June Moon* should be addressed to Samuel French, Inc., 45 West 25th Street, New York, N.Y. 10010.

Inquiries on productions of *Bravo!* and *The Late George Apley* should be addressed to the Dramatists Play Service, Inc., 440 Park Avenue South, New York, N.Y. 10016.

Graphic Design: Gautam Dasgupta

Printed in the United States of America

Publication of this book has been made possible in part by grants received from the National Endowment for the Arts, Washington, D.C., a federal agency, and the New York State Council on the Arts.

General Editors of The American Drama Library series:
    Bonnie Marranca and Gautam Dasgupta

Contents

Preface	7
JUNE MOON	11
BRAVO!	69
THE LATE GEORGE APLEY	123

Preface

I asked Performing Arts Journal Publications to publish these three plays of my father's (and his collaborators) for several reasons: the first and most practical reason is that they are all out-of-print. The second is that I think they are very good and should be read by students of the theatre. And the third reason is that, hopefully, some schools and/or regional theatres will like them well enough to produce them.

Two of the plays have been revived quite recently. In 1982, the Apple Corps Theatre in New York, directed by John Raymond, produced *Bravo!*. It was first rate. The actors and the material worked wonderfully together. They enjoyed acting in a play (so they said) with a beginning, a middle, and an end. Not a "modern" play to be sure, but one which, I feel, will last longer by the very fact of its structure.

June Moon is one of my favorite plays. The Manhattan Punch Line Theatre, directed by Steve Kaplan, gave it a wonderful revival in the winter of 1983-84. The actors were superb and understood the characters and situations perfectly. There are no hidden meanings, no complicated psychological claptrap—the play is there to be acted and enjoyed.

The Late George Apley has never been revived in New York. Perhaps people find the sensibilities and manners in the play old-fashioned. But I think they are mistaken.

Curiously, with these three plays, I think the collaborator had the upper hand. *Apley* was a dramatization of John Marquand's novel, and his brilliant Brahmin hand is everywhere in the script. But the structure was my father's, I'm sure. So too, with *June Moon*, which was based on a short story by Ring Lardner called "Some Like 'Em Cold." In the play, many of the characters speak in a Lardneresque fashion, but again, the shape and ultimate theatricality is pure Kaufman. Just as the idea for *Bravo!* seems to be very Ferber: sentimental, brave, and constantly talking about food—very un-Kaufman. But the craftsmanship! That's another story.

What is most interesting, however—I think my father was like a chameleon, taking on all the colorations of his collaborators, while keeping his own identity all the way through each work.

I think these plays stand up very well and hold their own with Durang, Kopit, Mamet, Norman, and Henley. As a matter of fact, I think that Ferber, Lardner, Marquand, and Kaufman are among America's most promising playwrights.

Anne Kaufman Schneider

May 1984
New York

JUNE MOON

A Comedy in a Prologue and Three Acts

Ring Lardner
&
George S. Kaufman

[1929]

June Moon was first produced at the Broadhurst Theatre, New York, on October 9th, 1929, with the following cast:

Fred Stevens	*Norman Foster*
Edna Baker	*Linda Watkins*
Paul Sears	*Frank Otto*
Lucille	*Jean Dixon*
Eileen	*Lee Patrick*
Maxie	*Harry Rosenthal*
Goldie	*Florence D. Rice*
A Window Cleaner	*Frank Conlan*
A Man Named Brainard	*Emil Hoch*
Benny Fox	*Philip Loeb*
Mr. Hart	*Leo Kennedy*
Miss Rixey	*Margaret Lee*

Music and lyrics by Ring Lardner
Staged by George S. Kaufman

THE SCENES

THE PROLOGUE
In a parlor car.

ACT I
Paul Sears' place. Ten days later.

ACT II
A room at Goebel's. A few weeks later.

ACT III
Still at Goebel's. About a month later.

DESCRIPTION OF CHARACTERS

FRED: *He is about twenty-four years old. Good-looking, unsophisticated, eager for life.*

EDNA: *She is twenty-one. Although inexperienced so far as life is concerned, she has a natural instinct for men, and her mind is shrewdly working even when her utterances are the most naive. An attractive and ingenuous little schemer.*

LUCILLE: *She is about thirty-two—a trifle faded. A woman who expected more from life than it has given her, and whose disappointment is reflected in her appearance.*

PAUL: *He is about thirty-four, and with the stamp of Broadway's Tin Pan Alley on him. An unsuccessful composer who continues ever hopeful, but on whose brow the grind is beginning to leave its mark.*

EILEEN: *She is good-looking, very blonde—in her early thirties. Has a lot of confidence in herself. A bit hard and a trifle worldly.*

MAXIE: *He is a man in his forties, easy-going, kindly; wears a dinner coat. He is an arranger for Goebel's and he knows the popular song business backwards.*

GOLDIE: *She is a blonde-headed young secretary.*

WINDOW CLEANER: *He is a tall, skinny, bald-headed man. Looks a great deal like a window cleaner.*

BENNY: *He is a young song-writer and a pest.*

HART: *He is a business-man. About forty-five.*

BRAINARD: *He is a middle-aged man with an umbrella and a dumb look.*

MISS RIXEY: *She is a very beautiful young lady.*

PROLOGUE

SCENE: *Two seats in a parlor car. Racks with baggage, sections of Sunday newspapers on the floor. The shades are pulled down.*

Fred Stevens in one seat. He is about twenty-four years old; good-looking, unsophisticated, eager for life. Edna Baker in the other. Edna sits with the back of her chair toward Fred. She is twenty-one. Although inexperienced so far as life is concerned, she has a natural instinct for men, and her mind is shrewdly working even when her utterances are the most naive. An attractive and ingenuous little schemer. There is a magazine in her lap, but she is not reading.

Fred is already a bit restless when the curtain rises. Peers down the car once or twice. Looks at his watch. Peers out the window at the side of the shade; cups his hands to shut out the light. Looks at time-table. Settles back again.

Edna swings her chair around once as though she wanted to look on down the car. Swings back again without ever having looked at Fred. Fred takes up a piece of newspaper; pretends to read, rattling the paper a bit too loudly. His eyes are on Edna by this time. Hums a little.

Edna swings her chair half-way around, as though seeking a more comfortable position. While settling herself in the chair at this angle, the least turn of the head enables her to meet Fred's eyes. Presently she does give her head that turn, but there is no flicker of flirtation in her glance. Nevertheless Fred is encouraged. He whistles a little. Another turn by Edna, this time the merest shadow of a smile.

Fred feels that the time has come to make the gesture. He gets up his courage.

FRED: Would you care to look at the paper?
EDNA: Oh, thank you very much. I don't think so, thank you.
FRED: I thought you might maybe want to read.
EDNA: No, thank you. (*A pause. She gives him a small smile.*)
FRED: We're due in New York at ten-three.

EDNA: Yes, I know.
FRED: You got on at Hudson, didn't you?
EDNA: Yes.
FRED: I seen you. (*A pause after this momentous remark.*) I been on ever since Schenectady.
EDNA: Really?
FRED: That's where I work. I mean, where I did work. At the G. E.
EDNA: G. E.?
FRED: General Electric. They call it the G. E. That's where their plant is, Schenectady.
EDNA: I've got a girl friend from Schenectady.
FRED: Is that so?
EDNA: She's in New York now, or at least she was the last time I heard of her. Working at Sax's. Grace Crowell.
FRED: I used to know a Mildred Crowell, but her name wasn't Grace.
EDNA: This was Grace. I haven't seen her for years, and I never did know her very well.
FRED: Mildred Crowell's brother was quite a billiard player. Three cushions. Eddie, his name was.
EDNA: That's my name, too. (*Laughs.*) Of course it isn't my real name. It's just my nickname. My real name's Edna.
FRED: Oh! (*A pause.*) Eddie Crowell used to pretty near live on the billiard table. Then finally his health broke down and he went out west somewheres. I couldn't tell you now if he's dead or alive.
EDNA: It's funny how we lose track of people. Some of the girls I used to go with, they still live there yet, but I never look any of them up, except Gertie Hutton. I guess it's terrible of me not to, because if a person's got good friends they ought to keep them.
FRED: I certainly got good ones. They showed that last night, at the banquet.
EDNA: Were you at a banquet?
FRED: I had to be. It was me they give it for. I mean I was the guest of honor.
EDNA: How exciting!
FRED: It was a farewell testimonial, on account of me going to New York. And then this afternoon ten or eleven of them come down to the station, and Ernie Butler had a hangover and bought me this seat in the parlor car; he said it would be a disgrace for me to ride in the day coach with this new bag. (*Indicates new bag.*)
EDNA: It's a beautiful bag.
FRED: They give it to me at the banquet. It's got my initials. F. M. S. Frederick M. Stevens.
EDNA: What's the M. for?
FRED: Martin.
EDNA: I like a man to have a middle name. Girls don't usually have them. I'm just plain Edna.
FRED: I wouldn't say "plain."
EDNA: You know how to make pretty speeches.
FRED: I bet you're used to them.

EDNA: There's another one. I'm not so used to them that I don't like to hear them, especially from people whom I think they're sincere.
FRED: I don't say things unless I mean them.
EDNA: I'm glad of that.
FRED: Talking about speeches, you ought to heard the speech Carl Williams made when he give me this bag. At the banquet, I mean. I guess he blushed, the things he said about me. A lot more than I deserve.
EDNA: I bet they were sorry to see you go. You look like the kind of man men would like. And girls, too.
FRED: I don't go around much with girls.
EDNA: I don't go much with men, either.
FRED: Neither do I. (*A pause; a moment of relaxation.*) It's comfortable in here, ain't it? Like being home. I never been in a parlor car before.
EDNA: My brother always insists on me riding in it. He says the day coach is generally dirty, for one thing, and another thing, the men that ride in the day coach are the kind that try and make up to pretty girls. That sounds like I was throwing a bouquet at myself, but I'm just repeating what Dick said. That's my brother's name, Dick. I guess a brother always thinks their sister is good-looking.
FRED: I believe in a man sticking up for their sister, or any woman. I got no use for a man that don't respect woman's hood. Where would a man be if it wasn't for their mothers and sisters and wives?
EDNA: Some men haven't got wives.
FRED: I haven't got one myself—yet. I ain't been lucky enough to meet a woman who would be a good pal as well as a sweetheart. I want my wife to be like mother used to be.
EDNA: I love to have a man love their mother.
FRED: I wished mine was still here. Like Carl Williams said in his speech last night—"If she was still here, maybe she would be a little proud of me."
EDNA: I bet she would.
FRED: He made quite a speech, all right. He said the boys expected me to make Irving Berlin jealous. I said I didn't want to make nobody jealous, but I wanted to make my friends proud. I said my only regret in going to New York was on account of leaving so many good friends behind, and as soon as my songs begun to sell up in the hundred thousands, and my dreams came true, I would invite them all down to visit me on Broadway and show them the sights.
EDNA: Is that what you are? A song-writer?
FRED: (*Nods.*) Not the music part; just the words. Lyrics, they're called.
EDNA: It must be wonderful to have a gift like that.
FRED: That's what Benny Davis called it—a gift. I guess you've heard of him—he's turned out a hundred smash hits.
EDNA: I guess I must have.
FRED: He wrote, "Oh, How I Miss You Tonight." It was a song about how he missed his mother—he called her his "Old Pal."
EDNA: That's sweet!
FRED: Well, he happened to be playing in Schenectady in vaudeville, and I happened to meet him and I happened to show him some of my lyrics. And he said a

man like I with the song-writing gift was a sucker not to go to New York, because that's where they have the Mecca for a man if you got the songwriting gift. So he give me a letter to the Friars Club, asking them to give me a two weeks' card, they call it. The Friars Club is where they have the Mecca for songwriters. And he give me a letter of introduction to Paul Sears, the composer. He wrote "Paprika." You remember "Paprika"? (*Sings a strain of it.*) "Paprika, Paprika, the spice of my life—"

EDNA: I think so.

FRED: When you write a song like "Paprika" you don't ever have to worry again. He's one of the most successful composers there is, Paul Sears. I bet you I and he will turn out some hits together.

EDNA: Are you going to be partners with him?

FRED: If he wants me to, and I guess he will when I show him Benny Davis's letter. That's the hard part, getting acquainted. I'd have broke away a long while ago only for my sister. I couldn't leave her alone.

EDNA: Is she in Schenectady?

FRED: (*Nods.*) She got married a week ago Saturday. A fella I been working with in the shipping department—Bob Gifford.

EDNA: She'll miss you just the same. I know how sisters feel, especially when their brother is like you or Dick.

FRED: Well, anyway, she got married, and I give them a pair of book-ends.

EDNA: She'll love them!

FRED: She always done everything for me—I mean, cooked my meals and sewed things for me. Look! (*Dives for his bag and starts opening it.*) She made me half a dozen shirts before I left. Different colors. Here's one of the blue ones. (*Brings it out.*) I bet if you was to buy a shirt like that you couldn't buy a shirt like that under a dollar seventy-five.

EDNA: I'll bet it would cost more than that.

FRED: Marion can sew, all right. My mother used to say she was a born seamstress.

EDNA: I love to sew. (*Looks at the shirt.*) Has it got your monogram, your initials?

FRED: No. She was going to put an "F" on the sleeve, but she was too busy.

EDNA: It's too bad you're not my brother and I'd embroider your whole initials.

FRED: You don't have to be a man's sister to embroider their shirt.

EDNA: I don't want you to misjudge me, Mr. Stevens. I'm not the kind of a girl that talks to strangers. My friends would die if they knew I was talking to a man whom I had not been properly introduced.

FRED: You don't need to be scared of me, girlie. I treat all women like they was my sister, till I find out different.

EDNA: A girl alone in New York can't be too careful, especially a girl in my position. You take at Dr. Quinn's where I work. He's one of the best dentists there is, and he has lots of men patients that would be only too glad to start a little flirtation. Why, even Doctor himself was fresh, the first day I met him. It turned out he wasn't really, but it seemed that way. He put his arm around my shoulders and I jumped away from him like he was a leopard or something, and I told him, I said, "Doctor, I guess I don't care to work here after all." Then he laughed and said forget it, that he was just testing me. He said he didn't want an assistant who was inclined to flirt. And from that day he's never made any ad-

vances, except once or twice.
FRED: He'd keep his distance if I was around.
EDNA: I wish you could be.
FRED: I got plenty of excuses for being there. (*Indicates his back teeth.*) There's a cavity back there as big as the Grand Canyon.
EDNA: (*Laughs merrily.*) You must forgive me laughing. Caroline used to tell me I had the keenest sense of humor of any person she ever met.
FRED: First thing you know I'll be coming to see Doctor What's-His-Name myself.
EDNA: He'll fix it for you. He's a wonderful dentist.
FRED: If I come, it'll probably be when he's out to lunch.
EDNA: Then what would you come for?
FRED: I'll let you guess.
EDNA: I'd rather you told me. I'm a bad guesser.
FRED: I might come to see you. Would you let me?
EDNA: I'd love it, if you wanted to.
FRED: I wouldn't say so if I didn't.
EDNA: You'll forget all about it.
FRED: No, I won't. Your smile will always haunt me.
EDNA: I'll bet you're a wonderful song-writer. No wonder your friends gave you that big dinner.
FRED: It certainly was quite a banquet. I bet some of my pals got a headache today, all right.
EDNA: I hope you haven't got one.
FRED: No. Liquor don't afflict me like most people.
EDNA: I hardly ever touch it myself, only once a great while, at a party.
FRED: Girls ought to lay off it entirely.
EDNA: I never touch it.
FRED: Take some of those women in Schenectady and they want to go out somewheres every night and guzzle. Married women, too.
EDNA: I don't see how they can, with a home to take care of.
FRED: Either they get all dressed up and drag their husband to a dance or a card party every night, or either they lay around the house in a wrapper.
EDNA: When I marry I'll be just as careful of my appearance as I am now. I believe a husband appreciates a wife dressing up for him.
FRED: If it ain't too expensive.
EDNA: The man I marry won't have any complaints. I make practically all my own clothes. Caroline—she's the girl I used to live with—she used to say I always looked like I had just stepped out of a bandbox, even if we were only sitting in our room. We hardly ever went out evenings; personally I prefer to stay home and read, or else just sit and dream. But still I always bathe and change my clothes even when I'm only going to cook dinner.
FRED: I think I'll take a room with a bathroom when I get to the hotel.
EDNA: Where are you going to stay?
FRED: The Hotel Somerset. They got rooms with a bathroom right in the room so you don't have to go out of the room. And it's close to the music-publishing houses and the Friars Club. Any place I want to go I can walk. Except to Paul Sears' place. He probably lives in some swell apartment or maybe a country

place in Great Neck or Jamaica.

EDNA: A successful man like he wouldn't live in Jamaica.

FRED: Well, some place. I don't know much about New York; I only been there once before, with Carl Williams. He's the fella that made the speech last night. It was the first time he's been away from home in the evening since he was married. He's got a wife and baby now.

EDNA: Oh, I'm dying to have a baby! Heavens! I didn't meant to say that! I love them so!

FRED: It's nothing against a woman to like babies. Carl's wife certainly likes hers. She's made him a nice home, too. He didn't have to buy hardly anything in the way of furniture; her grandmother gave her a bedroom suit and she bought some herself with money she saved while she was working at Berger's.

EDNA: She must be a good deal like myself. I could almost start housekeeping with the things I've got. I suppose I'm silly and old-fashioned, but I always thought a girl should bring her husband something besides herself. I even wouldn't mind going on working after I was married, till my husband established himself.

FRED: The girl I marry won't never have to work. I don't believe God ever meant for a woman to endure a life of druggery.

EDNA: Oh, Mr. Stevens, if only all men felt the same way!

FRED: (*Looks at his watch.*) It's nine twenty-six already.

EDNA: It's been a shorter trip than usual, for some reason.

FRED: (*Trying to peer out.*) I wonder where we're at now?

EDNA: Pretty near Yonkers, I guess.

FRED: (*Still peering.*) If we was on the other side we could see the Hudson River.

EDNA: (*Also peering.*) My, but it's dark!

FRED: There's a moon out.

EDNA: Yes, I love it.

FRED: June Moon.

EDNA: What?

FRED: I just said June Moon.

EDNA: It isn't June. It's October.

FRED: I know, but June and moon go together. They rhyme. I'm always thinking of words that rhyme, even when I ain't working.

EDNA: That'd be a catchy name, June Moon. For a song, I mean.

FRED: You could get other words to rhyme with it. Spoon, and croon, and soon. Marry soon, or something.

EDNA: And macaroon.

FRED: Yeah. I wish I had some. I'm hungry.

EDNA: I am, too, kind of. (*After a pause.*) Some day, when that song is published and people are singing it everywhere, I'll say to my friends, "I knew the man that wrote that. We were riding on a train and he looked out and saw the moon, and he thought of this song, and then the train got to New York and he never saw poor little me again."

FRED: You won't be telling the truth, because I'm going to see you again.

EDNA: You say that now. But you'll forget all about me.

FRED: No, I won't. Are you going right home when we get in?

EDNA: Why—I intended to.

FRED: I thought I'd go and get something to eat some place, only I wouldn't know where to go if I didn't have somebody with me that knowed where to go.
EDNA: I can tell you a place where I go once in a while, the Little Venice. Though most of the time I stay home and cook my own dinner, just because I love to cook.
FRED: It'll be too late to cook tonight. I was wondering if you wouldn't go along to this place, and maybe we could eat together.
EDNA: I'd love to.
FRED: It ain't a very expensive place, is it?
EDNA: Oh, no. The last time I went, there was two of us and we had hot roast beef sandwiches and peas and coffee, and it only came to a dollar-twenty.
FRED: All right. I guess we can each afford sixty cents.

BLACK OUT

ACT I

SCENE: *The scene is the living room in the apartment of Paul Sears.*
There is a hallway that leads to the outer door; a small door goes to the kitchen. An opening at right leads to bedrooms. It is a Riverside Drive apartment of the sort that may have been pretty good fifteen years ago. Now it is a little worn, and cheap. Parlor grand piano. Couch in front of the piano. Two small armchairs. A small stand. Occasional chairs, etc.
TIME: *The time is about eight-fifteen in the evening, a week or so after the Prologue.*
Paul Sears, in shirt-sleeves, is at the piano as the curtain rises, laboriously going over his newest composition. He is about thirty-four, and with the stamp of Broadway's Tin Pan Alley on him. Paul is a two-finger pianist, and when he plays the same phrase over and over it begins to get monotonous. Plays chord twice—starts to work.
Lucille, his wife, enters. She is about thirty-two—a trifle faded. A woman who expected more from life than it has given her, and whose disappointment is reflected in her appearance. Her mood, what with one thing and another, is not any too jolly. Paul plays the chord again twice. Lucille looks around for something, finds it—it turns out to be "The Graphic." She sits down with it; tries to read. The piano playing continues.

LUCILLE: What do you know about that! Myra Vale's engaged!
PAUL: I read it. Automobile man. Probably drives a truck. (*Plays two or three notes.*)
LUCILLE: If he does, at least she'll have something to go places in.
PAUL: I got Myra her first job; I introduced her to Dillingham.
LUCILLE: Yes, you did! (*Paul looks up.*) She was in "Nanette" with Eileen and me before you ever saw her.

PAUL: (*Belligerently.*) Who says so?
LUCILLE: Ask the door-man down at the Globe. He used to have to carry her in.
PAUL: She never took a drink when I knew her.
LUCILLE: I can vouch for that.
PAUL: (*Hits a chord; starts "Montana Moon." Crashes—rises.*) This is the last time I'll work with Fagan. I rewrite two whole bars of the melody for him, and when I ask him to change one word of his lyric, he squawks. He's got it "as a rose in June"—and I want him to make it "as roses in June." Listen—here's his way: (*Plays and sings.*) "As a rose in June." And here's the way I want it: (*Plays and sings.*) "As roses in June." All the difference in the world.
LUCILLE: It sounds just the same to me.
PAUL: (*Exasperated.*) My way gives me a triplet and makes it twice as effective. Listen! (*Starts hitting the same old notes.*)
LUCILLE: (*Wearily.*) Oh, isn't that enough? (*Paul stops playing.*) Must I sit around all night listening to that?
PAUL: Why don't you go out? You could go out if you want to.
LUCILLE: Who with?
PAUL: You could go out with Eileen. You and *her* could go somewhere.
LUCILLE: You know she's got a date with Hart. I suppose you want me trailing along.
PAUL: Well, I explained to you *I* can't go no place, with this fella coming up. I told you a dozen times.
LUCILLE: I don't expect you to take me anywhere, except maybe for a walk around the block. That's free.
PAUL: I don't enjoy laying around here no more than you do. I'm not a nun.
LUCILLE: That's the first I've heard about it.
PAUL: You wait till this number gets over. We'll go *everywhere* then.
LUCILLE: (*Tiredly.*) Oh, sure!
PAUL: You haven't heard it played yet. It'll be another "Paprika." Did I tell you what Dave Stamper said about it?
LUCILLE: Yes.
PAUL: He said it was another "Paprika." You wait till you hear it played. Dave Stamper says it's sure fire. (*Plays.*)
LUCILLE: The silliest thing in the world to me is a man trying to be a composer when he can't even play "Chopsticks."
PAUL: I can play as good as I need to. I can play as good as Berlin, and he's turned out twice as many hits as anybody.
LUCILLE: He knows what people want. He appeals to the women.
PAUL: It ruins a composer to play the piano too good. They depend on fancy harmony and tempo, instead of pretty melodies.
LUCILLE: (*Giving up.*) All right. (*Lucille rattles paper, turns page.*)
PAUL: (*Looks up.*) Did you read that thing from that Boston paper about "Pretty Polly"? They say Gershwin hasn't given them one tune. (*A pause.*) Ten years from now nobody'll know there *was* a Gershwin. He won't live. (*Plays.*)
LUCILLE: At least he won't starve to death.
PAUL: It was me that was responsible for Gershwin getting his start. I brought him and Georgie White together. (*Plays two chords.*)

LUCILLE: (*After a pause.*) Why can't you see this man in the daytime, instead of asking him up here?
PAUL: (*Rises.*) Because I don't want him to come in the office yet, that's why. I'm keeping him under cover till I get rid of Fagan.
LUCILLE: If there's one thing that'll round out my day, it's entertaining a lyric writer.
PAUL: This fella ain't like the rest of them. He's got a fresh slant. Take fellas like Fagan, that's been around Broadway all their life, and all their lyrics sound just alike. If Fagan gave me a new idea, I'd drop dead. But this fella's got a fresh slant.
LUCILLE: Fagan would drop even deader if you gave him a new tune.
PAUL: I gave him "Paprika," didn't I?
LUCILLE: That's so long ago I don't see how you remember it.
PAUL: Old man Goebel remembers it, and so does Hart. They made enough money out of it.
LUCILLE: Everybody makes money but you.
PAUL: (*Crosses up to piano; sits.*) Yes, they do! (*Turns to her.*) There's plenty fellas around the club that's just as flat as I am.
LUCILLE: That makes everything all right.
PAUL: I'll tell you who's got money, if you want to know, and that's Stevens.
LUCILLE: Who?
PAUL: This lyric-writer, Stevens. He's got money.
LUCILLE: A lot of good that'll do me.
PAUL: He's a nice kid, too. (*Hits a chord. Swings around from piano.*) If Eileen's got a date with Hart, why don't she keep it? It's half past eight.
LUCILLE: (*Paul rises.*) Don't you worry about that.
PAUL: What about him and her, anyway? If she's engaged to him, aren't they ever going to get married?
LUCILLE: You'll know as soon as there's anything to know.
PAUL: He'll wriggle off the hook some way. If you ask me, he's getting tired of her already.
LUCILLE: (*With sudden interest.*) What makes you think so?
PAUL: (*Turns upstage to piano.*) Just the luck I'm running in. If I ever marry *again*, it'll be a woman without a sister.
LUCILLE: She don't cost you much, and she's company for me.
PAUL: What's the matter with her getting a job somewheres? (*Telephone rings.*)
LUCILLE: Yeah. You ought to be able to place her, with your influence.

(*Eileen, wearing a kimona and carrying an evening gown, on which she is doing some sewing, appears in the doorway. She is good-looking, very blonde—in her early thirties. Has a lot of confidence in herself. She stops short as she sees that Paul is answering the telephone. It is obvious that she is expecting a call. Eileen crosses down by Lucille.*)

PAUL: (*At phone.*) Hello.—Oh, hello, Maxie! (*Eileen relaxes.*) Sure. Going to be here all evening.—All right.—Fine. (*Hangs up.*) Maxie's coming over. Wait till you hear him play it—(*A gesture toward the music.*)—then you'll see!

EILEEN: What time is it?
PAUL: (*Back at the piano.*) It's going to be another "Paprika."
LUCILLE: (*To Eileen, reaching for the dress.*) Want me to do that? (*It is perhaps a matter of a bit of lace to be sewn on.*)
EILEEN: I'll go crazy, waiting around here.
PAUL: (*Absorbed at the piano.*) If I team up with this new fella you'll hear some hits.
LUCILLE: (*To Eileen, handing over the paper.*) Did you see this? Myra Vale's announced her engagement.
EILEEN: Who to, for God's sake?
LUCILLE: Nobody we know.
EILEEN: (*Reading.*) No. (*Laying down paper, crosses up to piano.*) Nobody that knows her, either.
LUCILLE: Paul was trying to tell me he got her her first job; introduced her to Dillingham.
EILEEN: Oh, sure. He introduced Roebuck to Sears, didn't he? (*Sits on couch.*)
LUCILLE: (*Indicating the dress.*) This isn't going to last much longer.
EILEEN: I know it.
LUCILLE: Why don't you look around Monday? See what you can find.
EILEEN: Maybe I will. I've just been putting it off. I'm lazy, I guess. (*Rises.*)
LUCILLE: I'd never be too lazy to shop, if I had anything to shop with.
PAUL: You wait till this number gets over.
LUCILLE: By that time I'll only want a shawl.
PAUL: (*Hits dischord; jumps up from piano.*) There's nothing helps a man like being married to a woman that always encourages you and looks on the bright side. I'm going to write an article for the American Magazine, saying I attribute my success to my wife.
EILEEN: Why don't you try writing articles? They might be pretty near as good as your tunes.
PAUL: (*Turns to her.*) You don't have to worry about my tunes. Anyhow, I was talking to Lucille.
EILEEN: It's time you did something more for Lucille besides talk to her.
PAUL: If I was in your place, I'd keep pretty still in this house. That is, unless I was paying board.
EILEEN: (*Steps to him.*) Don't you dare say I'm dependent on you—because I'm not.
PAUL: Only for your meals and a place to sleep.
EILEEN: You wouldn't even have a job if it wasn't for me. Do you think Hart is keeping you on the staff because you wrote a hit three years ago?
LUCILLE: Now!
EILEEN: Well, make him lay off me, if he knows what's good for him. If he keeps riding me he'll be looking for a new job.
PAUL: Swell chance of them letting me out when I've got a number like "Montana." (*Starts off.*) I'd run right to Harms with it. (*Exits.*)
EILEEN: (*Calls after him.*) Harms wouldn't let you in their elevator.
PAUL: (*Off.*) I was in it this afternoon.
EILEEN: (*After a pause.*) Is Hart going to phone or isn't he? It gets me crazy, this

waiting. (*Sits.*)
LUCILLE: I wouldn't mind waiting if there was something to wait for. I nearly go out of my mind, just sitting. You hear women brag about the nice, cozy evenings they spend at home with their husband. They're not married to a piano-tuner with ten thumbs.
EILEEN: Maybe he didn't get back from Philadelphia. He might still be over there.
LUCILLE: What time was he going to call up?
EILEEN: Six o'clock. He said he'd call me the minute he got in. Maybe the train was late.
LUCILLE: They aren't late very often, from Philadelphia.
EILEEN: It's the only evening we'll *have* for three weeks, with him going away again tomorrow. (*Rises.*) If he was going to be late you'd think he'd try to reach me.
LUCILLE: Of course you know him better than I do, but when a man's really crazy about a girl, he calls her up, I don't care what he's doing. It's only when he begins cooling off that he finds excuses, like being in Philadelphia.
EILEEN: But he was in Philadelphia.
LUCILLE: I know, but they've got phones there now, too.
EILEEN: If you think he's cooling off, you're crazy. He's insanely jealous. When I told him I was thinking of going out with Bert Livingston—(*Sits.*)—he was sore as hell. He said, "All right. Go ahead and go out with him." I asked him if he meant it, and he said, "Sure! Go out with the whole Lambs Club!" He's insanely jealous and tries to hide it.
LUCILLE: I'd go out with the janitor if he asked me. God, I'm sick of this place!
EILEEN: Why don't you go to a picture?
LUCILLE: They charge admission. (*A little sardonic laugh.*) Remember the way I used to figure when Paul first came along? I thought marrying a song-writer meant going to all the first nights, meeting everybody that was worth while, going down to Palm Beach—
EILEEN: You would, too, if Paul was any good.
LUCILLE: I wonder what it'd be like if we'd stayed in Stroudsburg. I'd probably be married to Will Broderick, and we'd have a car—
EILEEN: To drive over to Scranton in.
LUCILLE: (*A sigh.*) I suppose I ought to get consolation out of one thing: I never expect a phone call or a mash note or an invitation or even a half-pound box of candy. Whatever happens is velvet.
EILEEN: You're a fool if you keep it up. You ought to break away while there's still time.
LUCILLE: That's an easy thing to say. I haven't got any grounds, in the first place.
EILEEN: You wouldn't need grounds. Just get him up in court and let the judge look at him.
LUCILLE: And even if I did get free, where am I? I'm not young anymore. No man under sixty would look at me.
EILEEN: Well, men over sixty are more liable to have money than boy scouts.
LUCILLE: I don't like old men.
EILEEN: Who does? Just the same, they've got their good points. They sleep eighteen hours a day. And they're like little kids—they believe everything you

tell them.
LUCILLE: I never could fool anybody. That's why I've been afraid to try anything with Paul. He knows when I'm lying to him, every time.
EILEEN: (*Rises.*) Him! He isn't even listening to you. You could have callers right in this room and he wouldn't hear them come in, not with all those God-given melodies ringing in his ears. (*Crosses up to piano; looks at music.*)
LUCILLE: What's the use of talking about it? There haven't been any volunteers. Women can't go wrong if they're not invited.
EILEEN: (*Sitting at piano.*) All I can say is, if you don't break away from him you're crazy.
LUCILLE: And if I did, do you know what would happen? He'd write ten smash hits in a week. That's my luck. (*Pause.*) God! It would be wonderful to have some clothes and hold up my head again!
EILEEN: (Rises.) I'm through arguing with you. You're hopeless.
LUCILLE: You'd better be thinking about Mr. Hart. You may be as bad off as I am.
EILEEN: Don't you worry about me. If he wasn't crazy about me, why would he be so insanely jealous? He's insanely jealous.
LUCILLE: Has he ever said anything half-way definite? About marrying, I mean?
EILEEN: Not in words, exactly.
LUCILLE: What did he say it *in*?
EILEEN: He must be thinking of it. He doesn't ever go out with anybody else.
LUCILLE: (*Trying to recall what Eileen had said.*) How long's he going to be gone this time—three weeks?
EILEEN: Yah—about. He's got to go to Chicago, and—a lot of places.
LUCILLE: What are you going to do with yourself all that time—just sit around?
EILEEN: Maybe he'll treat us to some shows—I'll ask him tonight. Maybe he'll get us seats for some shows.
LUCILLE: Do they still have seats at shows?
EILEEN: (*Restless again—crosses up to phone.*) Only I wish that thing would ring.
LUCILLE: Why don't you go out with Bert or somebody while he's gone? It might be a good thing for him.
EILEEN: Do you want me to get murdered? I tell you he's insanely jealous. (*Doorbell rings.*) Who's that?
LUCILLE: Maxie, I guess. (*Starting for door.*) Or maybe that lyric-writer.
EILEEN: Who?
LUCILLE: (*Disappearing into hallway, talking as she goes.*) You know, that's coming to see Paul. From Albany or someplace.
EILEEN: Oh!
LUCILLE: Of course he couldn't meet him in the daytime. He has to bring him up here in the middle of the night— (*Having opened the outside door.*) Oh, it's you.
MAXIE: (*Outside.*) Hello, there! (*Paul enters.*)
PAUL: Who is it? Maxie?
MAXIE: (*Enters, following Lucille.*) Yah, Maxie. (*He is a man in his forties, easy-going, kindly. Wears a dinner coat. He is an arranger for Goebel's and he knows the popular song business backwards.*)
PAUL: Hello!
MAXIE: Well! All staying home on a Saturday night?

LUCILLE: All nights are alike up here.
EILEEN: You didn't come right up from the office, did you?
MAXIE: (*Lighting a cigar.*) Do I look it? (*A gesture toward his clothes.*) I'm playing down at the Orchard this week. Pounding the piano for a lot of morons. I envy you people that can spend an evening at home.
LUCILLE: (*Sits as she reaches chair.*) Yes. It's a great treat.
PAUL: (*To Maxie.*) I want the girls to hear the "Montana" number—the way it sounds when it's really played. (*Eileen starts to exit.*)
MAXIE: O. K. (*Sits at piano.*)
PAUL: (*To Eileen.*) Hey! He's going to play the "Montana" number. (*Maxie starts "Montana."*)
EILEEN: That's all right. I'll close the door. (*Exits.*)
PAUL: Go ahead, Maxie. She don't know anything.
MAXIE: Think of me slaving down at the Orchard while you people enjoy all the comforts of home. (*An impatient movement from Lucille.*)
PAUL: Go ahead with "Montana."
MAXIE: It certainly was a tough day for me when Edison invented the piano. Fixing up other people's tunes—there's a life work for you.
PAUL: Go on.
MAXIE: (*His fingers rambling over the keys.*) You know I might have been a song-writer myself, but I got stuck on my own stuff—I wrote tunes nobody ever heard before— They wouldn't stand for it. (*Runs notes.*)
PAUL: (*Prompting with a gesture.*) "Montana."
MAXIE: (*About to start, but resumes talking instead.*) That was a great idea of Fagan's, writing a lyric about Montana. I've often wondered why lyric-writers stayed out of the Northwest.
PAUL: Maybe Fagan was born there.
MAXIE: Naw! Shamokin, Pennsylvania. If song-writers always wrote about their home state, what a big Jewish population Tennessee must have. (*Plays piano. Plays "What Have You?" softly through these next telephone lines.*)

(*Telephone rings. Paul takes telephone from near keyboard. Eileen appears in the doorway. As soon as she finds out it is not for her, she disappears again.*)

PAUL: (*At telephone.*) Hello—this is him.—Oh, hello.—Where are you at now?—448 Riverside Drive. Tell him just above 116th Street.—That's it. (*Paul hangs up; lays telephone back. Addresses Maxie.*) That's Stevens, the lyric-writer I was telling you about, from Schenectady.
MAXIE: Thank God he can't get that in a lyric.
PAUL: He had the phone number but he didn't know the address.
LUCILLE: Why didn't he look in the phone book?
MAXIE: Do you want miracles?
PAUL: You'll like this fella. He's young yet. He's got a fresh slant.
MAXIE: What does he do—write about counties instead of states?
PAUL: I've been thinking maybe he and I could do something together, if I can get rid of Fagan.
MAXIE: Fagan isn't so bad. Only he's using up his ideas too fast. "Montana

Moon." He puts a state and a moon all in one song.
PAUL: Are you going to play it? (*Maxie starts. To Lucille.*) Listen. (*Maxie plays and Paul sings the song, the chorus of which is as follows:*)

"Golden West that seems so far away,
Golden Girl for whom I'm always pining—
Don't you know I miss you night and day,
But chiefly when the full white moon is shining?

"Montana moonlight, as bright as noonlight,
Oh, may it soon light my way to you.
I know you're lonely, my one and only,
For I am lonely, yes, lonely too.

(*Lucille sews.*)

My heart is yearning for kisses burning,
For lips as sweet—

(*Lucille stops sewing.*)

As a rose in June.
I'm always dreaming of your eyes gleaming
Beneath the beaming Montana moon."

(*Lucille sews. Paul beating time to Maxie's playing.*)

Doesn't it sound great? The way Maxie plays it?
LUCILLE: I don't think Berlin will kill himself.
PAUL: It's nothing like Berlin. Play it in two-four and it's a great dance tune. (*Paul gestures Maxie to play two-four time. Maxie is obliging. Paul sings a strain of it; the music dies down.*)
LUCILLE: You don't get Berlin's songs to dance to. You get them to cry to.
PAUL: All right. You can cry to this, too. "My heart is yearning for kisses burning." That's sad.
LUCILLE: Yes, but there's something behind his songs. (*Sighs.*) They're sympathetic.
PAUL: Do you want to know why? Because he gets a little sympathy now and then. He's appreciated at home. He doesn't sit around here night after night with you yapping your head off at him, telling him he's all through.
MAXIE: (*Rises.*) Now, now! You're going to write plenty of hits.
PAUL: (*Sits.*) Well, it makes a fellow lose confidence in himself.
LUCILLE: I'm trying to help you, not hurt you.
PAUL: You go about it in a funny way. (*Eileen enters.*)
MAXIE: She doesn't mean anything. Of course she wants to help you. But this number—I wouldn't count on it too much if I were you.
LUCILLE: What do you mean?

PAUL: Why not?
MAXIE: I just wouldn't—that's all. You can't tell which way they're going to jump these days.
PAUL: They'll snap this one up. Unless they're crazy.
LUCILLE: Keep still a minute. (*To Maxie.*) What's happened?
MAXIE: Nothing definite. Only they were talking about it—Hart and Goebel.
PAUL: When were they?
EILEEN: What did you say?
MAXIE: Huh? I said Hart and Goebel were talking about Paul's new number.
EILEEN: When?
PAUL: What did they say about it?
EILEEN: (*No longer to be denied.*) You mean they were talking about it today?
MAXIE: Sort of.
EILEEN: In the office, you mean?
MAXIE: Yah. Sure.
EILEEN: What time?
MAXIE: I don't know. Five o'clock.
EILEEN: Goebel and Hart both?
MAXIE: Yah. Why? (*Eileen takes a moment to digest this bit of information. Then, with a sudden movement, she turns and leaves the room. Maxie watches Eileen off, then looks at Paul. Lucille also goes off, trying not to make too much of a situation out of it. Maxie turns to Paul. His eyes following the girls.*) Did I say something dirty?
PAUL: That don't matter. What did they say about the song?
MAXIE: But I don't understand— (*A gesture.*)
PAUL: Listen—what did they do? Turn it down?
MAXIE: (*Reluctantly.*) Right now they don't want it.
PAUL: (*Hotly.*) When did they hear it? After I left?
MAXIE: They asked me, so there was nothing for me to do but give it to them. I had Nate sing it.
PAUL: It's the lyric kills it! The melody's sure fire! Even if it don't sell over the counter, it'll get a good mechanical break.
MAXIE: (*Brightly.*) Maybe you could sell it outside.
PAUL: It makes a man look like a fool, working for one house and selling your stuff to another. (*Sits.*)
MAXIE: You mustn't let it worry you. The next one'll be great, and you'll forget all about it.
PAUL: What else did they say—when they heard it? Anything about—me?
MAXIE: What could they say about you?
PAUL: (*Rises.*) If I don't deliver pretty soon they'll let me out. I'll be like all those fellows that come around every day with another tune. (*Doorbell rings.*) I guess this is Stevens.
MAXIE: Who?
PAUL: Stevens—that lyric writer.
MAXIE: Maybe he's just what you need. Maybe he'll make all the difference in the world.
PAUL: His stuff's pretty good—what I've seen of it. (*Disappears into hallway.*)

MAXIE: (*Cheerily.*) There you are! Everything'll be fine! You see!
PAUL: (*Off.*) Hello, Stevens! Glad to see you.
FRED: (*Off.*) Hello, Mr. Sears.
PAUL: Put your hat and coat on the chair. Come right in! (*Paul and Fred appear in the doorway—Fred ahead of Paul.*) This is Maxie—Mr. Schwartz. Shake hands with Mr. Stevens.
FRED: Glad to meet you, Mr. Schwartz.
MAXIE: Hello, Stevens. (*Lucille enters.*)
PAUL: And this is my wife. Dear, this is Mr. Stevens.
LUCILLE: How are you?
FRED: I'm all right.
LUCILLE: (*To Fred.*) Paul tells me you're a song-writer yourself.
FRED: Just the words.
LUCILLE: Well, that's all Paul needs. Isn't it, dear?
FRED: I've always been one of Mr. Sears' greatest admirers. I've admired Mr. Sears ever since he wrote "Paprika."
LUCILLE: (*Gently.*) You've got a good memory.
PAUL: Maybe Stevens and I will turn out another "Paprika."
FRED: I'm anxious to get started, all right. Since I got to town, all I've done so far is spend money.
LUCILLE: Well, you're quite a stranger.
PAUL: Sit down.
FRED: Thanks. I guess I'm a little late. I got off the wrong subway station, and there was an old woman there selling papers, and I stopped and talked to her because I knew she must be somebody's mother.
MAXIE: (*Who is playing the piano softly through this entire scene.*) A fresh slant.
FRED: I was right, too, because she told me she has six sons. I feel sorry for old women that has to earn their living.
LUCILLE: What do the boys do—rent her the stand?
FRED: No, most of them are in a hospital and two of them had their foot cut off. She told me all about it and I gave her a dollar.
PAUL: You want to be careful in a place like New York. There's all kinds of people waiting to take your money away from you.
FRED: It's a great city, all right. Today I took the ferry boat over to Staten's Island and back. It's an island and you have to take a ferry boat. But I suppose you been there.
LUCILLE: I go there a lot, just for the trip.
FRED: I seen the Goddest of Liberty, too—I mean the statue. It cost a million dollars and weighs two hundred and twenty-five ton.
MAXIE: She ought to cut out sweets.
FRED: (*A gesture in the direction of Maxie, who has been playing the piano through all of this.*) He can play the piano! And I seen some of the big ocean liner steamboats. I seen the President Harding just coming in from London or Europe or somewheres, and the other day I seen the Majestic tied up to the dock. She's pretty near twice as long as the President Harding and weighs fifty-six thousand ton. The President Harding only weighs fourteen thousand ton.
LUCILLE: Imagine!

FRED: (*To Lucille.*) Have you been through the Holland Tunnel?
LUCILLE: No, I haven't.
FRED: (*To Paul.*) Have you been through the Holland Tunnel?
PAUL: No.
FRED: Have you been through the Holland Tunnel, Mr. Schwartz?
MAXIE: (*Still playing, shakes his head.*) I've been waiting for somebody to go with.
FRED: I'll go with you.
MAXIE: Fine!
FRED: I want to go every place so as to get ideas for songs. I was telling Mr. Sears about one idea—I haven't got it written yet—it's a song about the traffic lights, green for "Come ahead!" and red for "Stop!" Maybe a comical song with a girl signalling her sweetheart with different colored lights in the window, a green light when it's all right for him to call—
LUCILLE: And a red one when her husband's home.
FRED: (*Shocked.*) No, I was thinking about her father. I wouldn't write about those kind of women—I got no sympathy for them.
LUCILLE: I guess you're right.
FRED: (*To Paul.*) I was thinking of another idea on the way up here. Maybe a song about the melting pots—all the immigrants from overseas who've come to the Land of Liberty. Take the Jews—do you know there's nearly two million Jews in New York City alone?
MAXIE: What do you mean, alone?
FRED: And then there's the Hall of Fame, up to Washington Heights. They got everybody up there. Washington, Lincoln, Longfellow—they got two dozen—what do you call 'em—busts?
LUCILLE: (*To Paul.*) That's the place for you, dear. (*Paul makes impatient move.*)
FRED: No. A man's got to be dead for twenty-five years.
LUCILLE: Well, that fits in.
MAXIE: (*A discordant bang; rises.*) I've got to be going along.
PAUL: (*Rises.*) Wait. I want Stevens to show you one of his lyrics. Have you got that one with you? About the game?
MAXIE: I've got to be downtown at ten.
PAUL: This won't take a minute. (*To Fred.*) Go ahead.
FRED: (*Taking lyric from pocket.*) I'll have to explain first, so you'll understand. The idea come to me at a football game between Syracuse and Colgate. They beat them, and they felt pretty bad, so the idea come to me for this little song. I call it "Life Is A Game."
MAXIE: A novelty!
FRED: Here's the verse. Are you ready?
PAUL: Yeah.
FRED: (*Singing.*)

"I don't know why some people cry
When things appear to go wrong.
I always say 'Laugh and be gay!
Things cannot always go wrong!'
No use to pine, no use to whine,
Things will come right if you just give them time."

That's the verse.
LUCILLE: Uh-huh!
FRED: Then here's the refrain:
"Life is a game; we are but players"—
MAXIE: Hey, bring it here! Maybe we can put some music to it.
FRED: Just play some chords.
MAXIE: I'll see if I know any.
FRED: (*Sings as well as he can to Maxie's improvisation.*)
"Life is a game; we are but players,
Playing the best we know how.
If you are beat, don't let it wrangle;
No one can win all the time.
Sometimes the odds seem dead against you;
What has to be, has to be.
But smile just the same, for life is a game,
And God is a fine referee."

(*Maxie and Fred repeat. Maxie finishes with a phrase of "All Those Endearing Young Charms."*)

I haven't got the second verse yet.
MAXIE: You won't need one.
LUCILLE: I like a song with a love interest.
FRED: Well, I've got an idea and a title for another one—I mean, of course, I've got lots of ideas, but this one, I told it to a party, and she— (*Catches himself, embarrassed.*) I mean, this party seemed to think it was pretty good.
PAUL: Let's hear it.
FRED: It's just a title. You told me you'd rather have just a title and then write the tune first.
PAUL: What's the title?
FRED: "June Moon." That's the title—"June Moon."
MAXIE: A war song.
FRED: No, no. The verse will be about a fella that's met a girl in June, when there was a moon shining, and then something happened so that she went away, or maybe he went away, and then whenever he looks up at the moon after that he thinks of her. In the second verse she'll be doing the same thing for him.
LUCILLE: That's fair enough.
PAUL: I don't know. Another moon song—
MAXIE: (*Sits at piano.*) "June Moon"—I've got it!
FRED: (*Starts to sing to Maxie's improvisation.*) "June Moon—" (*Telephone rings.*)
LUCILLE: (*Leaping to the telephone.*) I'll answer.
FRED: How I wish you so-and-so—how I miss my so-and-so, spoon. June Moon, so-and-so and so-so— (*He breaks off. Lucille telephoning as Maxie still plays, very softly.*)
LUCILLE: Hello—no, this is Lucille. Just a minute— (*Calls.*) Eileen!
PAUL: Well, I might be able to dig up something for that. (*Music stops.*)
FRED: I got the idea coming in on the train. I happened to look out of the win-

dow— (*He stops as Eileen enters. She has put on a dress, but, in view of the news Maxie had brought, not the evening dress. Paying no attention to anyone, she goes straight to the telephone. She looks attractive, and Fred is obviously interested.*)
EILEEN: (*At the phone.*) Hello—Oh, no—not at all.

(*Simultaneous.*)

EILEEN: What train?—You're sure of that, aren't you?—Nothing, only I thought you might be mistaken. Everybody makes mistakes, you know.—Yes, I can imagine. It must have been terribly tiresome in Philadelphia all day—

MAXIE: Well, I'm due at the Orchard. Good night, everybody! Good night, Mr. Stevens!
FRED: Goodbye! I hope I see you again.
MAXIE: Hope so. See you tomorrow, Paul. (*Exit Paul and Maxie.*)
PAUL: I'll go with you to the elevator. Now look—don't say anything to Fagan, because I don't want him to know until I've talked to the old man.

(*Eileen continues her phone talk, as Fred stands in embarrassment.*)

EILEEN: What?—Oh, really?—I thought you were leaving tomorrow.—What time tonight?—My, it must be important!—Then I won't have a chance to say goodbye before you go— Oh, no, don't trouble yourself—it's quite all right.—Yes, I'm sure you are.—No, I don't mind a bit. I'm just sorry you have to—spend the night on a train, that's all.—Oh, perfectly.—Have a pleasant trip.—Good-bye. (*She hangs up. A look flashes between her and Lucille.*)
LUCILLE: (*Going right ahead to cover the situation.*) Mr. Stevens, this is my sister, Miss Fletcher. Eileen, this is Mr. Stevens.
EILEEN: Hello.
FRED: (*Impressed.*) I'm glad to meet you, Miss Fletcher.
EILEEN: Thanks.
LUCILLE: Mr. Stevens is a lyric-writer. He's from Schenectady.
EILEEN: Oh, yes. Have you been in New York long?
FRED: Just a couple of weeks. I'm from Schenectady. I was with the General Electric Company, but I left them.
EILEEN: I suppose they've closed down.
FRED: No. I had a postcard today from a fella that works there.
LUCILLE: Mr. Stevens has been all over New York—getting ideas for songs.
EILEEN: Do you like it?
FRED: Yes, I like it fine, but it costs money to live here. For instance, I had breakfast in the hotel this morning and it was ninety cents for salt mackerel and potatoes and a cup of Instant Postum.
LUCILLE: No wonder you think New York's expensive! A few more breakfasts like that and you won't have any money left.
FRED: I still got plenty.

LUCILLE: Really? (*Look passes between Eileen and Lucille.*) I'll bet you haven't been to any of the real places, have you? It takes a New Yorker to find those.
FRED: I seen the Goddess of Liberty.
LUCILLE: Oh, I mean the night places!
FRED: I seen it at night.
LUCILLE: Oh, no! Restaurants!
FRED: Huh?
LUCILLE: Mr. Stevens would love those. (*To Eileen.*) Wouldn't he?
EILEEN: (*Slowly coming to.*) Yah.
LUCILLE: I'll tell you what! Why don't we make up a party—the four of us—and show Mr. Stevens the town?
FRED: You mean tonight?
LUCILLE: (*Rises.*) What do you say, Eileen? How about it?
EILEEN: (*Thinking hard; her eyes go involuntarily to the telephone.*) Why—sure! I don't know why not! Sure!
FRED: Well, wait! It'd be great to go, all right—only the trouble is I got another engagement.
LUCILLE: Oh, but you could put that off.
EILEEN: Of course you could.
LUCILLE: (*As Paul re-enters.*) Paul had another engagement, too. He broke it on your account, didn't you, dear?
PAUL: What?
LUCILLE: We thought it would be fun for the four of us to go out some place, but Mr. Stevens doesn't want to.
FRED: (*Looking at Eileen.*) It ain't that I don't want to, but—
LUCILLE: You know, you really ought to. Paul was just saying that what you needed was to go places where they do the latest numbers and hear what kind of songs are getting over. That's true, isn't it, Paul?
PAUL: Ah, yes! Sure!
LUCILLE: Of course it is. Are we all set?
FRED: Well, I want to go all right. It's only I don't know on account of this other engagement.
EILEEN: (*Vamping a little—crosses to him.*) But you could do something about that. You could go if you really wanted to. Don't you—want to?
FRED: (*Hesitating and falling fast.*) Well, I ain't dressed to go out. I mean, to some swell place.
EILEEN: We'll go where we don't have to dress.
LUCILLE: How about the Orchard? Wouldn't Maxie be surprised to see the four of us stroll in?
EILEEN: Lucille and I'll go right in and get our things on. (*A movement.*)
PAUL: Well, wait a minute. It's just that I didn't happen to bring much money with me—
LUCILLE: Oh, that's all right. Mr. Stevens can be the treasurer tonight and you can fix it up with him later.
EILEEN: As long as you're going to be partners!
LUCILLE: Come on! Let's hurry! (*Exit Eileen and Lucille.*)
PAUL: Is that all right with you?

FRED: (*Looking after the pair.*) Say, she's quite a girl, isn't she?
PAUL: Who? Eileen?
FRED: Does she live here with you all the time?
PAUL: Yah. She does.
FRED: She's a regular New York girlie.
PAUL: (*Gets idea of cultivating Fred. Doing a little work.*) Maybe it wouldn't be a bad notion for you to knock around a few nights—I mean, before we start working. Might give you some ideas.
FRED: I'm willing.
PAUL: Great!
FRED: (*Starting to telephone.*) Say, can I use your phone a minute?
PAUL: Sure. Do you want the book?
FRED: No. I know the number. (*Takes receiver off.*) Rhinelander four-one-six-O.
PAUL: I'd better clean up a bit.
FRED: Look! They was talking about this Orchard. That ain't one of them expensive places, is it?
PAUL: No. Just about average.
FRED: Hello.—I want to speak to Miss Edna Baker, please.—Yes. (*To Paul.*) I mean, what do you think it would be likely to come to for the four of us? More than ten dollars?
PAUL: (*Vaguely.*) No—not unless we go on to some other place. You've got more with you, haven't you?
FRED: What other place?
PAUL: One of the other clubs.
FRED: But I don't—hello. Hello, Eddie? I want to tell you something.
PAUL: I'll go and wash up. (*Exits.*)
FRED: Well, I'm up there now, but that isn't—Yeah, it looks all right.—No, I'm still here. There was a piano-player here from Goebel's. He liked my stuff and made up a tune to some of it.—Yeah.—He said it was all right. But that isn't—No, what I called up to say was I can't get around there till late—No, it'll be later than that. There's no telling what time it'll be.—We got to study some songs.—Paul Sears and his wife.—No, no, don't think that. It's a business proposition. They're taking me to a place where I'll get some ideas.—Just the three of us.—But you know I'd rather be with you. (*Eileen re-enters with hat and coat.*) But I can't—I can't.—*They're* taking *me*. I'll tell you all about it in the morning.—That's all I can say now.—I can't.—In the morning. Goodnight. (*Hangs up.*)
EILEEN: You seem to be having your troubles.
FRED: No, that wasn't anything. Just a—friend of mine.
EILEEN: Is she nice?
FRED: It isn't—anybody. Just a little girl I happened to meet.
EILEEN: I understand.
FRED: She's just a—a girl from a little town. (*Lucille enters.*) I mean, she's not like—you—
LUCILLE: (*With hat and coat.*) Listen—it's kind of early for the Orchard anyhow. So why don't we take in the second show at the Capitol?

	PAUL: (*Enters.*) Is everybody ready?
	EILEEN: Oh, that's fine! And I know what you'd love! After the Orchard, what do you say we go to the Cotton Club? (*She throws a quick explanation to Fred.*) That's Harlem!
(*Simultaneous.*)	

LUCILLE: Great!
EILEEN: They've got a wonderful tap dancer up there. Better than Bill Robinson.
PAUL: But say, the Cotton Club don't get hot till three.
FRED: What time?
EILEEN: Oh, that's all right! We can go to the Madrid or Richman's in between.
LUCILLE: Oh, great!
PAUL: But say, Richman's burned down the other night.
FRED: Let's not go there.
LUCILLE: I'll tell you where I haven't been for a long while. The St. Regis Roof!
EILEEN: Grand!
LUCILLE: They've a wonderful view.
FRED: Where?
LUCILLE: The St. Regis Roof.
FRED: I get dizzy if I climb a ladder.
LUCILLE: Come on, everybody. All aboard for Broadway.

	PAUL: Say, I wonder where we can pick up a bottle of gin? You know if we buy it in one of those joints you can't tell what you are getting!
(*Simultaneous.*)	LUCILLE: Say, what's the name of that new place on 53rd Street? Clara Briggs was there the other night and says they've got a wonderful floor show.
	EILEEN: Come on, Charlie. Say, what is your first name, anyway?

CURTAIN

ACT II

SCENE: A room at Goebel's publishing house. Doors on either side of the room and centre door at back. Large double window. Parlor grand piano. Keyboard to window. Chair back of keyboard. Small table against wall above piano. Leather armchair, wooden armchair. Table with music on it against wall. Large music bookcase alongside wall, full of music. Music on piano and on tables.
TIME: About a month after Act I. Afternoon.
AT RISE: *Maxie is at the piano, playing "La Boheme."*
After end of first part of music, Goldie, a blonde-headed young secretary, enters and goes to music case.

GOLDIE: (*Looking at some music.*) "There Never Was a Girl Like Mother."
MAXIE: Maybe it's all for the best.—How's the boss? Did he have a good trip?
GOLDIE: He says not. He says in the Middle West they're still wild over "The Rosary."
MAXIE: That looks like a hit.
GOLDIE: Did Benny find you? He was looking for you.
MAXIE: Not yet.
GOLDIE: He's got a new song.
MAXIE: (*Stops playing.*) That's good. I was afraid he was written out.
GOLDIE: You'd better hide if you don't want to hear it.
MAXIE: No use—he always gets his man. (*Pause.*) Besides, I've got to stick around and play Paul's new one, "June Moon."
GOLDIE: Is it any good?
MAXIE: It's got a chance. It's a tune that's easy to remember, but if you should forget it it wouldn't make any difference. (*Fred enters.*)
FRED: (*To Goldie.*) Ain't Mr. Hart back yet?
GOLDIE: Not yet.

FRED: Don't you even know what time he's coming?
GOLDIE: (*Maxie starts playing.*) Can't tell. His first day back in town—he's probably got a lot of things to do. (*Exits.*)
FRED: It's pretty near half past four. He said he was coming back at two o'clock.
MAXIE: You get used to waiting in this game. I've been in it twenty-two years and nothing's happened yet. (*Plays.*)
FRED: Paul's coming right in. We want to play the song once before Mr. Hart hears it. I made a change.
MAXIE: Whereabouts?
FRED: In the refrain. We had it "Sweet nightbird, hovering above," now it's "winging aloft." You see, "aloft" means the same like "above."
MAXIE: Only higher.
FRED: I wish I'd known Mr. Hart was going to be late. I could have slept some more. I had to get up at twelve.
MAXIE: (*Rises.*) That must be tough after working for the General Electric, where a man's hours are practically his own.
FRED: (*Starts to chair.*) No. I had to be on the job at eight, every morning. But I went to bed about ten, except—(*Sits.*)—Saturday nights, when I seen a picture or something. I didn't know what life was, in Schenectady.
MAXIE: I'll bet it's an open book to you now.
FRED: Imagine—only going out one night a week and then just to a moving picture show! Down here it's like as if every night was a special night—there's always new places to go to. Miss Fletcher—she's always locating new ones. We was in three last night. Wound up at half past seven this morning, in the Bucket of Blood. There's a lovely place. We was the last ones there. Paul and Lucille, they went home at seven, but I and Miss Fletcher stayed and she made the proprietor sell me six bottles of gin. It's real gin—what they call pro-war. You got to have good gin. It's one of the things they put into what they call a Bronx cocktail.
MAXIE: Is that so?
FRED: Didn't you ever have one?
MAXIE: I don't drink. After I listen to songs all day I don't want liquor. I just go home and take a general anaesthetic.
FRED: I like Bronxes best. They're nothing but gin and orange juice. I don't know why they call it a Bronx.
MAXIE: It's great orange country up there. (*Sits.*)
FRED: Anyway, I got a bargain—six bottles for sixty bucks. I gave Miss Fletcher three bottles for a present, because if it hadn't been for her I wouldn't have got them. She made the man do it. When you're around with her you just can't resist doing things.
MAXIE: I know. That's why I don't carry a gun.
FRED: Huh? She's a great sport, all right. She'd make a wonderful wife—she's such a good pal. I think a man's wife ought to be their pal as well as their sweetheart.
MAXIE: That's worth thinking over.
FRED: (*Rises.*) Say—how much money do you think a fella ought to be making before he could get married? In New York, I mean?
MAXIE: It depends on the girl.
FRED: Buddy De Sylva makes pretty near half a million dollars a year out of just

writing lyrics. I guess a man could support a wife on that!

MAXIE: If she was satisfied to ride a bicycle.

FRED: Well, suppose "June Moon" is a big smash? What's the most we could make out of it?

MAXIE: It's hard to say. Take a song like "Swanee River" and it's still going big.

FRED: Yeah, but that's because it was in a big production like "Show Boat."

MAXIE: How's that?

FRED: And with that girl to sing it, that sits on the piano.

MAXIE: You're thinking of Sophie Tucker in "Strange Interlude."

FRED: Well, whoever it was. (*Turns away; suddenly remembers.*) Oh, say! I was over to the tailor's today. I'm getting a new suit. Miss Fletcher took me.

MAXIE: That so?

FRED: It's a blue search, with a hair-bone strip. He took my measures all over. Like I was a fighter. I'm thirty-eight inches around my chest, and thirty-three around my stomach, and—I forget my thigh. Anyway, he's got it all wrote down.

MAXIE: I must get a copy.

FRED: If they like "June Moon"—I'm going to have an evening dinner-coat made, with a tuxedo. I been wearing an old suit of Paul's, but it's too big. Miss Fletcher says it would hold two like me.

MAXIE: There couldn't be two.

FRED: She was just joking.

MAXIE: I see.

FRED: They've given me a wonderful time, all right. They've introduced me to all the big stars. Gil Boag, and Earl Carroll, and Texas Guinan! I met Texas Guinan.

MAXIE: She's kind of hard to meet, isn't she? (*Maxie sits.*)

FRED: No. She's one of the friendliest women I ever seen. When the girls told her who I was she said it was a big night in her life—she said she'd always wanted to meet a lyric-writer. I wonder what my friends in Schenectady would say if they knew I sat around and talked to Texas Guinan. I didn't know nothing when I lived there. Even the first few weeks I was in New York I was kind of a sap.

MAXIE: That sounds incredible.

FRED: (*Leaning on piano.*) I went sightseeing to places like the Aquarium, Grant's Tomb and the Central Park animal zoo and thought I was having a great time. A little friend of mine, she took me around places she'd been to and I thought I was seeing New York because I didn't know no better. She was from a small town, too—she didn't know no better either. Only now I've learned.

MAXIE: What's become of her? Did she go home?

FRED: No, she lives here. She works for a dentist. I must call her up some time and see how she's getting along. (*A Window Cleaner enters. He is a tall, skinny, bald-headed man. Looks a great deal like a window cleaner.*) What are you going to do?

WINDOW CLEANER: Wash the windows. (*Crosses to window.*)

FRED: (*By piano.*) But we're going to try a song here. Can't you go somewheres else first?

WINDOW CLEANER: First! I'm pretty near through for the day. Besides they're

singing songs all over the building. That don't bother me.
FRED: But we're going to sing a new one for Mr. Hart.
WINDOW CLEANER: How much does a man get for writing songs?
FRED: It depends on the song.
WINDOW CLEANER: Say a big hit like "Nearer My God To Thee"?
PAUL: (*Enters.*) Are you ready?
FRED: Yah. (*To Maxie.*) Let's do the song now.
MAXIE: Plenty of time.
FRED: I wish Hart would come, so I can get my advance royalty check. Say, where will I get it cashed? At the American Express Company?
MAXIE: Or the 59th Street Bridge.
BENNY: (*Enters. Benny is a young song-writer, and a pest. To all.*) Where's Hart?
FRED: He ain't back yet.
BENNY: (*To Maxie.*) I've got it, this time! "Hello, Tokio!" How's that for a title? They wanted a novelty number. I guess I've give it to them.
FRED: I and Paul have got a hit.
PAUL: Yeah.
FRED: We think so, anyway.
BENNY: In the verse I've got a fella here in New York that sees a pitcher of a Japanese princess and he's nuts over her, but he can't afford a trip to Japan just on a chance. So he calls her up—get it? "Hello, Tokio!" Get this! (*Crosses to piano.*) Now here's the refrain. After he calls her up. (*Plays and sings.*)
"Hello, hello, Tokio!
Girlie, you'll excuse it, please,
If I no spik Japanese.
This little call will leave me broke-e-o,
But I simply had to say 'I love you so!'
(*Fred looks at Paul. Maxie smokes fast.*)
Believe me, dearie, it's no joke-e-o;
I'd gladly fly through fire and smoke-e-o,
To share with you the marriage yoke-e-o,
Fairest flower of Toki—oki—okio."

(*They all think he is through, but he swings into the refrain again. Second Chorus, Window Cleaner begins to beat time with sponge; puts sponge in front of Benny until Benny looks at him. On "girlie you'll excuse it, please" Window Cleaner drops back. At finish Window Cleaner joins in.*)

What do you think? (*Paul and Fred rise.*)
MAXIE: It would sound better in Japanese.
BENNY: How about it, Paul?
PAUL: It's a pretty good number.
BENNY: It's a great number! Here's another one. It just came to me last night. (*Starts to play a refrain. It is so familiar that Maxie pushes him off the bench and finishes it for him.*) Oh, you're too wise. (*Exit Benny.*)
MAXIE: (*Starts to play.*) All right, boys.
PAUL: Drop it down a tone, will you?

MAXIE: O. K. (*Starts to play. The Window Cleaner opens the window and a gale of wind blows the music off the piano.*) Hey!
FRED: (*Picking up music.*) What are you trying to do?
WINDOW CLEANER: I'm sorry. I didn't realize it was blowing so hard. Gee, I'm glad I ain't out on a boat.
MAXIE: I wish you were on the Hesperus. Come on! (*Maxie plays and Fred sings "June Moon."*)
FRED: (*Singing.*)
  Summer winds are sighing in the trees, my dear;
  I am sure I know what makes them sigh;
  They are sad on moonlit nights like these, my dear;
  They are lonely for you, same as I.
  Sweetheart, how can you resist their plea
  And the moon you used to share with me?

(*Window Cleaner exits through window.*)

  June Moon, shining above,
  Will my true love come soon?
  June Moon, I am so blue;
  I know that you long for her, too.
  Sweet night-bird, winging aloft,
  Singing a soft love tune—
  Tell her to come to me here,
  To me and her dear June Moon.

(*Edna enters at the end of the first chorus; waits through a repeat. Maxie plays tune through after Fred finishes singing. Maxie sees Edna as he finishes playing.*)

MAXIE: You got an audience.
FRED: (*Turns.*) Hello there, girlie!
EDNA: (*Ill at ease.*) Hello!
FRED: I wasn't expecting to see you. Ah—this is—you met Mr. Sears. This is Miss Baker, everybody. And this is Mr. Schwartz.
MAXIE: How do you do, Miss Baker?
EDNA: Hello. They told me to come in, but I'm afraid you're busy.
MAXIE: Not a bit.
FRED: We were just polishing off our number, "June Moon."
EDNA: You've finished it, haven't you? It's beautiful.
PAUL: Did you like the melody? (*Goldie enters; goes up to music bookcase.*)
EDNA: I loved it. And I love Fred's words. I think everybody will.
MAXIE: Are you fond of music?
EDNA: I love it.
MAXIE: We'll send you some good stuff. (*Goldie starts off.*) Goldie! Get Miss Baker's address before she leaves—we'll send her some music.
GOLDIE: Oh! Yeah? (*Exits.*)
EDNA: (*An embarrassed pause.*) I don't want to interrupt. Maybe I'd better be

going.

MAXIE: No, no! We'll go. You stay right here!

FRED: But look, if Mr. Hart comes in—

MAXIE: We'll be in Benny's room. Goodbye, Miss Baker.

EDNA: Goodbye, Mr.—

MAXIE: Schwartz. Maxie Schwartz. It's a Greek name. (*Exit Maxie and Paul.*)

EDNA: (*When she and Fred are alone.*) Hello!

FRED: (*Not at ease.*) I'm fine. Are you?

EDNA: We're all alone, Fred.

FRED: Huh?

EDNA: Nobody's looking.

FRED: Oh! (*He kisses her.*)

EDNA: My, it seems nice again.

FRED: You bet!

EDNA: Fred, what's been the matter?

FRED: Nothing. I just been busy, that's all. I was going to call you as soon as I wasn't busy.

EDNA: I thought maybe you were sick or something. I tried to call you up two mornings—I mean, at your hotel—and they said you couldn't be waked up before one o'clock, I think it was.

FRED: That's only because I been up late the night before, working. We got the song all finished.

EDNA: It's beautiful. I had no idea it would turn out so beautiful. It's beautiful.

FRED: We're going to sing it for Mr. Hart as soon as he gets here.

EDNA: It's a beautiful song. Up to now I felt it was sort of ours together. I mean, the way it started when we were on the train, and then you telling me how it was getting along every day, and now all of a sudden it's finished and I haven't got anything to do with it any more.

FRED: Yes, you have. When it's published I'll make them put your name on the cover—"Dictated to Miss Edna Baker."

EDNA: Oh, Fred, I'd love that. But I'd love something else better.

FRED: What's that?

EDNA: It's been two Sundays since we went anywhere together. Remember the day we took our lunch, and went over on the Palisades all day, and then in the evening we went to the amusement park and went on all the rides! We didn't get home till pretty near twelve o'clock. And then we were going again the next Sunday, only—we didn't.

FRED: But that's because I been working. I told you.

EDNA: You don't have to work days and nights both.

FRED: I have to work when Paul feels like it. Music writers don't keep no hours—they work when they're inspired. And it ain't just writing the songs that takes time. You have to go around places, and keep in contract with the other boys, so you get new notions. You got to keep getting new notions in this game.

EDNA: What kind of places do you have to go to?

FRED: You know—places where they have music.

EDNA: You mean—night clubs?

FRED: Some of them.
EDNA: Just you and Mr. Sears?
FRED: Well, generally we all go together.
EDNA: Who else?
FRED: Paul's wife. Lucille, her name is.
BENNY: (*Starts to enter. Sees them; both look at him. Graciously.*) That's all right. (*Withdraws.*)
EDNA: Doesn't anybody else go along, to sort of even up the party?
FRED: (*A second's hesitation.*) Nobody you know. I hardly know her myself. She just comes along because she's Lucille's sister and lives there.
EDNA: Oh!
FRED: You can't leave her home by herself. She's timid.
EDNA: Does she know about—me, Fred?
FRED: Huh?
EDNA: Didn't you ever tell her about—me?
FRED: Well, you see, we just—it's only business, and there hasn't nothing like that come up.
EDNA: What's she like, Fred?
FRED: I don't know—she—
EDNA: (*Sighing.*) A girl like she has probably got lots of beautiful clothes. She probably makes little me look like nothing.
FRED: (*Turns to her.*) No, that part don't matter. It wouldn't make no difference to me if she had all the clothes in the world. Or if she was bare, either.
EDNA: Is she—very pretty?
FRED: Yah, she— (*A change of manner.*) I hardly ever noticed if she was pretty or not.
EDNA: What's her name?
FRED: Miss Fletcher.
EDNA: I mean her first name.
FRED: I think they call her Eileen.
EDNA: That's a beautiful name. It's a lot nicer than mine, don't you think?
FRED: It's just—a different name.
EDNA: Is she blonde or brunette?
FRED: Both—I mean she's blonde. That is, I never paid much attention.
EDNA: How old is she?
FRED: I don't know.
EDNA: Older than I am? (*Steps toward him.*)
FRED: A little bit, I guess. I guess she must be. She's been on the stage.
EDNA: (*Putting across a little mild horror.*) Honestly, Fred?
FRED: Yah, but don't think—I mean, that don't mean anything.
EDNA: Oh, Fred, you want to be careful. Because you take a woman like she, that's close to forty or more—
FRED: She ain't forty.
EDNA: Well, thirty-eight. And she sees a young boy who almost any woman would be proud to win your affections, and there isn't anything she might not stoop to, to entangle you.
FRED: There won't no woman untangle me.

EDNA: You can't tell, Fred—the most terrible things can happen. There was a near friend of mine, a man, and he was acquainted with a count, an international count, and he came here to New York and one night they went on a wild party and he fell in love with a beautiful chorus girl from the Metropolitan Opera Company—I forget the name of the opera. And he bought her pearls and diamonds, and in less than a week's time he found out they was both married. That's just what could happen to you, dear.

FRED: Who found out who was married?

EDNA: Both of them were married—the count and the girl.

FRED: (*Turns away.*) He must have been a fine count, not to know he was married.

EDNA: Fred, doesn't it cost an awful lot of money when you go around to all these places—or do they take you?

FRED: Well, that part's going to be all right, because as soon as they take our song I'll get what they call an advance royalties. And of course, after it's a big hit I'll have plenty of money.

EDNA: I see.

FRED: Only the first thing I'm going to do—I mean, when I get my advance royalties—I'm going to pay you back that little loan.

EDNA: That doesn't matter, Fred.

FRED: But I don't like owing money to a girl. Especially a girl.

EDNA: But it's all right when two people are like you and I. That makes it all right. I'd give you everything I've got, only I'm afraid I'm not going to have very much from now on.

FRED: What do you mean?

EDNA: (*Turns.*) I wasn't going to tell you, but I haven't got my position any more. I mean, with Doctor.

FRED: You mean you quit? (*Follows her.*)

EDNA: He discharged me.

FRED: What for?

EDNA: I made a mistake. I gave Mr. Mowrey's appointment to Mr. Treadwell, and Doctor scraped Mr. Treadwell's bones instead of Mr. Mowrey's.

FRED: I'm terribly sorry, Eddie. Gosh, I wish there was something I could do about it.

EDNA: There is, Fred, if you felt like doing it.

FRED: What?

EDNA: Are you going to be busy—after they hear the song?

FRED: Well, I'm afraid so—tonight. I got to work with Paul.

EDNA: Well, then, before that. After Mr. Hart hears it. Oh, Fred, couldn't I stay and hear it, too?

FRED: Oh, no, Eddie. When Mr. Hart's hearing a new number he can't have nobody around. He's got to consecrate.

EDNA: Oh!

FRED: I'll tell you what. You can wait in the reception room or somewheres, and the minute he's heard it I'll come and tell you what he says.

EDNA: Oh, Fred, that's grand! Then can we go somewhere together for a little while? Have a soda or something?

FRED: Yah, I guess so.
EDNA: Oh, Fred, I'm so glad! You do care a little, then? I mean, you do care whether you—see me?
FRED: Of course I do. Sure. Certainly.
EDNA: Oh, Fred! (*She presents herself impulsively. He kisses her.*) Everything seems all right again now. I don't care about losing my position any more.
FRED: Yah, but— (*Mr. Hart finally arrives. Business man type. About forty-five. He enters and starts for door. Running after him.*) Oh, Mr. Hart! Mr. Hart!
HART: (*Turns.*) What?
FRED: We've been waiting for you. We're all ready.
HART: Ready with what?
FRED: The new number. We'll go through it for you if you'll just wait a minute.
HART: What number?
FRED: "June Moon." The number I wrote with Paul Sears.
HART: Oh! (*Starts away.*)
FRED: I'll get he and Maxie and we'll run it through for you.
HART: That's very thoughtful. (*Exits.*)
FRED: Yes, sir. (*Turns.*) All right, Eddie. You go in there and as soon as the song's over I'll come and tell you. (*Paul enters.*)
EDNA: All right, dear.
PAUL: (*Crosses to Fred.*) Did Hart get back?
FRED: Yah. He went in there. I told him we was ready. Where's Maxie?
PAUL: He's coming!
MAXIE: (*Enters.*) Well! Are we all set?
FRED: He's here, but he went in there. He came in, and I talked to him, and he went out.
PAUL: What do you think we better do?
MAXIE: How about throwing a cordon around the building? (*Exits.*)
PAUL: Maxie'll bring him.
FRED: (*Trying his voice.*) "June Moon"— (*Suddenly sees Edna again.*) All right, Eddie, we're going to sing it now.
EDNA: All right, dear, I can wait happy now. (*Exits.*)

(*Window Cleaner opens window.*)

FRED: (*Singing—turns toward piano.*) "June Moon"— (*To Window Cleaner.*) Hey! You can't work here now.
WINDOW CLEANER: What? (*Hart and Maxie re-enter.*)
MAXIE: Here we are!
HART: All right—let's have it. What's the name of this song?
BENNY: (*Bounds on, following Hart.*) Are you ready, Boss?
HART: What?
BENNY: For "Tokio"?
MAXIE: Listen, Joe—these boys have been waiting since two o'clock.
HART: All right, all right. Let's have it. What's the name of it?
FRED: "June Moon." (*Maxie sits at piano.*)
BENNY: Great idea!

GOLDIE: (*Enters.*) Pardon me, Mr. Hart. Mr. Wayburn's on the wire.
HART: Can't talk to him now. Go ahead, boys! What's this song called?
GOLDIE: He wants to know if he can use the Java number tonight. It's a benefit.
HART: Who for? Him?
GOLDIE: I think he said the widows of New Jersey commuters.
HART: Oh, sure. Tell him he can have it if he pays for it.
GOLDIE: Yes, sir! (*Goldie exits.*)
HART: That's a great number, "Java." Great number.
BENNY: Yes, sir.
HART: Do you boys want a sure-fire idea?
PAUL: Yes.
BENNY: Yes.
FRED: Yes, sir.
WINDOW CLEANER: Yeah.
HART: Write a war song. Just have it ready—in case.
FRED: Is there going to be a war?
HART: (*Taking them all in.*) I won't say yes and I won't say no. But in this little swing around the West I had a chance to sort of feel out the common people. (*Grows very confidential.*) I'll tell you something. I'm not a bit comfortable about the Mexican situation.
WINDOW CLEANER: Me neither.
HART: It's a dangerous situation. I don't like it. I don't like it a bit. (*A long low whistle from Benny.*) Wouldn't surprise me at all if something happened and happened soon. And when it does, the first fellow in the field is going to clean up. You boys want to watch the papers—be ready for an emergency. Not only war, but these aeroplane flights all over the place— (*Brainard turns doorknob; enters. A middle-aged man with an umbrella and a dumb look.*) —television—all the big inventions. (*To Brainard.*) What is it?
BRAINARD: Have you seen a couple of men?
HART: What?
BRAINARD: Have you seen a couple of men? One of them had his appendix out.
HART: What men?
BRAINARD: From our office.
HART: What office? Where are you from?
BRAINARD: (*Reaching for a card.*) Devlin, Devlin, Stewart and Devlin.
MAXIE: How did Stewart crash in? Marry one of the Devlin girls?
BRAINARD: No. Only one of the Devlins has got a daughter. She's—
HART: For God's sake! Get out of here, will you?
BRAINARD: But I got to find them.
HART: Well, they're not here. What would they be doing here?
BRAINARD: This is their day in this building.
HART: We're busy now. Come in tomorrow.
BRAINARD: They won't be here tomorrow.
HART: Listen to me. I don't know who you are or where you're from—
GOLDIE: (*Enters.*) Beg pardon, Mr. Hart.
HART: Now what?
GOLDIE: George Gershwin's out there.

HART: George Gershwin?
GOLDIE: Yes, sir.
HART: My God! (*He hurries out.*)
FRED: Who is it?
WINDOW CLEANER: George Gershwin. (*He also hurries out.*)
BRAINARD: Yeah? (*Brainard, after a second's hesitation, also exits, hurrying a little. Benny is next to go.*)
PAUL: (*To Fred.*) Did you ever see him?
FRED: (*Starting for the door.*) No.
PAUL: He stole my rhapsody. (*Exits. Fred follows. Maxie runs notes on piano.*)
GOLDIE: Aren't you going out to see him?
MAXIE: (*Rises.*) Let him come to me. (*Exits.*)
LUCILLE: (*Off stage.*) Well, maybe they're in here— (*Eileen and Lucille enter. Eileen leads the way; she is thoroughly at home.*)
EILEEN: Where's everybody?
LUCILLE: Hello, Goldie!
GOLDIE: Good afternoon, Mrs. Sears.
EILEEN: (*To Goldie.*) I see you've moved the piano.
GOLDIE: Not me. (*Exits. Eileen takes off coat and hat; lays them on chair.*)
LUCILLE: (*Sits.*) Well, here we are. Why don't you go in and say hello to Hart?
EILEEN: I'd rather run into him accidentally. It looks better.
LUCILLE: You're not as sure of him as you let on.
EILEEN: Yes, I am! Why shouldn't I be?
LUCILLE: Well, the way he went away, in the first place. And he didn't exactly keep the wires hot while he was gone.
EILEEN: He wrote to me, every place he went.
LUCILLE: Yah, if you call picture postcards writing.
EILEEN: He was busy most of the time. It was a business trip.
LUCILLE: He certainly sent you a beautiful view of the Detroit Athletic Club. (*Eileen glares at her.*) And that new waterworks in Cleveland. A man that didn't care about you would have sent a picture of the *old* waterworks. He's kind of a Latin type. Hot-blooded.
EILEEN: You can say all you want to. Just the same, when he finds out I've been going out with Stevens he's going to be insanely jealous. You watch him.
LUCILLE: Well, maybe. But he didn't even wire you for a date tonight. It's the first time he hasn't done that.
EILEEN: (*Sits.*) He's taking it for granted. That's even better. (*Benny enters.*)
BENNY: Hello, there!
LUCILLE: Hello.
BENNY: George Gershwin's outside.
LUCILLE: Yeah?
BENNY: Don't you want to meet him?
LUCILLE: It's too late now.
BENNY: No—he's still there.
LUCILLE: Yah, but I'm not.
BENNY: I was telling him about my new number—"Hello, Tokio!" He said it was a great idea. But I forgot—you ain't heard it. (*Benny dashes to piano.*)

LUCILLE: It's all right. I'll take Gershwin's word.
BENNY: He said it would make the knuckles of a great musical show. It's about a fella that falls in love with a pitcher of a Japanese Princess and he calls her up on the long distance phone.
LUCILLE: Is she sitting home?
BENNY: Yah. Why?
LUCILLE: I just wondered if things were the same over there.
BENNY: Of course in a musical show he and she have got to get together. (*Gets a sudden idea; a snap of the fingers.*) I got it—he flies there! That's what he does—he flies there! (*Now working as if in a trance.*) And he arrives in cherry blossom time!
LUCILLE: Is that a record?
BENNY: What a part for Lindbergh—if he could only sing. (*Benny exits.*)
LUCILLE: We'd better be moving. We're kind of exposed here.
PAUL: (*Paul and Fred enter.*) Oh, hello!
FRED: (*Crosses to Eileen.*) Hello, there! Gee, I'm glad to see you!
EILEEN: Hello!
PAUL: You two can't stay here. We're going to do the song.
FRED: Mr. Hart ain't heard the song yet. Gee, I hope he likes it.
EILEEN: He'll like it, all right. Lucille and I have brought you luck.
LUCILLE: Yah. I'm a born rabbit's foot.
PAUL: We don't need luck, with this number.
FRED: If they take it, we'll have some celebration tonight. Won't we?
EILEEN: We can decide that later. I don't know—I may not want to go out tonight. (*Hart enters.*)
FRED: Why not?
PAUL: Here we are!
FRED: Oh, Mr. Hart! (*Crosses up to him quickly.*)
HART: (*A little flustered.*) Well! I didn't know we had visitors. Hello, Lucille.
LUCILLE: Hello! (*Hart turns to Fred.*)
FRED: This is Miss Fletcher, Mr. Hart. Miss Fletcher's Paul's sister-in-law.
HART: (*Going through with it.*) Yes. I've already met Miss Fletcher.
EILEEN: Yeah!
FRED: Mr. Hart's been off on a trip.
EILEEN: That's very interesting.
FRED: He's been in all the big cities. Chicago and Cincinnati, and Cleveland—
LUCILLE: I understand Cleveland's got a new waterworks. (*Hart looks at her dumbly.*)
FRED: Are you ready for our song now, Mr. Hart? I mean "June Moon"?
HART: (*Turns to Fred.*) In a minute. (*Eileen steps in front of him.*) I've a little work to do.
EILEEN: (*Quickly.*) Fred's been trying very hard to learn the business.
HART: (*Arrested.*) Yes?
EILEEN: I guess we've been pretty nearly every place, haven't we, hearing the new songs? (*Hart looks at Fred.*)
FRED: You bet! Miss Fletcher's taken me every place. I think I know now what people want, all right.

HART: Oh! So you are a friend of Miss Fletcher's?
FRED: We ain't been acquainted long, but—well, we're pretty good friends. (*To Eileen.*) Aren't we?
EILEEN: Yah!
HART: (*Turning to Fred.*) Suppose you boys come in my office and we'll run this song over.
FRED: You mean right away?
HART: Yes, of course.
FRED: That's fine. (*Rushing to piano.*) Where's the lead sheet and the lyrics?
PAUL: Here they are. (*Paul hands lead sheets to Fred.*)
FRED: Shall we go right in?
HART: Yes, of course.
FRED: But where's Maxie? We got to have Maxie.
HART: I'll send for him. Now, then, who wrote this song?
FRED and PAUL: (*Together.*) I did. (*Exit Fred, Paul and Hart.*)
EILEEN: (*As the door closes.*) Did you see that? He's insanely jealous.
LUCILLE: (*Rises.*) Well, if that's jealousy I'll take a plain lemonade.
EILEEN: You don't know him the way I do. He's burning up.
LUCILLE: He controlled it pretty well. He didn't say anything about a date tonight.
EILEEN: How could he, with Stevens here? (*Puts out cigarette.*)
MAXIE: (*Enters.*) Well, it won't be long now. He's going to hear it at last.
LUCILLE: Yah. We're waiting for the verdict.
MAXIE: It's Stevens' first offense. He'll get away with a small fine. (*Exits.*)
LUCILLE: You know, if they buy that limerick Stevens'll be getting up a party for tonight. He was talking about it already.
EILEEN: I know.
LUCILLE: What are you going to do about him, anyhow? He's going to be kind of a nuisance with Hart back.
EILEEN: (*Sits.*) I can handle him. He's so far gone you can tell him anything.
LUCILLE: We certainly do attract song-writers, we Fletcher girls. It's a curse.
EILEEN: He's not a bad kid. I kind of like him. And he might make a lot of money in this game. Plenty of others have done it.
LUCILLE: I wonder if that damned song *is* any good. All of Paul's stuff sounds just alike to me.
EILEEN: Maybe Stevens' lyrics are just silly enough to get over. I've got kind of a hunch that they are.
LUCILLE: Even if they buy it, it won't mean anything to us. Paul's so far ahead of his royalties they'll never catch up. He could write "Madame Butterfly" and it wouldn't even get me a new step-in.
EILEEN: Anyway, I've got Stevens broken in right, whoever gets him. You've got to give me credit for changing some of his ideas. I imagine every week was Thrift Week in Schenectady.
LUCILLE: It's Thrift Year for me. Year after year. (*Crosses to Eileen—sits by her.*) And I'm getting pretty sick of it.
EILEEN: Why don't you do something?
LUCILLE: Maybe I am.

EILEEN: You are? What?
LUCILLE: (*Shakes her head.*) That's all right.
EILEEN: Don't be a fool. What's happened?
LUCILLE: Nothing exactly yet.
EILEEN: Well, what's going to happen?
LUCILLE: I don't know. Nothing.
EILEEN: (*Pleading.*) Will you tell me?
LUCILLE: Remember—Ed Knowlton?
EILEEN: Yes. What about him?
LUCILLE: I ran into him Friday, on Madison Avenue.
EILEEN: Why didn't you tell me?
LUCILLE: Because I knew what you'd say and I wanted to think it out for myself.
EILEEN: What's it all about? What's he doing here?
LUCILLE: He's left Chicago for good. They're living on East Fifty-seventh—he and his wife and the two kids.
EILEEN: Well?
LUCILLE: He still likes me, and I like him.
EILEEN: Has he got any money?
LUCILLE: He makes a lot, but he spends it.
EILEEN: If he likes you, that's not a fatal drawback.
LUCILLE: He likes me, all right.
EILEEN: Can he get rid of her?
LUCILLE: (*Shakes her head.*) No. It's her uncle or something owns the business. (*A pause.*) But he saw I wasn't happy, and—well, we had a couple of drinks and talked. He kept saying I ought to have nice things—(*Slowly rises.*)—and that he was willing to give them to me.
EILEEN: Don't tell me you aren't going to do it?
LUCILLE: I'm kind of afraid. Suppose Paul gets inquisitive?
EILEEN: Paul! He doesn't know silk from asbestos. To hell with him anyway. It's time you had some luck.
LUCILLE: I don't know what to do. You and I look at things different. But Ed's so nice. The things he says—they make me feel young again. And it's such a relief to just talk to a man that hates music.
EILEEN: Listen, if you don't do this— (*Fred enters, excited.*)
FRED: They're going to take it! They've took it! They're crazy about it!
EILEEN: Well, that's fine. I knew they'd like it.
FRED: It's my first song. My first one to be published.
EILEEN: That's wonderful.
LUCILLE: It's quite thrilling.
FRED: They're making me out a check for two hundred and fifty dollars. That's just what they call an advance royalties.
PAUL: (*Enters.*) They took it, all right.
LUCILLE: So Fred said.
EILEEN: Yes!
PAUL: You should have heard what Hart said about the melody.
FRED: (*To Eileen.*) Aren't you glad about the song? Aren't you excited?
EILEEN: (*Her mind beyond the door.*) I should say so.

HART: (*Enters. Expansively.*) Well, what do you think of this young man? Making good in his first attempt!
EILEEN: It's wonderful.
LUCILLE: Yes, indeed.
HART: And Paul, too. He's written a nice little melody. (*Maxie enters.*) Did you get your check, Stevens?
FRED: No, sir. Not yet.
HART: Goldie'll bring it to you.
MAXIE: Well, thought you people would be on your way by this time.
EILEEN: We are waiting for Fred's check—
MAXIE: I'll bet you are! (*Exits.*)
FRED: Mr. Hart! We were all planning on going some place, to celebrate the success of the song. (*Eileen moves as if to interrupt.*) We'd love to have you come along with us, if you can. (*A moment of embarrassment. Eileen just waits.*)
HART: Well, now, I'd like to do that, but I'm very sorry. (*Hart starts talking to Fred, but shifts his gaze to Eileen.*) You see, I just got back from this trip, and I'm tied up with Mr. Goebel tonight.
FRED: Oh, that's too bad.
EILEEN: (*With more meaning.*) Yes, it is.
HART: I'm sure you'll have a wonderful time. Can't tell you how much I'd like to be along. But of course, business comes first. (*A very beautiful young lady enters. Her name is Miss Rixey.*) Oh—
MISS RIXEY: Hello, Joe. Am I late?
HART: (*After clearing the throat.*) Miss Rixey, isn't it?
MISS RIXEY: (*Puzzled at this reception.*) What?
HART: Ah—they told me you were coming.
MISS RIXEY: You knew damn well I was coming.
HART: Did you bring those orchestrations?
MISS RIXEY: (*Holding up a bundle which obviously contains two bottles of liquor.*) You mean this?
HART: (*Sunk by this time; quickly crosses to her and grabs her by arm; rushes her to door.*) Ah—just step into my office and we'll talk business.
MISS RIXEY: Listen, Joe, that driver of yours is so damn dumb—
HART: (*Loudly.*) Yes, we publish that. Right this way. (*Hart and Miss Rixey exit.*)
LUCILLE: (*Airily.*) Well, well, well!
FRED: It's too bad he can't go, but the four of us can have a good time.
EILEEN: (*Recklessly.*) Have a good time! You bet we can. We're going to have the best time any crowd ever had. Aren't we, Freddy boy? (*Throws arms around him and kisses him.*)
FRED: We sure are, girlie! (*Goldie enters.*)
GOLDIE: Here's your check, Mr. Stevens.
PAUL: Great!
EILEEN: Hooray! Here's the check! (*She takes it.*)
FRED: Just in time!
EILEEN: Two hundred and fifty dollars! You've just got to give me a great big kiss.
LUCILLE: Oh, you two! (*Circles chair to piano and picks up bag. Fred kisses Eileen.*)

EILEEN: Do you love me?
FRED: You bet I do.
LUCILLE: Where'll we go for dinner?
PAUL: I want a good steak.
EILEEN: (*Breaks from Fred.*) How about the Park Casino?
LUCILLE: Oh, fine! I've never been there. I hear it's marvellous.
PAUL: We've got to stop for a bottle of that gin.
EILEEN: They've got the most wonderful band. You'll love it, Freddie boy.
FRED: I will if you're along.
EILEEN: I'm going to be. Don't you worry about that. Wherever you are, that's where I'm going to be.
FRED: That suits me all right.
LUCILLE: Come on, everybody.
PAUL: Don't forget we got to stop at the Astor. (*Paul and Lucille exit first. Fred and Eileen cross to door.*)
EILEEN: (*Waving the check.*) I should say not. We're not going to forget that, are we, Freddy boy?
FRED: You bet we aren't. (*They have been moving out during these lines. But by this time their voices have died away in the hall.*)

(*Goldie remains on the stage after delivering the check. When the four are gone, Goldie turns up to the music shelves; gets a sheet of music; turns to go. Edna enters.*)

EDNA: Do you know if they've heard Mr. Stevens' song yet? I mean "June Moon."
GOLDIE: (*Stops.*) Yah. They did.
EDNA: (*Starting brightly forward.*) Was it all right? Did they like it?
GOLDIE: (*Surveying her.*) They took it.
EDNA: (*Crossing further, in pleased excitement.*) Really! I'm— Where are they? Still in there?
GOLDIE: Not any more. They've all gone.
EDNA: What?
GOLDIE: They went out just a couple of minutes ago.
EDNA: Mr. Stevens, too?
GOLDIE: Yah. With Mr. Sears and the two girls.
EDNA: Oh! Thank you very much. (*Goldie goes out. Edna stands a moment.*)

(*Window Cleaner enters; looks at Edna. Edna exits. Window Cleaner goes to piano—hesitates, touches a note three times. Sees music on piano, drops sponge on window shelf, goes to piano; starts to pick out "Tokio" with one finger. Second time starts to sing "Hello, hello, Tokio!" Maxie enters; listens to him; sees the sponge, picks it up and starts to wash window.*)

CURTAIN

ACT III

SCENE: *The scene is still at Goebel's. The time about a month later. Morning. At the rise, Goldie comes on and goes to the music racks. While she is searching for songs, Benny enters.*

BENNY: Where's Hart?
GOLDIE: He's out somewhere. (*Takes music to table; sits in chair and sorts it.*)
BENNY: Did you tell him I wanted to see him?
GOLDIE: Yes, but he was on his way out.
BENNY: What did he say?
GOLDIE: Nothing. He just hurried.
BENNY: I've got to see him. I've got a number that will knock his eye out.
GOLDIE: Like "Tokio"? (*Sitting in chair by table, sorting music.*)
BENNY: Don't kid me about "Tokio." If ever a man got a crooked deal! Listen—
GOLDIE: I've heard it.
BENNY: You ain't heard it all because I didn't know it myself till last night. Harry Ruby told me at the Friars. It seems that the night I played it there there was a fella named Stein hanging around.
GOLDIE: At the Friars?
BENNY: Well, he hears my number, and he tells these other fellas, and they turn out their damn "Hello, Shanghai" and beat me to it. It's incredible, but that's what happened. And on top of that Maxie says their number is better than mine because Shanghai's further away than Tokio. I'll kill the two of them the first time I get them alone together. I don't care if they got a thousand friends with them. And that ain't all. They stole my song and I'm going to sue them for perjury.
GOLDIE: I think you'll get it.
BENNY: And it wasn't only a song they stole—it was a whole production. A musical

comedy. That's where the big money is. And that's what I'm going to get into. I'll tell you something. (*Confidentially.*) I'm not going to be with Goebel's much longer.
GOLDIE: I heard that.
BENNY: Who from?
GOLDIE: Mr. Goebel.
BENNY: You couldn't—he doesn't know it yet.
GOLDIE: Oh!
BENNY: I'm quitting and they can see how they like that. They can get along with Stevens and his brilliant ideas. "June Moon"! The lucky saphead.
GOLDIE: It was on five different stations last night.
BENNY: The oldest idea in the world! And I write a great novelty number and it's stole off me!
PAUL: (*Enters. To Goldie.*) Have you seen Stevens?
BENNY: Want to hear a great song?
PAUL: (*Still to Goldie.*) Have you?
GOLDIE: He hasn't come in.
BENNY: Get this, Paul! Tell me if you don't—(*Hart opens door. Goldie rises.*)—think it'll slaughter them! (*Benny hits one chord. Hart enters.*) Hello, Boss! You're just in time.
HART: (*A wave of the hand that takes care of Benny for the moment.*) Where's Stevens? Is he in yet?
PAUL: (*Shakes his head.*) I'm waiting for him myself.
HART: (*To Goldie.*) Call his hotel. See if he's there.
GOLDIE: I did a while ago. He was out.
HART: See if they know where to get hold of him. (*Goldie exits.*) How are you coming with the new numbers?
PAUL: (*Uncomfortably.*) Pretty good, only Fred doesn't seem to want to work lately. He was going to meet me here at eleven.
HART: He ought to be getting busy. He's not going to work on his honeymoon.
PAUL: No, sir.
HART: When he comes in, tell him I'd like to see him.
PAUL: Yes, sir. (*Goes out.*)
BENNY: (*Stopping Hart.*) Listen, Mr. Hart. It won't take me two minutes to show you this number. It's sure to hit you.
HART: Anything like "Tokio"?
BENNY: I had a tough break on that, Mr. Hart—that "Hello, Shanghai." Why, do you know what? There ain't even a telephone between New York and Shanghai.
HART: Well, we'll have one put in. (*Maxie enters.*) Oh, Maxie, I was just going to send for you. There's a young fellow outside with a song.
MAXIE: Who is it?
HART: That's just the point. Somebody my sister-in-law sent, so do whatever you can for him. He's only sixteen years old.
MAXIE: And still grinding them out?
HART: It's probably one of those things, but *you* know—you never can tell. Anything can happen, after "June Moon."
MAXIE: As long as you've brought that up, would you mind answering me a riddle?

HART: What is it?
MAXIE: Did you have any idea it was going to be a hit? Honestly, now?
HART: Well, I—I'll tell you, Maxie—
MAXIE: That's all I wanted to know.
HART: Do whatever you can for the lad, Maxie. He came all the way from East Orange.
MAXIE: He'll get home safe. (*Exits.*)
BENNY: Listen, Mr. Hart. Won't you hear this?
HART: Hear what?
BENNY: This number. The title is "Give Our Child A Name." It'll make "June Moon" sound like a dirge. It's a couple that give birth to a little one in two-four tempo.
HART: It won't do you any good knocking Stevens' number.
BENNY: I ain't knocking his lousy number, but get this, Mr. Hart. (*Jumps to piano.*)
"Should a father's carnal sins
Blight the life of baby-kins?
Mister, won't you give our child a name?
I mean a last name."

(*Breaks off; bangs keyboard when Fred and Eileen enter. Benny exits hurriedly.*)

HART: Well! Here's the groom at last.
EILEEN: You can blame it on me. I've been making him get some new clothes.
HART: Well, you two are certainly to be congratulated.
EILEEN: Thanks.
FRED: Much obliged.
HART: But don't forget your work. And when do you sail?
EILEEN: Saturday.
FRED: We sail Saturday.
HART: I certainly envy you. I wish I could go along.
FRED: There's no chance, I suppose.
HART: Not this time of year. (*Visibly enjoying the situation.*) If you could postpone it a month—
FRED: (*Brightening.*) Yah, that might be a good idea.
EILEEN: Don't be silly!
FRED: I forgot. Eileen wants to be on the Riveeria in the season.
HART: I see. Well, I hope they don't take you at Monte Carlo.
FRED: If they don't take us there we can go somewhere else.
HART: Anyhow, be sure to get your work done. (*Starts away.*)
EILEEN: Oh, Mr. Hart!
HART: (*Turns.*) Yes?
EILEEN: Fred wants to speak to you about something else.
FRED: No, I don't.
EILEEN: But you do, dear.
FRED: (*To Hart.*) I'll ask you later.
HART: Is anything the matter?

FRED: No, no! It wasn't—I just—
HART: Well, I'll be in my office, if you want me. (*Exits.*)
EILEEN: Why didn't you ask him when you had a chance?
FRED: They've advanced me so much already.
EILEEN: But sweetheart, you promised me. You said you'd ask him today.
FRED: I will, after a while. I got to find Paul now—to go to work.
EILEEN: Oh, don't go to work yet. (*Fred sits. Eileen sits on arm of chair.*) You never have any time for me. You don't realize I want to be loved once in a while.
FRED: I held your hand in the taxi.
EILEEN: Just think! Only three more days till we belong to each other. Isn't it marvelous?
FRED: It's four, ain't it?
EILEEN: Four till we sail. Only three till we get married.
FRED: I wished it wasn't quite so soon.
EILEEN: What?
FRED: I mean, on account of those two numbers.
EILEEN: Don't forget—you're to ask him for a thousand dollars advance on each of them.
FRED: But that's too much! I've borrowed thirty-five hundred dollars off them already on "June Moon." Maybe more than my royalties will amount to altogether.
EILEEN: Don't be ridiculous! That number will still be selling when you're dead.
FRED: I won't care so much then.
EILEEN: Your children will. (*Fred is embarrassed.*) Don't you want children, dear?
FRED: I don't get along with them very good.
EILEEN: You would with your own.
FRED: No. I figure I'd get along better with other people's, because they'd go home once in a while.
EILEEN: We needn't think of that now. Let's just think of you and me, all alone on that big boat.
FRED: We won't be alone. The fella said it would be pretty near full.
EILEEN: But we don't have to see anybody. A bride and groom don't generally go around much—they're supposed to be so awfully in love.
FRED: I'll want to eat once in a while.
EILEEN: They'll serve us in our cabin.
FRED: It'll be kind of close quarters. Maybe I could go in the dining room and order you a meal sent up.
EILEEN: And leave me all alone? I'd be scared to death. (*Rises.*)
FRED: (*Rises.*) It's just as dangerous in the dining room as the bedroom. If the ship sinks, pretty near all the rooms will be under water.
EILEEN: Let's not think about such things. Just think of the pleasant side, London and Paris. I'm glad we're going to Paris first, so I can get some clothes.
FRED: Clothes? What have you been buying?
EILEEN: They're all right for the ship, dear, but not the Riviera. Don't you want to be proud of me—the way I look?
FRED: But if you're going to stay in your cabin all the time you won't need nothing —(*Maxie enters.*)—but a Mother Hubbard.

MAXIE: Well! All ready for the big trip?
FRED: Pretty near. The boat sails Saturday.
MAXIE: I don't know what you want to go to Europe for.
EILEEN: (*Bristling; turns to him.*) Why not?
MAXIE: Because he's never been there. A songwriter never goes anywhere for the first time—they're always going back to places—back to Indiana—back, back to Baltimore.
EILEEN: Fred, are you going to talk to Mr. Hart?
FRED: Yes, ma'am.
EILEEN: (*Irritated.*) Well, this would be a good time. (*She exits.*)
FRED: I'd like to be going back to Schenectady, but Eileen's got her heart set on Europe.
MAXIE: I hear it's quite a place.
FRED: Yes, I guess so. I was kind of excited about it, at first, but now—I don't know. I don't want to go so bad. I'm kind of tired, I guess—the way we been going it lately. I'm kind of behind on my sleep.
MAXIE: But you've been having a lot of fun. All those night clubs.
FRED: I did at first—dancing and everything—but now my feet's so sore I have to take a bath every day. You might as well take a whole bath as just your feet. And they ache so I can't sleep in them. Gosh, I'm so tired all the time, I don't have time to sleep, anyway. We shop till the stores is closed, and then we get dressed up for dinner and the evening. (*Sits on arm of chair.*) If I don't get some rest soon I'll have a nervous break-up. And everything costs so much. Eileen wants a taxi if she's only going in the other room.
MAXIE: This trip to Europe—that's going to be kind of expensive, too, ain't it?
FRED: Yes! I always thought I'd save my money, if I ever got any.
MAXIE: You picked out a thrifty girl, all right.
FRED: I kind of get thinking sometimes, maybe a man like I that's just breaking in, maybe he shouldn't get married so soon, especially a woman that's got to have so many clothes. Sometimes I think it would be better if I hadn't got engaged.
MAXIE: I read of a case once, in Michigan, where a man was engaged to a girl and didn't marry her.
FRED: I didn't read that. Have you got the clippings?
MAXIE: No. But my memory's pretty good. For instance, I remember a mighty nice young girl—(*Fred rises.*)—that was here to see you one time. I even remember her name—Miss Baker.
FRED: Maxie, you haven't seen her or anything, have you?
MAXIE: Me? No. Why?
FRED: (*Uneasily.*) I guess I shouldn't be thinking of her at a time like this—
MAXIE: Are you?
FRED: I don't know. Sometimes I— (*Goldie enters and goes to shelves.*) I got to find Paul. I got to do some work. (*He exits, uneasy. Maxie looks after him.*)
MAXIE: Just one of the Happiness Boys. He and Pagliacci.
GOLDIE: (*Examining songs.*) Mother song and mother song and— Oh! Why don't they ever write about their uncle?
MAXIE: Suppose I told you I was thinking of doing something about him?
GOLDIE: What?

MAXIE: Suppose I went even further and told you I'd already done it?
GOLDIE: What are you talking about?
MAXIE: I'm talking about a little girl that came in here to see Stevens about a month ago. The one you sent the music to.
GOLDIE: Oh!
MAXIE: She's the one he ought to be marrying, instead of this whatever-she-is.
GOLDIE: My God, what's the difference who marries a lyric-writer? (*Exits. Maxie, deep in thought, drifts to the piano. His fingers run over the keys. Lucille enters. A changed Lucille, fashionably dressed. A deliberate entrance, designed to show off the clothes.*)
MAXIE: Hello!
LUCILLE: Where's everybody?
MAXIE: Paul's outside somewhere. I think he's working.
LUCILLE: Has Eileen been here?
MAXIE: She's around.
LUCILLE: Thanks.
MAXIE: All dressed up today.
LUCILLE: Not especially.
MAXIE: You look like a bride yourself. (*Eileen enters.*)
EILEEN: Hello. I thought I saw you.
MAXIE: (*Rises.*) Well, I've got to get busy, if you'll excuse me. (*Exits.*)
EILEEN: (*Observing the dress.*) Oh, say, it's a peach!
LUCILLE: Do you like it?
EILEEN: You bet! (*Looks.*) Have you got a date?
LUCILLE: I think so. I'm to phone his office later on. (*She is not at ease.*)
EILEEN: (*A look at her watch.*) What do you say we have lunch? (*Starts up.*)
LUCILLE: Wait a minute.
EILEEN: What's the matter?
LUCILLE: I don't want to go out there yet.
EILEEN: Why not?
LUCILLE: I don't feel like running into Paul.
EILEEN: Aren't you ever going to get over that? What is there to be afraid of?
LUCILLE: I don't know. I'm just nervous.
EILEEN: He'll never guess anything. He's blind and always has been.
LUCILLE: Thanks.
EILEEN: You know what I mean. All he thinks about's his tunes. We've got a chance to be happy, you and I—for a while, anyhow. Let's take it.
LUCILLE: You're a funny one to figure out.
EILEEN: Why?
LUCILLE: Taking up with Stevens this way. You always lectured me about Paul— his being a songwriter. And now you're going to go and do the same thing.
EILEEN: Stevens is different. He's a nice kid. Of course, he's not what you'd call— bright.
LUCILLE: Bright? He's not even born yet.
PAUL: (*Enters.*) Oh, hello.
LUCILLE: Hello.
PAUL: What's that—a new dress?

LUCILLE: This?
EILEEN: I'll meet you outside, Lucille.
LUCILLE: Wait a minute—I'll go with you.
PAUL: No, I want to talk to you.
LUCILLE: (*Scared.*) What?
PAUL: Ah— (*Looks at Eileen.*) Stay in here a minute.
LUCILLE: What for?
EILEEN: I'll go out. I want to talk to Fred. (*Exits.*)
LUCILLE: What's the matter?
PAUL: (*On the dress again.*) That *is* new, isn't it?
LUCILLE: Don't you think it's about time?
PAUL: How much was it?
LUCILLE: It won't come due for a while. I may take care of it myself.
PAUL: I can take care of it if it ain't too soon.
LUCILLE: I've got to go on out. Eileen's waiting.
PAUL: Hold on! (*Lucille turns, not knowing what to expect.*) That's what I want to talk to you about.
LUCILLE: What?
PAUL: About her and Fred.
LUCILLE: Oh!
PAUL: She's got him so he can't hardly work at all. I don't know when we're going to finish the new numbers.
LUCILLE: Of course you can finish them.
PAUL: But taking him off on this trip! It's going to cost him a million dollars. And just when we're beginning to work good together!
LUCILLE: You can write other numbers while he's gone.
PAUL: But that's not the point. I mean—do you think they ought to do it?
LUCILLE: Do what?
PAUL: Do you think they ought to go ahead and get married? He's a hell of a nice guy—I've kind of got to like him.
LUCILLE: What of it? Eileen's a nice girl.
PAUL: But—you know what I mean. Isn't it kind of a dirty trick—I mean, after the way Eileen—Well, Hart and everything?
LUCILLE: (*A look around.*) You ought to have more sense.
PAUL: Just the same, I don't feel right about it. And the way she's throwing his money around—like it was confetti. Spending every nickel she can get on herself! Clothes, clothes—
LUCILLE: You can't go to Europe in a life belt.
PAUL: Do you know what she spent in one afternoon, yesterday? Close to four hundred dollars. He pretty near cried when he told me. And I don't blame him. He's too nice a kid.
LUCILLE: She doesn't spend that every day.
PAUL: She shouldn't have spent it at all. You should have had more sense than to let her.
LUCILLE: (*Flaring a little.*) How could I stop her? I wasn't there.
PAUL: Yes, you were. You were with her all afternoon.
LUCILLE: (*Quickly recovering herself.*) Oh, yes. I thought you meant the day be-

fore.
PAUL: It was Sunday, the day before.
LUCILLE: Yah—I just got mixed up, that's all.
PAUL: Anyhow, something ought to be done about it. She's got him in debt enough.
LUCILLE: (*Nervously.*) I'll talk to her about it. (*Turns back to him.*) Don't you say anything to her. Don't say anything about— I mean, what she spent yesterday afternoon. I'll go and talk to her. (*Lucille exits, glad to escape. Paul takes a breath, straightens up, starts toward door. Benny bounds in.*)
BENNY: Can you listen to that number?
PAUL: (*Turns.*) What?
BENNY: Can you hear that number now?
PAUL: Aw—I got to work, Benny. (*Exits. Goldie immediately enters.*)
BENNY: Where's Hart?
GOLDIE: Can't you think up a new question?
BENNY: Where is he?
GOLDIE: He's out getting a permanent. (*Exits. Benny again gives up; is about to exit. This time, through the door, there comes the beautiful young woman known as Miss Rixey.*)
BENNY: (*Without much hope.*) Say, do you want to hear a new song?
MISS RIXEY: Sure!
BENNY: (*Very much surprised.*) What?
MISS RIXEY: I said sure.
BENNY: (*Darts to piano and starts. He plays and sings.*)
"Should a father's carnal sins
Blight the life of baby-kins?
All I ask is give our child a name."

(*On second line Miss Rixey listens a moment, and in the middle of verse dances off, doing Buffalo step. Benny sits in dejection. Edna enters, a highly uncertain Edna.*)

BENNY: Hello, kid!
EDNA: Hello!
BENNY: Want to see somebody?
EDNA: I'll be going.
BENNY: Wait! You want to hear a great song? You know who I am, don't you? I'm Benny Fox, the hit writer. I write words and music both. I'm like Berlin, only more pathetic. Now I got a new one. It's about a couple that have a baby without benefit to a clergyman, and you can dance to it. (*Plays and sings.*)
"Should a father's carnal sins
Blight the life of baby-kins?
All I ask is give our child a name,
I mean a last name.
I don't ask to share your life,
Live with you as man and wife,
All I ask is give our child a name—
Not just a first name."

(*Maxie enters.*)

Hello, Maxie. I'll start over so you can get this. (*Begins to play.*) "Should a father's carnal sins—"
MAXIE: (*Looking at Edna.*) Wait a minute! Isn't this—Miss Baker?
EDNA: And you're Mr. Schwartz.
MAXIE: Correct!
BENNY: Come on, Maxie! Get a load of this!
"Should a father's carnal sins—"
MAXIE: Go back to your cell! We want to talk!
BENNY: But she wants to hear this number!
MAXIE: Listen! You don't know who she is.
BENNY: No.
MAXIE: Well! Remember what happened to "Tokio." (*Benny goes quickly to door and exits.*) My, but I'm glad to see you!
EDNA: (*Pleased.*) It's nice of you to say so, anyway.
MAXIE: I guess it was kind of nervy of me, calling you up that way. Hope you don't mind.
EDNA: Why—no. I—I thought it was very friendly.
MAXIE: Of course it ain't really any of my business exactly, but—nobody else was doing anything, so I thought I would. Probably you can guess who it's about.
EDNA: Tell me about him. What's happened? What's happened to him?
MAXIE: Do you mind if I ask a question? I think I know the answer.
EDNA: What?
MAXIE: You're in love with him, aren't you? (*Edna turns away.*) You know, you can tell me. I'm for you—I want to help you. You do—love him? (*Edna nods.*) Enough to keep him from—ruining himself?
EDNA: How do you mean?
MAXIE: He's engaged to be married—you know that?
EDNA: I—supposed that was it.
MAXIE: But he's not happy. He's not in love with her.
EDNA: I can't do anything. He doesn't love me. He never did.
MAXIE: Somebody's got to do something. He's not a fellow that can think for himself. They left that out.
EDNA: Oh, why did you make me come here? I shouldn't have done it—I don't know why I did. I've been trying every way to forget him—I went away, and I didn't see anybody, and then I went around with lots of people—it only made it worse. I kept wanting to call him up, and once I did, only—I hung up before he could come to the telephone.
MAXIE: Let me bring him in here.
EDNA: No, no! I don't want to talk to him. I mustn't!
MAXIE: But he's in trouble. You're the only one that can help him.
EDNA: He don't want to see *me*.
MAXIE: Let me tell him you're here. It can't do any harm. (*Edna is silent; turns away.*) You needn't answer. Only promise me one thing.
EDNA: What?
MAXIE: No matter what happens, come and see me afterwards. Will you? (*Edna*

nods.) The second door on the left, down that hall. (*Maxie exits. Edna is alone for a moment. Fred enters.*)
FRED: Hello, Eddie!
EDNA: Hello!
FRED: I'm awful glad to see you, Eddie. Gee, but I'm glad to see you.
EDNA: I didn't really come to—I mean, it was Mr. Schwartz that made me talk to you.
FRED: My, but it's great to see you again. I didn't know how great it would be. (*Comes closer.*)
EDNA: I'm glad to see you, too, Fred. I'm glad you're well and that you're going to be—happy.
FRED: (*Edges nearer to her.*) I been thinking about you, Eddie—an awful lot, lately. I been waking up in the morning, thinking about you.
EDNA: Are you waking up in the morning again, Fred?
FRED: I been going to call you up to tell you about it. We used to have a lot of fun together. Remember that day in Van Cortlandt Park when I lost my watch and that little boy found it?
EDNA: You gave him a nickel.
FRED: It was a dime. And he said, "Keep it and buy your wife a radio set." He thought we was married. (*He laughs, as though trying to induce a mood of merriment in Edna.*)
EDNA: I remember.
FRED: You was embarrassed, all right. You got red.
EDNA: (*She turns.*) Any girl would.
FRED: And then coming back we forgot to change at Seventy-second Street. That is, you forgot. I didn't know any better.
EDNA: (*Backs a bit.*) I just wasn't thinking.
FRED: (*Follows her.*) We had to go all the way down to Times Square. That's when we saw the flea circus.
EDNA: You said one of the fleas reminded you of a man in Schenectady.
FRED: Yeah. Perry Robinson. He always walked like he'd just picked up a nail. (*Edna laughs. Fred, in sudden realization of the situation, grows serious.*) Eddie, did Maxie say anything to you? About me.
EDNA: He said you were going to be married, Fred. I should have congratulated you.
FRED: (*Suddenly.*) I don't want to any more, Eddie. I know it now. I don't want to.
EDNA: Don't say that, Fred! Don't! (*A pause.*) Don't say it unless you mean it. I couldn't stand it.
FRED: But I do mean it, Eddie! I mean it more than anything in the— (*Eileen enters.*) Oh!
EILEEN: (*Rather gayly.*) I'm sorry.
FRED: No—don't go away. This is—Miss Fletcher.
EILEEN: (*Appraisingly.*) Hello!
FRED: And this is Miss Baker. She's the little girl—I mean, I used to know her when—
EDNA: (*Crosses to door.*) I'll be going if you don't mind. Goodbye, Fred.

FRED: No—look! Don't go away!
EDNA: Yes, I must! I— Goodbye, Miss Fletcher. (*Exits. Fred moves defiantly to follow her.*)
EILEEN: Fred!
FRED: Huh?
EILEEN: Why, what's the matter with you? One would almost think it was her you were going to marry instead of me.
FRED: (*Crosses to her.*) I got to tell you something.
EILEEN: Why, what is it?
FRED: I don't want to get married. I mean—you and I!
EILEEN: Do you know what you're saying?
FRED: I can't help it! I shouldn't ever have done it. I didn't realize.
EILEEN: Well! This is a fine time to tell me. Why didn't you wait till Friday?
FRED: I just now realized it.
EILEEN: I see! And you think all you have to do is tell me and that settles it. Well, it doesn't quite work that way.
FRED: What?
EILEEN: You think I'm going to stand by and let you throw me over for that little snip!
FRED: She is not.
EILEEN: Not by a damned sight! I'll sue her for alienation. That's what I'll do.
FRED: You can't! She was born right here in New York State.
EILEEN: You seem to have forgotten something. Did you beg me to marry you or didn't you?
FRED: But I didn't know then—
EILEEN: You seem to have forgotten that I was engaged to another man, and that you took me away from him. What about that?
FRED: I can't help it.
EILEEN: But that isn't the main thing. I love you, Freddy. You made me love you. I didn't at first, but you made me. And now you want to leave me.
FRED: But you don't want me to marry you, if I feel that way—
EILEEN: What would you think of a man that made a girl love him, when she was already engaged, and then threw her over? Do you think that would be quite—honorable?
FRED: (*With sudden inspiration.*) Honorable! That's just what I got to be. That's why I can't marry you.
EILEEN: That little kid? (*A gesture.*)
FRED: Yes!
EILEEN: You mean you've got her in trouble?
FRED: Yes! That's it!
EILEEN: I don't believe you. I'm going to call her back.
FRED: (*Stopping her.*) No, no, no! You mustn't tell her that.
EILEEN: Why not?
FRED: I—I want to surprise her.
EILEEN: (*Calm again.*) Did you think I was going to fall for any story like that? (*Fred turns away.*) I'm the one you're engaged to, and I'm the one you're going to marry.

PAUL: (*Enters.*) Not interrupting, am I?
EILEEN: (*Slowly, and narrowly observing Fred.*) No, I was just going. (*With great deliberation.*) We understand each other, don't we? (*She watches Fred; gets no response; exits.*)
PAUL: What's the matter?
FRED: (*Dully.*) Huh?
PAUL: You haven't had a fight, have you?
FRED: (*Shakes his head.*) There ain't anything the matter.
PAUL: I—I thought maybe we might get after one of those numbers.
FRED: I don't feel much like working.
PAUL: I'm sorry if—anything's happened.
FRED: It ain't nothing. I'll be all right soon.
PAUL: The only thing is—there isn't much time left if we're going to finish before you go. Here it is Tuesday.
FRED: How about starting in early tomorrow morning?
PAUL: What are you doing this afternoon?
FRED: I got to go to the French passport place.
PAUL: I thought you went there yesterday.
FRED: I couldn't. I told you I went with Eileen while she was shopping.
PAUL: Oh, yah! Four hundred dollars!
FRED: She certainly knows how to spend.
PAUL: (*After a second's thought.*) You must have had a swell time running around with two women all yesterday afternoon.
FRED: No, I wasn't. What two women?
PAUL: Her and Lucille.
FRED: Lucille wasn't along. Just I and Eileen.
PAUL: Yesterday?
FRED: (*Nods.*) We was together from one till five-thirty. (*Paul turns thoughtfully away.*) Why?
PAUL: Nothing, only—was it yesterday she spent the four hundred?
FRED: It was three hundred and eighty-seven.
PAUL: That's funny.
FRED: What's the matter?
PAUL: I don't know. I guess I got things kind of mixed up.
FRED: What things?
PAUL: Didn't Lucille ever meet you, during the afternoon?
FRED: No. Why? (*Eileen and Lucille enter.*)
LUCILLE: We're going out to lunch. Want to come along?
PAUL: I want to talk to you.
LUCILLE: What?
PAUL: I said I want to talk to you.
LUCILLE: What about?
EILEEN: (*Catching a note of something in Paul's manner.*) What's the matter with him? (*Stepping closer to Lucille.*)
PAUL: Where were you yesterday afternoon?
LUCILLE: (*Trying to do some quick thinking.*) I was—out.
PAUL: (*Quiet, but terrifying.*) I said, where were you?

LUCILLE: Do I have to report all my movements?
PAUL: You do when I catch you lying. Where were you?
LUCILLE: I had an engagement. It was—with an old friend of mine, and I thought you might not want me to do it, and so I told you I was with Eileen.
FRED: *(Beginning to understand.)* Oh!
LUCILLE: I know it was foolish of me. I was going to tell you later.
EILEEN: She was going to tell you tonight. She told me so.
LUCILLE: *(More to Eileen than to Fred.)* Yah!
PAUL: Yah? *(After another terrible pause.)* Where'd you get that dress?
LUCILLE: What? I bought it.
EILEEN: I treated her to it, if you want to know.
PAUL: Is that so? That isn't what you told me.
LUCILLE: I was afraid you wouldn't let me take it.
PAUL: Where'd you go, yesterday afternoon? With this fellow?
LUCILLE: We went to a matinee.
PAUL: On a Monday?
LUCILLE: It was at the Palace. We went to the Palace.
PAUL: *(Taking plenty of time.)* Who was there?
LUCILLE: What?
PAUL: On the bill. Who were the headliners?
LUCILLE: I don't see what difference that makes.
PAUL: You—dirty—lying—double-crosser!
EILEEN: That's not true!
LUCILLE: *(Stopping Eileen.)* Keep still! *(She faces Paul.)* I'm sick of the whole thing. *(A pause.)* Yes! *(Pause.)* Yes, if you want to know. *(Another pause.)* Yes, and to hell with you. Did you think I was going to wait around forever for you to give me the things I wanted? God knows I waited long enough! And then—I just didn't wait any longer. That's all. What do you know about that? Huh? What do you know about that? *(Paul is stunned. Turns slowly away.)* So—that's the way that stands! *(She turns. Eileen goes to her, puts arm around her. Maxie enters.)*
FRED: But—but you mean to say that when you were married to *him*— *(He takes a moment, trying to realize it. Then to Eileen.)* But you must have known she was doing it.
EILEEN: What? Why—no, I didn't.
FRED: Yes. You said you bought her the dress.
PAUL: *(A scornful laugh.)* Hah! Known she was doing it! She put her up to it!
EILEEN: That's not true.

(Simultaneous.)	PAUL: No? Well, then, I'll tell you something that is true. EILEEN: Don't you believe him, Fred. PAUL: And thank God I've got courage to tell you at last. EILEEN: He's just a liar, that's what he is! I tell you he's a liar!

FRED: Why, what is it?

PAUL: You didn't know your fiancee had a lover, did you?
FRED: What?
EILEEN: I tell you it's a lie. He's just trying to separate us.
PAUL: Am I?
EILEEN: Don't you believe him, Fred—he's just making it up.
PAUL: She told you she was engaged to be married. Well, she wasn't. He was her lover, and he kicked her out, and that's why she took up with you. I'd have told you long ago if I hadn't been a coward.
FRED: (*Staggered, turns to Eileen.*) Is this true?
EILEEN: (*In final realization that the game is up.*) Of course it is, you little fool.
FRED: (*Paul sinks into chair.*) Gosh!
EILEEN: That's probably a pretty big shock to those fine upstate morals of yours.
FRED: Then I been going around all this time with a—bad woman? (*Edna enters.*)
EILEEN: And now have we both got permission to go, or does somebody else want to speak? (*Spotting Edna.*) Maybe your little girl friend would like to say a few words?
FRED: If she does, she'll say them to me. And I'll know I can believe them, too.
EILEEN: I'm sure you'll understand each other. And what's more, you are probably the only two people in the world that would. Come on, Lucille. I want to come and visit that child of yours next month. (*Lucille and Eileen exit. Paul has dropped into a chair, his head buried in his hands.*)
FRED: (*Turning to where Edna and Maxie stand.*) Eddie, I—I don't have to marry her.
EDNA: I'm so happy, Fred.
FRED: I'm sorry, Paul, about—everything.
PAUL: (*Rises, crosses to door.*) That's all right. I'm glad if I helped to fix things for you. I should have told you long ago. (*Exits.*)
FRED: Only look! I've still got the ticket for the boat, and it says "Frederick M. Stevens and Wife." I wonder if the steamship people allow you to change your wife?
MAXIE: Yes. If you don't do it in midstream.
EDNA: If your wife is the right kind she won't let you take her on an expensive trip. She'll make you put everything into a home. I don't mean a big home—just a little bungalow would do.
FRED: Bungalow! A bungalow for two! That'd be a great title!
MAXIE: And I've got a great tune! (*Maxie plays; starts "Button Up Your Overcoat." After the first phrase sings "In a Bungalow For Two."*)
FRED: Say, that's great.
MAXIE: I thought you'd like it.

END

BRAVO!

Edna Ferber
&
George S. Kaufman

[1948]

Bravo was first produced at the Lyceum Theatre, New York, on November 9th, 1948, with the following cast:

Vilna Prager	*Janet Fox*
Rudy	*Oliver Cliff*
Martin Link	*Edgar Stehli*
Zoltan Lazko	*Oscar Homolka*
Rosa Rucker	*Lili Darvas*
Lew Gilbert	*Arthur Havel*
Jimmy Flint	*Morton Havel*
Kurt Heger	*Kevin McCarthy*
Stephanie	*Zolya Talma*
Anna Zinsser	*Elena Karam*
Lisa Kemper	*Christiana Garutoff*
Jeffrey Crandall	*Frank Conroy*
Sophie Marelle	*Fritzi Scheff*
A Man from Downtown	*King Calder*
Another Man from Downtown	*George Cotton*
Jane Velvet	*Jean Carson*

Staged by George S. Kaufman

THE SCENES

The scene is an old brownstone house in the West Sixties, New York.

ACT I
December.

ACT II
February.

ACT III
April.

ACT I

SCENE: *An old brownstone house in New York's West Side. Once handsome, it has fallen into shabby estate. Remnants of its past day still remain—the chandelier, the fine windows, the wainscoting. The furniture is a bit from here and there. A battered white-and-gold grand piano. The whole has the effect of comfortable decay.*

TIME: *It is the end of a late winter afternoon.*

AT RISE: *Vilna Prager, a girl in her twenties, arresting-looking in a sulky way, is perched on the piano bench, manicuring her nails. She is wearing a somewhat haphazard costume of slacks, mules, jersey shirt. She has her tray of implements easily within reach on the piano top. Rudy is coming downstairs, carrying mop and pail. Crosses to kitchen. Immediately there is heard a peremptory masculine voice shouting from upstairs: it is the voice of Zoltan Lazko.*

ZOLTAN: Kaffee! Kaffee! Wo ist meinen kaffee! Ich will meinen kaffee haben! Fast funf uhr und noch kein kaffee! Du weist ganz genau dass ich um funf uhr meinen kaffee haben muss! Verdammt, was ist denn! (*A rather rakish man of thirty-five enters—or at least as rakish as a man can be who is in his shirt-sleeves and is wearing a kitchen apron. His name is Rudy.*)
RUDY: (*As he enters.*) English! English!
ZOLTAN: Auch recht—English! Coffee! I want my afternoon coffee!
VILNA: The way he shouts orders around here you'd think he was somebody.
RUDY: He is.
VILNA: He was.
RUDY: I don't know why they let you stay here. Lying in bed until the middle of the afternoon. Why don't you go out and get yourself a job? (*Martin Link comes in from kitchen carrying, on a tray of metal, freshly made candy, which he places on table. He is a short, distinguished looking man of about sixty. A gray*

mustache, an old-fashioned high cut vest, a figure of shabby elegance.)
MARTIN: Anybody like a piece of candy? It is, I am afraid, not quite cool yet.
VILNA: (*A disdainful glance at it.*) I wouldn't spoil my figure with that stuff.
MARTIN: They are better than they look. I think I know why the other ones they would not buy. Here in this country they like in a piece of candy a full meal. Nuts, cherries, maple sugar, caramel. Here it must be munchy, crunchy, bunchy, lunchy—
RUDY: Zoltan! Coffee! (*To Martin.*) Those messes of yours are all over the kitchen. I hardly have room to— (*Again calls upstairs.*) It will get cold!
MARTIN: Afternoon coffee is very important, but with candy I earn a living. (*He sits, picks up law book.*)
RUDY: (*Pouring himself a cup of coffee.*) You're supposed to have your stuff out of the kitchen by four o'clock. That's our agreement.
MARTIN: (*Becoming suddenly judicial.*) What's an agreement? A covenant or treaty duly executed, and therefore legally binding. Was such an agreement duly executed? *Res ipse loquitur.*
RUDY: *Flagrante delictu* to you, Your Honor. You're not a high judge in Vienna anymore, remember. You're a candy peddler.
MARTIN: (*Sardonically.*) Four years at Heidelberg, four years at the University of Vienna, graduate of the University of Prague—all to learn how to make cocoanut opera creams. A career.
VILNA: I've tasted them. You should have gone to the Sorbonne, too.
RUDY: (*Turns on Vilna.*) You're always fooling around with those nails of yours—sawing and smearing.
VILNA: They break off.
RUDY: Not from housework.
VILNA: I'm not strong. You know that. I have not been able to dance all winter.
RUDY: You can't dance sitting down.
VILNA: And now when that girl comes I must climb up four stairs, not three only. A servant room it must have been.
MARTIN: My dear child, all of us in this house would prefer to live at the Ritz.
VILNA: Don't you worry, I'll be living there yet. (*She stops as Zoltan Lazko, an imposing figure in a shabby, once splendid, dressing gown, descends the stairs. A man of about fifty, his dark hair strongly streaked with white, a well trained monocle, the air of one who is accustomed to being looked at and listened to. He is smoking a cigarette in an impressive holder. Under his arm is a worn, tooled manuscript case.*)
ZOLTAN: (*Consulting his watch.*) Half-past four in the afternoon. (*A peremptory gesture that waves Vilna off the piano stool.*) Geh weg! (*Vilna scurries away.*) Half-past four in the old days! That was a thing to look forward to. (*Slaps the manuscript in his hand.*) A time of refreshment! A time of exhilaration! The car rolls up to the coffee house. I enter like royalty. The doorman—the vestiaire—the Maitre d'hotel! (*He makes a deep bow by way of illustration.*) The orchestra starts up my favorite waltz. As I make my way through the tables a hundred hands reaches out for mine. Lazko! Lazko! The new play! Superb! The prettiest in the room smiles up at me! (*Vilna, assuming the role, smiles up at him. Zoltan dismisses her attempt with a wave of the hand.*) My favorite table

awaits me. Cafe Melange. Sacher torte. (*Peers at the cake on the table. Repeats, doubtfully.*) Sacher torte. (*Looks at it with dislike.*) From Schrafft's. (*Drops it back on the plate. He picks up his glass of coffee.*) Where is the cream? The whipped cream!
RUDY: We haven't had any for six months.
VILNA: Cream costs money.
ZOLTAN: In my country the mountains were *capped* with whipped cream! (*The telephone rings.*)
MARTIN: (*Answers phone.*) Yes! . . . Gilbert Flint . . . Gilbert *and* Flint . . . Wait a minute. (*With a shrug that says, "I don't know who it is," he hands the receiver to Zoltan.*)
ZOLTAN: (*Takes phone. To whom the phone is nothing to be taken lightly.*) Here is Zoltan Lazko! (*He winces slightly as a torrent of nasal talk comes over the wire.*) Who is talking to me? (*A fresh torrent.*) I am sorry, it is for me difficult to telephone. Write me please a letter. I will say good-bye. (*He hands Martin the phone, who puts it back on the piano.*) About one of my old plays something. Not a word did I understand. (*Martin sits, picks up law book.*)
RUDY: You ought to get out and around more. Improve your English.
VILNA: At home in Poland I always had an English governess.
RUDY: Of course I was educated in England.
ZOLTAN: English! When I was in Paris I spoke of course French. In Budapest, naturally Hungarian. (*He sits at piano.*) Vienna! Of course! (*He plays a Viennese waltz.*) But here I am like a little boy. Before the war, a man who every mot he utters is the next day repeated on the boulevard, I come here to America and what is my conversation? "Where is the pen of my uncle's wife's cousin who is in the garden?" Phooey! (*He slams his hand on the piano keys.*) In those days what did I need with English? They came to me. (*He plays through the following.*) My plays were translated in every language.
MARTIN: (*Still sitting.*) I happened to be in Paris the night *Toujours* opened. You would think a Judge of the Oberste Gerichsthof would have a choice seat. (*A gesture.*) I was lucky to be up there. (*Zoltan stops playing.*)
ZOLTAN: That was a night, eh! (*Embellishes the picture for Rudy's benefit. He rises.*) When I came before the curtain the audience went wild. They stood in the aisles. Bravo! Bravo! The women stripped off their bracelets and threw them at me.
RUDY: You haven't got one on you, have you?
MARTIN: It is not possible, perhaps, a few of the bracelets were intended for Rosa?
ZOLTAN: Rosa! What an actress. Tragedy, comedy, anything. Rudy, you were at the Schloss that summer in Salzburg. (*Turns to Martin.*) We put on, just among ourselves, for fun, a production of Tolstoi's *War and Peace*. I dramatized it. But Kolossal! Eh, Rudy?
RUDY: (*Dryly.*) Five hours.
ZOLTAN: It was that last summer. Forty-fifty guests—Rachmaninoff—Churchill—Picasso—
VILNA: I could tell stories, too. When I was in the Royal Ballet—
RUDY: We know, we know.
VILNA: You know, you know! *Vy paskudno psy!*

RUDY: (*The classic gesture of contempt that always accompanies this bit of vituperation.*) Ah, tu me barbe!
VILNA: They are well rid of you in your filthy little country.
RUDY: (*Rises.*) Polsky! Barbarian!
MARTIN: (*Takes candy.*) You two! You two! Always quarreling. (*Exits.*)
ZOLTAN: Quiet! (*The slam of the door.*) Ich muss quiet haben! (*He sits. Rosa Rucker comes in from the hall. She is in street clothes. A zestful high spirited woman, not the beauty she was twenty years ago, but still handsome and even romantic looking in a worn way. A rather ratty coat that was in its prime when Rosa Rucker was. She had dressed up for an audition. The effect is flamboyant, and slightly of another day. She moves swiftly, gracefully, seems to be in two places at the same time. In one arm is a huge string bag from whose top protrude carrots, lettuce, a loaf of bread. In the other hand she carries a small paper bag. Her hat is slightly askew, she looks cold and nipped and weary, but still vital.*)
ROSA: (*Crossing to Rudy, gives him string bag.*) Rudy, the schnitzel is for tonight, it's too late for the goulash.
ZOLTAN: Rosa! (*Rudy exits.*)
ROSA: (*Gives Zoltan small bag.*) Zoltan, something you love! Black cherries!
VILNA: Black cherries in winter! You must have got the job!
ZOLTAN: You did!
ROSA: (*Throws her arms wide in a gesture of triumph.*) No! (*Rudy re-enters.*) Not only did I not get the job, but I now believe that I have never stood behind the footlights. Rosa Rucker never existed. (*Takes off coat, crosses to hall rack, hangs it up.*)
ZOLTAN: You mean—this canaille—they did not know you!
ROSA: They did not even know I was there. (*She puts an academic question.*) Did you ever visit the Club Schizophrenia—Uptown? Night club at two in the afternoon. Romantic as a dishrag. The boss with the cigar, like a cartoon out of *Simplicissimus*. Twenty girls, each one sixteen, and all in uniform. Mink! Blue minks, blond minks, platina minks. I was at least different. Well, I sang.
ZOLTAN: You sang! But you cannot sing.
ROSA: Nevertheless, I sang! (*Ironically.*) The cigar was talking to another cigar. And the minks were doing this. (*She illustrates with an acrobatic twirl of her leg.*) I finished. I stood. Silence. The man with the cigar turned his head at last to look at me, and he said to me those four hideous words—"Thank you very much."
ZOLTAN: A man of great restraint.
ROSA: Ah, well! One can only try.
RUDY: (*As he passes Vilna, still sitting indolently in the most comfortable chair in the room. Swings legs over arm of chair.*) You're going to wear out your behind. (*Exits to kitchen. He has gone with his coffee cup.*)
ROSA: Yes, Vilna. In this room, general conversation, quarreling and Viennese pastries. Upstairs the finger-nails, toe-nails and bathing.
VILNA: (*Gathering up her manicure implements and tray.*) In that box under the roof I can hardly turn around.
ROSA: Anyhow, it is a roof. And all of us are under it, thank God. Look at Rudy

and Martin—they are in boxes, too. Do they complain?
ZOLTAN: (*Quietly.*) Yes, they do.
ROSA: All right, we all complain. Look, my girl, we are glad to have you here. So long as you are without a home you may stay. But please, be happy once in a while. Not always Lady Macbeth.
VILNA: (*Indicating a little door at one side.*) What about *that* room? Why can't I have that?
ROSA: (*Outraged.*) That room is Mr. Lazko's study!
VILNA: (*Contemptuous.*) Study!
ROSA: (*Controlling herself.*) All right, you are moving to another room, perhaps not quite so pleasant. But this girl who is coming—
VILNA: This girl, this girl! Always Lisa Kemper! *I've* had trouble, too! (*She storms out of the room and up the stairs.*)
ZOLTAN: What a wife for some lucky man!
ROSA: Poor creature.
ZOLTAN: Look, Rosa, I want to read this to you.
ROSA: Well? There's been a telegram? From Lisa?
ZOLTAN: Nothing. But it is early yet.
ROSA: We should have heard by now. The ship is in. One of us should have gone to Boston.
ZOLTAN: A girl who has battled her way from Budapest to Shanghai—she can get from Boston to New York.
ROSA: I am almost afraid to see her. That horrible night in Vienna. A thousand times I have thought of her. Running out of the theatre—all of us—I in my costumes—the ride to the airfield—would we be stopped?—then hoping—hoping until the plane left the ground that Lisa and Friedrich would be there. We should have made her go with us, Zoltan.
ZOLTAN: Rosa. You have tortured yourself all these years. The child would not leave her father.
ROSA: And in the end—poor Friedrich.
ZOLTAN: Poor Friedrich. Only today, as I sat writing, I thought here is a part that only Friedrich should be playing. The Gluckman part. In America there are no actors.
ROSA: How do you know? You never go to the theatre.
ZOLTAN: Ach, here is no temperament, no purple! But Friedrich. Who could handle as he did that scene in *The King's Mistress*—the third act. "Go back to your master and tell him this one word. NO!" I think the greatest play I ever wrote.
ROSA: Showy, but not sound.
ZOLTAN: (*Advances on Rosa in quiet resentment.*) *Where* is it not sound?
ROSA: The woman. I played her months and months, and every time I came to the second act—
ZOLTAN: (*With quiet fury.*) Maria Forstner in *The King's Mistress* ranks with Magda, Nora, Juliet, Ophelia. She is studied in universities—in Prague, Oxford, the Sorbonne, Harvard.
ROSA: (*Standing her ground, even maddeningly sweet.*) But she is not sound.
ZOLTAN: And now, twenty years later, at half-past five in the afternoon, in a house with the plumbing broken in West Sixty-second street, America, you tell

me that she was not sound!
ROSA: One of your greatest faults, Zoltan—
ZOLTAN: *My* greatest faults! Did it ever occur to you, my dear Mrs. Lazko—
ROSA: Who? Since when am I an appendage! Like a middle class housewife! I am Rosa Rucker!
ZOLTAN: Rosa, I meant no harm. After all, you *are* Mrs. Zoltan Lazko.
ROSA: Since when?
ZOLTAN: Sei nicht kindisch, Rosa.
ROSA: Even if I had married you, to the world I would still be Rosa Rucker.
ZOLTAN: We were married in Prague—wasn't it—the year I wrote *Katina*?
ROSA: That was Katy Detman. Why else did you call the play Katina!
ZOLTAN: (*She has a point. He tries again.*) Paris! That spring in Paris. *Long Live the King.*
ROSA: That was Vera the Russian.
ZOLTAN: You mean it, Rosa? We were never married?
ROSA: (*With a shrug.*) There was always a rehearsal—you were writing—I had a costume fitting—with us it does not matter, Zoltan.
ZOLTAN: (*Who has been deep in thought.*) Twenty years almost. This is the longest affair I ever had.
ROSA: Or ever will have, my poor darling.
ZOLTAN: (*With mock formality.*) Mademoiselle Rucker—or, if I may be so bold—Rosa! For a long time now I have admired you from a distance—well, maybe not always a distance. But anyhow, I have a question. Perhaps you can even guess. Rosa, will you marry me?
ROSA: (*The shy miss.*) Herr Lazko, this takes me by surprise. But first I must speak to my guardian.
ZOLTAN: Good. Maybe a little cash comes with you. . . . Now, Rosa, let us sit quietly. I want you to hear this. (*He opens his manuscript. Enter Martin with candy boxes.*)
MARTIN: Now if I only had one of those red carriages with the horses. (*He is talking as he crosses the room into the hall.*) Not only would it be easier, but I could charge three times as much for the candy.
ROSA: Martin, what a lot of boxes! Big business! Will you be back for dinner?
MARTIN: Just the stores in the neighborhood. (*Pointing to the boxes.*) Something new. (*He goes.*)
ROSA: (*Looking after him.*) Candy! For such a man. (*Enter Rudy.*)
RUDY: The stove is kaput again.
ROSA: We'll manage. We always do.
RUDY: And two doctors just went in next door. The old man must be worse again.
ROSA: Oh, no!
ZOLTAN: Last year too he was worse in January. In the spring he is always better.
ROSA: But this time he may not get better. Then what happens to us?
RUDY: Then we are out on the sidewalk with one white-and-gold piano, two dozen plays by Zoltan Lazko, and about sixty-five pounds of peanut butter crunch. (*He turns to go. Gets tray, starts out.*)
ROSA: Rudy! I forgot. The new job—the Automat! How did it go?
RUDY: (*Turns back.*) Success! I am first helper to the man who slides the sand-

wiches into the slots. American cheese, two nickels—tuna fish salad, three nickels—liverwurst and currant jelly, four nickels. Clank! Gulp! The meal is finished.

ROSA: Oh, but it's fun. It's like roulette—you never know what color's coming out.

RUDY: Anyhow, it's a job. What was my education—flirting, skiing, and driving a racing car. (*He is off.*)

ZOLTAN: Everyone is more important than I am. Stoves, doctors, *tuna fish!*

ROSA: (*Stirs coffee.*) All right, Zoltan, I am listening. (*Zoltan, a monument of irate impatience, regards her silently until she feels his gaze upon her, hastily stuffs the paper into her bag and snaps the bag shut.*)

ZOLTAN: Endlich! . . . As you know, they are in the hunting lodge, Rupert has just learned from the lady-in-waiting that Herta has been false to him. Herta, not knowing this, comes in. Now! (*He finds his place in the manuscript, preparatory to reading. He clears his throat, adjusts his monocle.*)

ROSA: (*Gently.*) Zoltan, you know you mean everything to me. I am interested only in your success—and mine.

ZOLTAN: What are you saying?

ROSA: Zoltan, we have nothing. We live in this house from week to week—day to day, almost. Everyone brings in a little, and so, somehow we manage. But you heard what Rudy said. The old man next door is worse. He may die. And if he does then *his* house will come down, and this house, and the whole row. They are only waiting. Where can we go? Rudy, Martin, Stephanie, Kurt—and Anna. I have in my purse perhaps five dollars. And now Lisa is coming. For ten years in Europe she has been running from hole to hole—here she must have security.

ZOLTAN: What dummheit are you talking? In a month—six weeks—my play is finished, Jeffrey produces it, we leave this rat-hole and we live as two great artists are supposed to live.

ROSA: Zoltan, in these past years in America you have written two plays. Jeffrey Crandall produced them beautifully, and I played in them. But you know what happened.

ZOLTAN: (*Hotly.*) Before the war Jeffrey Crandall also produced in New York twenty of my great successes. On my plays he made his reputation.

ROSA: Yes, Zoltan. But a hundred years have gone by in the past ten. And this play you are writing now—forgive me, dear—but hunting lodges and kings and satin and gold braid—they are finished, Zoltan. All over the world they are finished.

ZOLTAN: (*With enormous scorn.*) Finished! My plays, which for thirty years in every civilized country—they are finished!

ROSA: (*With great conviction.*) Yes! This is another world, the old one has been torn up by the roots. All life has changed—do you think the theatre alone has stood still! It is reaching out in every direction—new forms, new ideas!

ZOLTAN: (*A sardonic laugh.*) You mean like that great play that Jeffrey sent us seats for! That you dragged me to! Where they are all living together in a subway washroom, and she is in love with her uncle and he is in love with the turnstile! What was it called again? "Let's Sit on the Third Rail." No, Rosa, no! (*He has walked away from her, seats himself at the piano.*) My world is gaiety and color and romance. It is not finished! It still lives if I make it live! (*He begins spiritedly to play and sing, "Wien, Wien, Nur du Allein" as if in defiance of Rosa.*)

ROSA: "Wien! Wien! Nur du allein!" Vienna, city of your dreams! Nightmares, that's what they were! What did your dream cities do for you? Vienna, Budapest! We had to run for our lives! Reinhardt and Thomas Mann and Einstein . . .

ZOLTAN: Aber! Rosa! . . .

ROSA: *Here* must be your dream now! Here is a new career for you—and you sit mourning over the ashes of the old!

ZOLTAN: *Um Gottes willen*—what do you want of me!

ROSA: I want you to stop hiding from life! Get out into the world and see what it is like. Open your mind. There has been a revolution! You are no longer king! You do not read an American paper, you do not read books, you do not meet people! You do not even leave the house!

ZOLTAN: That is not true. Every day I walk to the corner.

ROSA: Yes. And then, like a frightened child, you run back. Your days are all alike. You get up at noon. You have coffee and coffee and coffee. You come downstairs. More coffee. You have made of this place a small Vienna. You cannot face the world, so you stay in the house.

ZOLTAN: Where am I to go? A strange city, a strange land. It is not like the old days.

ROSA: Haven't I known the old days! Silken dressing rooms and maids and secretaries and Madame-will-not-need-the-car-until-three. But here I am in and out and up and down. Fifth Avenue—Sixth Avenue—Broadway. Subways—buses—battling with agents—trying to see producers—stage—radio—anything.

ZOLTAN: And what has come to you from all this running? Nothing!

ROSA: At least I am alive—I see—I feel. Life here is just as funny and just as tragic and just as rich as it was over there. People are people.

ZOLTAN: Ah! Here is no romance—no color. It is sordid. Dull!

ROSA: And I say it is not! If you are going to write plays you must stop pulling the covers over your head.

ZOLTAN: You tell *me* how to write plays! You are only the actress! I am the playwright! (*The ring of the doorbell. Rosa to door.*) Zoltan Lazko is Zoltan Lazko in any country. I will not starve, and you will not starve, and Lisa will not starve. And I will tell you something else, Madam—

VOICE: We're looking for Mr. Zoltan Lazko.

ANOTHER VOICE: We have an appointment. Gilbert and Flint.

ROSA: Oh, yes. (*Rudy has appeared from the kitchen, seens that the door is being answered, and exits. Rosa precedes two men into the room. The two men look strangely alike, though in coloring and even manner, they are different. Their step is springy, their clothes too tailored, they personify Broadway. Rosa, hesitantly.*) Zoltan, these are—

GILBERT: (*Taking off coat.*) Gilbert and Flint. We had an appointment through the Jackson office. We telephoned.

FLINT: (*Taking off his coat.*) I'm Jimmy Flint, this is my partner, Lew Gilbert. I do the music and he writes the lyrics.

ZOLTAN: Oh, yes. Yes.
GILBERT: Hiya, Mr. Lazko! (*They both hand their coats and hats to Rosa.*)
ROSA: Gentlemen, Rosa Rucker! (*They give her the curtest of nods, intent on their business.*)
GILBERT: Hi!
FLINT: Certainly had a time getting to you, Mr. Lazko. Never see you around. Guess you don't do the hot spots. (*Rosa takes coats and hats—puts them on hall table.*)
GILBERT: You know why we're here. Course we know all about you. And I guess maybe you've heard of us.
FLINT: Two shows on Broadway, kind of hard to get away from us. Ever listen to the Hit Parade?
ZOLTAN: I am sorry—I live a very quiet—
ROSA: Of course! Number one! "Rustle Your Bustle!" Is that yours?
GILBERT: Natch! Who else!
FLINT: Two million copies.
ZOLTAN: (*To himself.*) Natch.
GILBERT: (*To Rosa.*) Anja see *Jamboree* last year? That was ours, too.
ROSA: I'm afraid I—
GILBERT: You didn't! It's in Chicago now. Did forty-two last week with Chi spotty.
ZOLTAN: Chi spotty. I am sorry—my English is—what does that mean—chi-spotty?
FLINT: Chi. Spotty. Means business is lousy in Chicago. See?
ZOLTAN: Ah, yes. Yes.
ROSA: It is so interesting to hear about your marvelous success. Of course, Mr. Lazko's work in the theatre is so different that we were wondering—
FLINT: Different—nothing! (*Interlaces his fingers.*) Meshes like this.
GILBERT: Here's the dope. You got an old play, *The Mountain Maiden*. Bet you forgot you ever wrote it. Jimmy and I are stuck on it.
FLINT: Make a great musical. You got this dame up on the mountain—Princess Gizzle or something. This guy skins up the side of it to pitch a little woo. Same time this shepherd—he's stuck on the dame too—he gets hep to what's cooking and tries to bollix it up. Remember? Hell, you wrote it!
ZOLTAN: (*Dazed.*) I wrote this!
GILBERT: 'Course the mountain angle—that's old stuff, we'd throw that out. We figger she's a girl up on top of the Empire State Building. She works for this airplane company and the boss is nuts about her. He's the menace.
FLINT: He makes her work late one night—says it's important business—so the two of them are up there alone.
GILBERT: Now, the kid that runs the elevator, he's the love interest.
FLINT: (*Enter Rudy.*) But the heavy has put the elevators on the blink so he can't get up there to save her.
GILBERT: The kid's no fool, he gets into his airplane—and— (*To Rudy.*) Heh, boy! Gimme an ash tray, will you! (*Rudy puts down the plates, picks up an ash tray.*) Shake a leg! (*Rudy courteously proffers the tray.*)
ROSA: (*Deciding to entertain herself.*) Rudy, I think you would be interested to

meet these two gentlemen. Mr.—uh—
GILBERT: Lew Gilbert.
FLINT: Jimmy Flint.
ROSA: (*Very grand.*) Mr. Lew Gilbert and Mr. Jimmy Flint. Gentlemen, His Royal Highness Prince Rudolph Maximilian Hertwig von und zu Schlesingen Hohenburg.
RUDY: (*Clicks his heels, bows with great formality.*) Would the gentlemen care for anything else?
GILBERT: For Chri—you really a prince! (*Rudy bows and leaves.*)
FLINT: Heh, Lew! That's one on you, all right.
GILBERT: Yeah. Now, where were we?
FLINT: The kid gets into his airplane, goes up.
GILBERT: By this time, she's hanging out the window, yelling for help.
FLINT: He zooms right up to the window, scoops her up into the plane—
GILBERT: And they do this big dance number—*Stepping High.*
ZOLTAN: In the airplane!
GILBERT: Don't you love it!
ZOLTAN: But who is steering the plane?
FLINT: Automatic control.
GILBERT: Wait'll you hear it. Kill you. (*He plays a double vamp of a lively number.*)
FLINT: (*Going into the lyric. Very nasal.*)
　We're stepping high,
　Up in the sky,
　Just you and I
　O me, O my!

She says—

　I got a guy
　He's kinda shy,
　But I can try
　To get his eye.

Catch on?
ROSA: (*Mockingly, she does a little improvisation of her own. Singing.*)
　I think that I
　Will say good-bye.
FLINT: Yeh, yeh. Whaddyou say, Mr. Lazko? Cute, eh?
ZOLTAN: (*Still mystified.*) Quite. Quite.
GILBERT: (*Springing up from piano.*) Suppose we get down to cases. You let us make a musical out of your play, we pay you one percent of the gross.
FLINT: It does forty grand, you get four hundred a week.
GILBERT: You don't have to do a thing.
FLINT: Just sit on your can.
ZOLTAN: (*Ponders this bonanza.*) Four hundred a week! You mean dollars!
GILBERT: Sure—dollars.

ZOLTAN: (*There is a tense silence. He looks at Rosa, then, for guidance.*) Rosa!
ROSA: (*Dropping into the security of the Viennese patois for a rapid fire private conversation.*) Zoltan, du wirst doch die Leit' net ernst nehmen. Des kommt doch gar net in Frage!
ZOLTAN: Also bitte mein kind—vier hundert Dollar in der Wochen! Du sagst mir doch, mirmis sen des Geld hab'n!
ROSA: Du bist wohl net ganz beinand! Mit solche Schlieferln wirst du di einlassen!
ZOLTAN: Also ein' Moment sagst mir so und im nachsten Moment grad des Gegenteil.
GILBERT: Heh, let us in on this. We don't speak French.
ROSA: (*To Zoltan.*) Before I would let you do such a thing I would go out and work as a cook. At least it would be honest cooking. A man like you cannot degrade himself in this way.
FLINT: Degrade! Wait a minute!
ROSA: I am sorry. Your work is, of course, your own affair. But Mr. Lazko is not interested in your offer.
FLINT: Well, pardon me, but who are you? Can't he talk for himself?
ZOLTAN: You are quite right! I speak for myself. I regret that I must decline.
GILBERT: But we're offering you dough!
ROSA: Thank you, but Mr. Lazko is very busy with his new play. It is about to be produced. You are gentlemen of the theatre, you understand.
FLINT: (*A contemptuous look around the room.*) Well, if you don't need it, you don't need it.
GILBERT: See you around. (*The two stare at each other a moment, Flint shrugs his shoulders. "I give up." They exit singing "Stepping High." Slowly Zoltan and Rosa turn and face each other.*)
ZOLTAN: I only did not want you to worry so. It was for you I wanted to do it.
ROSA: (*A tender smile comes to brighten her face.*) You are a very charming man, Zoltan. If I ever marry *anyone*—
ZOLTAN: Tomorrow morning we will be married. We will go down to the place—it takes here three or four days, but we will be married.
ROSA: All right, Zoltan—married. (*Gently she kisses him.*) But now I must cook the Wiener Schnitzel.
ZOLTAN: (*Looking down at his dressing gown, which he evidently intends to change.*) I come out in a minute and shell the potatoes.

(*Enter Vilna. He goes into his study as Rosa disappears into the kitchen. Vilna descends the stairs. She has changed to a bright and becoming blouse and skirt, her hair has been freshly done, she is wearing smart pumps. She carries a lurid paperbound book. She glances quickly around the room, then goes to the window, peers out searchingly. Disappointed, she seats herself, opens the book. Rudy, coming in from the rear of the house, brings cutlery for the table.*)

RUDY: He's late tonight. If you're not careful you could set the table. (*He throws the cutlery on the table. Goes. Vilna half-heartedly places a few pieces of cutlery, but as soon as Rudy is gone she gives up the pretense and darts again to the window. Now her vigil seems to be rewarded. She skips back to her chair, is absorbed in her book. The sound of the front door opening. A moment later Kurt Heger stands in the doorway. A somewhat haggard but arresting-looking man of about thirty, thin, very alert, quick. He is wearing a rather shabby leather windbreaker. A taxi driver's cap is on his head, pushed back a bit. His shield is on his lapel. He brings an evening paper which later he tosses on a chair. He steps into the room rather eagerly, brightly whistling a tune of the moment. The whistle stops abruptly at the sight of the waiting Vilna.)*

VILNA: *(Speaking in a low voice, intense and urgent.)* Kurt! You must take me away from here. Tonight.

KURT: *(Sighting a crisp roll on the dinner table, goes toward it.)* Sure. Palm Beach or Nassau?

VILNA: I cannot stand it any longer. They torture me!

KURT: What are they using? Hot irons? *(Buttering a roll with considerable relish.)*

VILNA: Funny! Funny! I tell you they hate me! They make of me a drudge with the housework—if I sit down even a minute they—do you know what they have done to me now!—I am driven out of my room for this girl—I must sleep in a— *(She can no longer endure the sight of Kurt calmly munching his roll.)* Stop eating when I talk to you! *(She slaps him smartly across the face.)*

KURT: *(Goes on eating, unruffled.)* Watch your head, lady.

VILNA: I wish to God I had died that night. Why did you ever drag me out of that river?

ZOLTAN: *(He is on his way to the kitchen. His dressing gown has been discarded for a short house-jacket. As he crosses the room.)* A very good question!

VILNA: *Each do diabwe!* [Go to the devil!]

KURT: *(Very quietly.)* Look here, my gal. Just because I fished you out of the river doesn't mean I have to wet-nurse you the rest of your life. Just say the word, I'll drive you down to the foot of Seventy-ninth Street, drop you in again.

VILNA: In the beginning you seemed to like me, you liked to be with me.

KURT: Now wait a minute! I took you to a movie now and then. I'd come home, you'd be draped over a chair feeling sorry for yourself, so I'd take you to a movie.

VILNA: You brought me here! You brought me to this miserable house, full of hateful people.

KURT: Where did you want to go? The police station? Sure I brought you here, got my taxi all wet doing it, and you've been here ever since. Two months now. What you need is either a kick in the pants or a good psychiatrist, and a psychiatrist's too expensive. So where does that leave us?

VILNA: I warn you, whatever happens to me, it will be your fault! *(She runs out of the room and up the stairs. Kurt, with a sigh, and a shrug, goes back to the table and another roll. Enter Rudy.)*

RUDY: Don't fill up on bread. We've got a good dinner.

KURT: I'll eat it. Taxi drivers eat all the time. Don't you know that?

RUDY: I think I'll try that racket some time—driving a cab. Out in the open air, girlies hopping in and out all day, cab full of Chanel Number Five.

KURT: Oh, it's a dreamy job. "Driver, turn here, catch the light on Madison, turn again and catch it on Fifth." You listen to everybody's troubles—their wives and their kids and their business. . . . For a fifteen-cent tip you're supposed to be Siegmund Freud. (*As he talks he drifts over to a small table by the doorway, on which the day's mail is always placed. Giving it a quick glance, he picks up a bulky envelope.*) Well, I might as well open it. (*The sound of the front door closing, and a woman, alert, well-dressed, fortyish, comes briskly along the hallway. Her name is Stephanie.*)

STEPHANIE: Anything for me?

KURT: Couple. Sweden. Switzerland.

STEPHANIE: Thanks. (*She goes up the stairs—exits.*)

KURT: (*Having opened envelope, MS. in hand.*) "Yellow Cab," by Kurt Heger. (*His eye slides over the accompanying letter.*) "Absolutely magnificent . . . strength of Hemingway . . . brilliant dialogue . . ."

RUDY: Say! Congratulations!

KURT: No. Here it is. Must have been too good. (*Throws script on table.*) My father always said I'd never be a writer. Don't embroider, he used to tell me. No fancy work.

RUDY: Old Eckstein at Heidelberg used to worship your father. Made us read every editorial he ever wrote.

KURT: He was a wonderful man, all right. *Ein grosser mensch.* I'll never measure up to him.

RUDY: Sure you will. You're trying to do too much. Driving that hack all day, going to those college courses at night.

KURT: I've got time to spare now. (*Rudy stops.*) They just gave me a vacation—without pay.

RUDY: You got fired?

KURT: I pull into the garage at four, and I show twenty-two dollars on the clock. Ten hour day—you're supposed to clock twenty-five, but you don't always get the breaks. So the checker says— (*With a gesture of his thumb he indicates that he is on the carpet.*) and I go in. The boss is sitting there behind the desk. And then he starts in, smooth as oil. "Tell me," he says, "how was the movie?" I say, "What movie, boss?" That's what you're supposed to call him—boss. And he says, "The movie that you saw this afternoon." I say, "I didn't see any movie, boss!" "Oh! Maybe you're not feeling well." "I feel fine, boss." "Maybe you're tired. Haven't got the old pep." "I got plenty of pep, boss." "How's about going away for a week, couple weeks in the country. Get your strength back." You get called in twice, and the third time you're out. (*A snap of the fingers to indicate the finality of his exit.*)

RUDY: Why don't you get out and stay out? If you're a writer, why don't you write?

KURT: Even a writer has to eat. Besides, it's fun. You meet all the kinds of people there are, and they do the damnedest things. And have I learned a lot! (*He goes up the stairs. Zoltan comes in from kitchen, bringing with him a great pan of potatoes and a paring knife. He is wearing a kitchen apron.*)

RUDY: (*Surveying this odd sight.*) Not the great Lazko?

ZOLTAN: (*Seats himself.*) The pen has not been lately so mighty with me, I thought I would try the sword. (*And by way of illustration he digs the paring knife into the first potato. Rudy is gone by this time, and Zoltan sets to work in earnest.*

His method would make any housewife shudder—it is really amateur butchery. What started out to be a large potato is found to be so full of imperfections that it is gradually reduced to a marble. There is the sound of the outer door, and Anna Zinsser enters. Her clothes are plain and almost frumpy, but her face is one of rare dignity and intelligence. She is perhaps thirty-five or forty.)

ANNA: Zoltan, hello!

ZOLTAN: Anna, my girl!

ANNA: *(Regarding his struggles with the paring knife.)* At the finish, Zoltan, the potato should be bigger than the peeling. *(Takes off hat.)*

ZOLTAN: *(As Anna merely smoothes her hair with the palms of her hands, carelessly.)* Anna, of all the women I have ever known, only you take off your hat without once looking in the mirror.

ANNA: *(She has taken the knife and potato from Zoltan's hands and is expertly paring as she stands.)* I see so many strange things in the microscope all day, I do not care to see another one at night.

ZOLTAN: Tell me, Anna, what miracle did they make in the laboratory today? A machine, maybe, that makes a round trip to the moon every hour, builds a house in twenty minutes with dinner waiting on the table, and can also be used as a nail file? Huh?

ANNA: *(Grimly humorous.)* And destroys continents, of course.

ZOLTAN: Anna, you have a rare scientific mind. You are a great woman, in your field a genius. The stove is kaput again; they are waiting for you to fix it.

ANNA: *(Picks up the pan of potatoes as she starts to go.)* Ah, that is *really* important.

ZOLTAN: Anna. *(She pauses.)* It goes better? The work? I mean, naturally, by now they realize what you can give—a woman who stood as you did in Europe.

ANNA: *(Simply.)* So far, the things that I do, I could be a school girl in a chemistry class. But at night sometimes I can stay alone in the laboratory. *(A light comes into her face.)* Then I work!

ZOLTAN: Three, four o'clock in the morning you have been coming in. We thought, hello! *Amour* has come to Anna.

ANNA: It is not a bad union—science and *amour*. With Mme. Curie it brought forth radium.

ZOLTAN: *(Mischievously.)* And Eve Curie. *(A little laugh. She is gone. As Zoltan turns away Martin is seen peering cautiously into the living-room.)* Martin! Already back! They liked it, eh?

MARTIN: *(Finding that only Zoltan is present, he advances a few steps into the room, a dejected figure. He is carrying the bundle of candy boxes, untouched.)* The neighborhood stores, people buy a newspaper, a five-cent candy bar. Tomorrow, I will go more downtown. *(Rather shamefacedly he conceals the stack of boxes in a corner behind the piano.)*

ZOLTAN: Martin. *(Martin slowly turns toward him.)* I have been thinking. Why can you not, in this country, use something of your great legal knowledge? Even if it is only a clerk in a lawyer's office. But something.

MARTIN: Mm . . . a doctor, yes. Lungs are lungs, a heart is a heart, the world over. But a lawyer, here I would have to start school from the very beginning. And next week I will be sixty-five.

RUDY: (*Comes in from the kitchen regions carrying a tray of wine glasses and a bottle of red wine. He is humming a familiar radio wine-selling jingle.*) Just the other day—I heard a lady say—te tum-ta-ta-ta-tum, ta-dee da da da dum. (*Exits. Zoltan strolls over to the piano, his fingers drift over the keys. Stephanie comes swiftly down the stairs and into the room. She is wearing a simple smart dress. A brilliant silk scarf hangs over her arm. She carries a sewing bag.*)

STEPHANIE: Where's Rosa? Is Rosa in the kitchen? Rosa, can I help with the dinner?

ROSA: (*Comes in from the kitchen.*) No, no. I've just put the vegetables on, there's plenty of time. Oh, Stephanie, what a smart frock!

STEPHANIE: I couldn't resist it. I snatched it right off the rack first thing this morning, before the customers came in. Of course we're not supposed to. (*Folds the scarf about Rosa's neck.*) And this I bought for you.

ROSA: Stephanie, how lovely! But so extravagant.

STEPHANIE: It's the winter sales. And with the employes' discount, it's nothing. (*Sinks into a chair.*) I'm dead. On my feet all day trying to tell sixteens they can't wear fourteens without wounding their vanity.

ROSA: From Koniglich-Hapsburg to Bergdorf-Goodman—it's quite a trip, Stephanie.

STEPHANIE: (*Nods.*) They used to come in to stare at the fallen Arch-Duchess, but now they look at the price tag.

ANNA: (*Entering from the kitchen, a glass of milk in her hand.*) The pilot light was out. You could all have been asphyxiated.

MARTIN: (*Quietly.*) Not a bad idea.

STEPHANIE: (*Fishes a bit of silken needlework out of her bag as Anna settles herself in a corner with a book.*) Yes, Arch-Duchesses are a dime a dozen these days. And a king's ransom is fifteen cents, two for a quarter. (*Enter Rudy.*)

ANNA: (*Glancing up from her book.*) What does it matter! We are all the same. Every human being is ninety-six percent water.

ZOLTAN: Not Lazko! Liebfraumilch and champagne, perhaps. But not water. Water is for washing.

STEPHANIE: I want to ask you all something. Would you think it mad of me if I were to open my own *maison de couture*? A dressmaking Duchess carries a certain cachet. All you need is enough gall.

RUDY: And a bankroll.

STEPHANIE: Funny—how things link up. When I was a little girl I had a governess, her name was Gromchen. And I hated her because she made me learn to sew. I used to kick and scream and threaten to have her head cut off when I grew up. But she made me sew. (*A little sigh of recollection.*) And it's kept me alive.

ROSA: Zoltan, we sit here—what has happened to Lisa? Why hasn't she telephoned?

ZOLTAN: You still think she is a child. Ten years have gone by. She is a grown woman. Surely she can take care of herself. But now she is not ill, she has been a year in London, you—

ROSA: She has been ill, she has been through hell, strong men have been destroyed by less. (*She sits.*)

(*Their mounting voices are cut off by a sharp voice from the stairs, almost a command. It is Kurt dashing down the stairs, and firing questions as he descends. He has shed the taxi driver's habiliments, has done a quick job of washing and shaving, looks surprisingly young and fresh.*)

KURT: (*Very peremptory.*) Rosa! Who was the first president of the United States?
ROSA: Mr. Washington!
KURT: Zoltan! Who wrote the Declaration of Independence?
ZOLTAN: James Jefferson.
ROSA: Thomas!
ZOLTAN: (*Quickly.*) Thomas!
KURT: Rosa, what was the cause of the Civil War?
ROSA: Wait a minute—uh—Liza and the bloodhounds— (*She is now on the right track.*) yes—and Abraham Lincoln and then that man Wilkes Booth— Imagine an actor doing a thing like that!
KURT: Close enough. You'll pass.
ZOLTAN: If only the judge asks us the right questions? *Thomas* Jefferson. *James* Mendelssohn.
ROSA: Madison.
ZOLTAN: Madison.
KURT: (*His inquisition ended, has picked up his newspaper and is sprawled in a chair.*) Seems to be some history going on in Europe, too.
ROSA: In Europe the answers are not so easy.
ZOLTAN: (*Peering at paper over Kurt's shoulder.*) We had better start to learn them. Whatever happens in Europe—war or starvation or influenza or what—sooner or later it jumps the ocean and comes here.
KURT: That's a pretty thought. I can't wait.
ZOLTAN: (*Looking more closely at paper.*) Who is Betty Grable? (*He pronounces the name with a short "a."*)
ANNA: (*Correcting him.*) Gra-ble.
ZOLTAN: Grable, Gra-ble. How does such a person make in a year, it stands here, four hundred and eighty-seven thousand, six hundred and twenty-four dollars?
ANNA: She is a cinema actress.
ZOLTAN: Oh, yes . . . But why does she get more money than anybody else?
ROSA: Legs.
ZOLTAN: Oh! Like Mistinguett. But even Mistinguett never— (*He gives up.*) This girl must be a centipede.
STEPHANIE: Something wrong, Martin?
MARTIN: J'ai le cafard.
ZOLTAN: This piano that Jeffrey has loaned us—it must have been used in *The Merry Widow*, nineteen hundred and seven.
RUDY: (*Seated near window, he stretches out a hand to part curtains and peer out.*) Those two doctors haven't come out yet. Their car is still outside.
STEPHANIE: What doctors?
ROSA: The old man next door is worse again, malheureusement.
ANNA: Two doctors!

KURT: I'll be sleeping in my taxi yet.
MARTIN: The house is falling down anyhow. Stove—plumbing—plaster.
STEPHANIE: Rosa, why don't you make him some strong broth—chicken and mutton bone and barley? All simmered together for hours.
KURT: It might be a good investment.
MARTIN: They used to make it at Zanger's—remember? A bowl like this!
ZOLTAN: (*He stops playing.*) Zanger's Am Danube. I had almost forgotten. Old Zanger himself, with his Franz Joseph whiskers; the apfel charlotte, the musicians in their red coats . . . (*He bounces into the "Blue Danube." As he plays he booms out the tune with relish.*)
ROSA: Zoltan! Stop! Vienna waltzes! Strauss, Strauss! Always the past! Why not today! Why not—Gershwin! Besides, old Zanger was a robber, I can make better *apfel charlotee* myself, the musicians played off key, and the Blue Danube is not blue, it is yellow! Yellow as death! (*There is a moment's rather mystified silence. Doorbell rings. At the same time Vilna appears, descending the stairs.*)
VILNA: Aren't we ever going to have dinner?
RUDY: (*To Vilna as he goes to door.*) You've certainly earned it.
STEPHANIE: I must say, Rosa, that was quite a speech.
ANNA: You'll feel better now. Relieves the adrenal gland. (*Zoltan looks transfixed at a new figure, who has come into the archway. The others slowly follow his gaze. The girl who stands in the doorway is Lisa Kemper. She is a lovely and radiant girl who, surprisingly enough, shows no apparent effects of the hazardous and cruel life through which she has passed in the last ten years. Her dress is very plain, even shabby. In one hand is a small battered suitcase. She stands a moment looking at the group, wide-eyed.*)
ROSA: (*With growing emotion.*) Lisa. Lisa, Lisa! Lisa! (*The two women come together in an embrace. Lisa's suitcase drops from her hand.*)
LISA: (*Emerging from Rosa's arms, now turns toward Zoltan.*) Papa Zoltan! (*They embrace.*)
ZOLTAN: We thought, after everything, a little sick kitten—but look! (*He turns to the others in triumph.*)
ROSA: (*Takes her hand.*) This is our Lisa. I will tell you who your new friends are. The Arch-Duchess Stephanie—
LISA: Eurere Kaiserliche Hoheit. (*She drops a low curtsey.*)
STEPHANIE: No, no! Not here! (*Rosa raises her up, tenderly, turns toward the others in further introduction.*)
ROSA: The famous Anna Zinsser . . . Miss Vilna Prager, the—the ballerina. Prince Rudolf of Schlesingen . . . Kurt Heger and Judge Martin Link. To you they are Stephanie and Anna and Martin and Kurt and Vilna and Rudy. And this is our home, Lisa—and your home.
ZOLTAN: Come, child. Take off the coat. You are going to stay a long time. (*Lisa takes off her coat.*)
ROSA: We will send for your trunk. Did you get a trunk check?
LISA: (*A little trill of laughter.*) I have no trunk.
ZOLTAN: Look, Rosa! When she laughs it is Friedrich all over. (*To the others.*) Her father was Friedrich Kemper.
LISA: To think that I am really here!

ROSA: Lisa, you're quite well again? You look so wonderful.
ZOLTAN: In England she has been months in a nursing home. You would not imagine, huh?
VILNA: They said you had been through so much. But then, they always exaggerate.
ROSA: All that is finished, she has put it out of her thoughts—haven't you, Lisa? Here you will be gay and happy and busy among people who love you.
LISA: Yes! Yes! (*Suddenly her hands cover her face, she is sobbing a little silently.*)
ZOLTAN: *Kindchen!*
LISA: No. Pay no attention. I am just so happy to be here. This beautiful house. You must be rich to live in such a house. (*She begins to circle the room, looking all about her. She throws her arms wide as though to embrace the house and all the people in it. As she stands there motionless, face uplifted, Kurt walks swiftly over to her. He has seen a familiar mark. He pushes back the sleeve from her wrist.*)
KURT: (*Very tense and low.*) How long were you there? (*Lisa looks down at her wrist, then up at him. Shakes her head. She does not answer.*)
ROSA: Lisa, you're probably tired. We'll have dinner in half an hour. If you want to go to your room—
LISA: I am not tired! I am not hungry! I am just here! It is all so exciting. Everything is so—I had of course pictured, but—the—the taxicab just now—enormous like a room, and shining, and great red leather, and I am all alone in it, and buildings like mountains, and I can look through the top—
KURT: (*The expert.*) Sky-View.
LISA: Yes, yes, the sky, too. And I look out of the window and every woman has a fur coat. And the train is all silver—and in the restaurant in the train there is everything in the world to eat, and I said to the man, whether to have bread or meat, and he said, Have anything you want, lady—have the whole— (*She reaches for the word.*) works! So I had the works!
KURT: Heh! It's going to be fun to take you around.
LISA: It is all so marvelous, so exciting!
ZOLTAN: *Unglaublich!* Friedrich Kemper all over! I only hope you have inherited some of his talent.
LISA: It has been so long. So far away from me—the theatre. How do I know what I am!
ZOLTAN: (*Half in jest.*) Listen, young lady. From you I expect the name in electric lights. To bring you here I have signed a paper like this— (*Indicating its length.*) the government thinks I have bags full of money in the bank. (*A little sardonic laugh.*) Money! I only hope they do not come for me with handcuffs.
KURT: And you're not kidding!
LISA: Papa Zoltan, if it could be one of your plays! Your wonderful plays! What a triumph you must have had here in America. And Rosa! What are you playing in now? Could I see it tonight?
ROSA: It is not quite the way it was in Europe, Lisa. . . .
LISA: Tell me, is it a play about America?
ZOLTAN: Well, I have been seriously thinking about writing a play about America. I have been for some time now observing the moods, the customs, the American

tempo, the patois—in short, the whole American scene.
KURT: American scene! You think Madison Square Garden is where they grow flowers.
ZOLTAN: Oh, you think I do not know, h'm? I am familiar with bits of the American language which you have never even—for example: *Chi spotty*. You do not know what that means, do you! Well, *I* do. That means business is lousy in Chicago! Natch! (*He strikes a triumphant attitude.*)
ROSA: (*Between amusement and irritation.*) But, Zoltan!
ZOLTAN: You see! I have been until now preparing myself, and now I am ready! I write an American play! A play about America. In the American language. Buses, not schlosses. Gershwin, not Strauss! What did he write, anyhow, Gershwin?—Ach ja! (*He dashes to the piano, plunges into a spirited performance of "Dixie."*)
ROSA: Zoltan! No, no! (*But he pounds on.*)

CURTAIN

ACT II

SCENE: *The living-room is the same. Lisa Kemper is now part of the household.*
TIME: *Two months have passed.*
At rise: Lisa is standing on a footstool in the center of the room. She has lengthened the skirt of the simple black dress she is wearing, and is now up for inspection before Anna Zinsser. In her hand Lisa dangles a filmy diminutive white apron such as waitresses wear. Anna is standing a few feet away, her eye judicial, a tape-measure in her hand.

ANNA: (*Measuring.*) Eleven inches. That ought to satisfy them.
LISA: I'll put the apron on. It takes it up in the waist. (*Ties on the apron.*)
ANNA: (*Standing off to look at her.*) It does make it a bit shorter.
LISA: The woman at the agency—she seemed to think waitresses should have no legs. (*Looks down at her own very satisfactory pair. Vilna comes downstairs. She is popping a last bite of something delectable into her mouth as she walks.*)
VILNA: Oh, that's your uniform! You look charming! It's very becoming to you.
LISA: Thank you. I would exchange it for sables.
VILNA: (*Helps herself to a cigarette from a box on the table.*) I think it's very brave of you, Lisa, serving all those horrible people at their filthy luncheons and dinners. I would rather die.
LISA: I would rather live.
VILNA: (*Carelessly, over her shoulder.*) Chacun a son gout. (*She is gone.*)
ANNA: It *is* brave of you, Lisa. That girl with the stiletto, she does not mean it, but I do. Why do you do this work? You are an actress.
LISA: (*Slowly.*) I am afraid to try. In your work, Anna, everything is so mathematical, so certain. You put something into something else, and you hold it over that little flame, and suddenly, there it is!
ANNA: Not so suddenly. You work your whole life through—days, nights—even to

buy a pair of shoes, it takes too much time, so you wear the old shoes. Finally, what you have done is a great success, it gets the Nobel prize, and you have been dead only twenty years.

LISA: Anna, do you know you are really beautiful? The planes of your cheeks . . . if you would let me just make you up a little it would be an entirely different face.

ANNA: No, no! It is like the shoes. I wear the old one. (*From the stairway comes the sound of Kurt's voice. He is talking as he descends. He is carrying a portable typewriter. Anna, at the sound of his voice, whisks up an empty milk glass and plate that stand nearby and goes to the kitchen.*)

KURT: I'm going to work in the kitchen. The temperature up in my room is exactly two. I just planted a flag and claimed the whole thing for America. (*He is striding across the room—a figure in sweater, muffler and gloves. Suddenly he is aware of Lisa in her service dress.*) I hate that dress!

LISA: You look dazzling!

KURT: I'm working!

LISA: So was I! (*She is nervously playing with the tape-measure in her hand.*)

KURT: That stinking job!

LISA: Taxi driving is chic!

KURT: Don't compare that with your job!

LISA: You don't mind taking tips.

KURT: I do when it's less than a quarter.

LISA: Lovely! You're beginning to talk like them. (*The two stand glaring at each other. Kurt plunks the typewriter down to the table, unwinds the muffler from about his neck, removes the gloves finger by finger, with exaggerated elegance. Then in one quick swoop he takes her in his arms and kisses her very hard. Lisa angrily pushes him away.*) I've told you and told you!

KURT: Tell me again.

LISA: You just must not do this!

KURT: But why! Why! Why!

LISA: Because I love you.

KURT: That's a hell of a reason. (*Vilna enters quietly from the kitchen.*)

LISA: I'm—I'm so mixed up. Kurt, you should understand that. After what you went through over there.

VILNA: Oh! I'm just going up to my room. (*As she goes up the stairs, Lisa stands waiting. Kurt turns away and walks a few steps abstractedly.*)

KURT: All right, it was tough. But that's finished! You've got everything— you're young and beautiful—why, that day you walked into this room—And you were fun! So what happens! You turn on the tragedy and take a job serving soup to nuts.

LISA: What do you want me to do?

KURT: I want you to marry me!

LISA: (*Helplessly.*) Kurt, I'm not trying to be difficult. I just can't make up my mind about anything. Even you. I'm afraid.

KURT: Afraid of what, for God's sake!

LISA: Afraid of everything. That is why I am doing this work. They say to me, do this, and I do it. I pick up the plate, and I put down the other plate. The soup,

the entree, the salad, the dessert. There is no deciding.
KURT: What do you want to do—go on living and avoid life! I'm a very fine type guy. You'd better decide while you can get me. And what about the theatre! You're an actress. Suppose a job comes along. You'll have to decide about *that*, won't you?
LISA: Stop deviling me! I'm doing the best I can. I can only—

(*Rosa and Zoltan are heard at the front door. Their voices are high and gay, there is a snatch of unfinished sentence before they call out to whoever may be in the house.*)

ROSA: (*Off.*) If he had worn a powdered wig. But that shining bald head.
ZOLTAN: (*Off.*) Who is *zu hause!* Martin! Anna! (*In the doorway.*) Ah! Kurt and Lisa! (*Just beside him is Rosa. The two are arresting, though somewhat bizarre figures. Zoltan's cape is thrown over his shoulders. He is wearing a romantic soft black hat with an over-size brim. Rosa's clothes are, as usual, rather flamboyant elegancies salvaged from the old days. She is wearing a small American flag pinned to her coat.*)
KURT: You made it!
ZOLTAN: (*Impressively. He makes a gesture toward Rosa.*) Citizen Rosa Rucker!
LISA: Oh! I congratulate you! (*Anna enters from the kitchen at the sound of their voices.*)
ANNA: Hello! How did it go?
ZOLTAN: With Rosa it went fine. But me—I must go back again next time. Something with my papers, the man said. A comma is missing there, I wrote on the wrong line here—anyhow, I must go back in two more weeks.
ANNA: Oh, Zoltan, how disappointing!
ZOLTAN: It is nothing.
ROSA: That even *I* am a citizen is a miracle. Four hundred people in the courtroom and Zoltan tells the judge what to do.
KURT: Maybe that's why you didn't get your papers.
ZOLTAN: No, no. This was after. But the whole business—never in my life have I seen such a bad production of a good script. The room—but enormous—windows . . . (*With a sweeping gesture.*) to the floor! But no drama—no emotion—nothing! A judge I would not cast for a grocery clerk. Two flags like little handkerchiefs.
ROSA: That is true, Zoltan. But you should not have stood up and told the judge that Max Reinhardt could have done it better.
ZOLTAN: He would have had anyhow some excitement—a band playing. Drama! There we were—all those people—saved from God knows what. We have waited years to be American citizens, and in here is a feeling, we want to cry, we want to shout, and a man says gobble-gobble-gobble—responsibility—gobble-gobble-gobble—you're an American citizen. *Fertig!*
KURT: That's all right. Hitler did the flags and the music—remember.
ROSA: Here you are supposed to feel it yourself, from the inside out. Not because a band plays.
ZOLTAN: All right, all right. Anyhow you are now an American citizen, and you

can vote for President, and have sinus trouble. . . . Where is my coffee? I want my coffee!

ANNA: You drink too much coffee. You should drink milk. It contains all the necessary ingredients to maintain life. It is a whole food. (*Exit Anna.*)

LISA: Oh, Papa Zoltan! I forgot. They telephoned. Mr. Crandall's office telephoned. He's coming to see you.

ZOLTAN: When does he come?

LISA: Soon. Now.

ZOLTAN: Rosa! You hear! Jeffrey is on his way up. Last night only I sent him the play. A producer does not come running unless . . . It must mean he likes it.

ROSA: Let's not jump too fast, Zoltan. We don't know yet.

ZOLTAN: But you heard. He is coming up quick. Did he rush up last time when he read *Spring Carnival*?

ROSA: He was in Sun Valley.

ZOLTAN: He is always somewhere, but if he likes it he gets here.

ROSA: Let's hope.

ZOLTAN: Here you have proof, Rosa. An artist is an artist, I don't care where he is. America or Shangri-la, Zoltan Lazko is still Zoltan Lazko. I have written an American play.

ROSA: (*As she goes toward kitchen door.*) Oh, Lisa! Some of the Dobosche Torte when Mr. Crandall gets here. He loves it. . . . After all, a producer looks out for himself. The playwright is . . . (*Again calling to Lisa.*) It's in the tin box on the second shelf behind the corn flakes . . . because again and again he has . . . (*To Lisa again.*) only it's marked pretzels! . . . Well, maybe it's a good sign. (*She carries her hat into the hall.*)

ZOLTAN: (*A contemplative figure as he leans against table, absorbed in thought. When he sits, he is speaking really to himself.*) Katharine Cornell . . .

ROSA: (*With a dreadful sweetness and calm, emerging from hall.*) What did you say?

ZOLTAN: H'm? Oh, I was—just thinking out loud.

ROSA: *Too* loud.

ZOLTAN: (*An elaborate but unconvincing series of shrugs. Mumbling.*) Where are we! Russia!

ROSA: (*With great calm.*) In what connection are you thinking of Miss Katharine Cornell?

ZOLTAN: Rosa, this is an American play—these people are in a log cabin on the prairie, the woman she is a rancher's wife, she goes out and ropes horses . . .

ROSA: (*Standing her ground.*) If Katharine Cornell can rope horses, *I* can rope horses!

ZOLTAN: Rosa, you are the greatest actor of your day. There is no woman living who can— (*The sound of the outer door. A resplendent Rudy stands in the hallway. He is wearing a camel's hair top coat, a lemon yellow scarf, and as he removes his coat we see a smart tweed jacket and trousers correctly not matched. He strikes the traditional pose of the professional model.*)

ROSA: Rudy! How magnificent!

RUDY: (*Walks impressively over to her.*) Feel it. (*She strokes it.*) Unborn cream puff.

ZOLTAN: Such a thing is anyway a month's salary.
RUDY: Celebrating! Out of the Gent's Wear into the Ski Department. Fifth Floor! Skis and ski-ing accessories! Ski boots, ski jackets, ski pants, ski gloves, ski glasses—and me.
ROSA: You see, my princeling! Something you learned in your misspent youth turns out to be valuable.
RUDY: You wouldn't believe what comes in to buy skis. Stenographers, Bronx housewives, shipping clerks—and who walks in a half an hour after I'm on the job but Jane Velvet.
ZOLTAN: What is that? Jane Velvet?
RUDY: Movie star. Merely one of the top ten. In five minutes she'd bought two thousand dollars' worth of ski junk, in seven minutes she had me out in Sun Valley as ski master, and in ten minutes she dated me for dinner tonight. What is technically known as a fast worker. I'm scared to death.
ROSA: You are really a very attractive fellow, Rudy, but you have an inferiority because you're a prince.
RUDY: (*As he bounds up the stairway.*) All I know is, she's a man eater. If there'd been a leopard skin in the store I wouldn't be here to tell the tale. (*He is off. Lisa comes from the kitchen carrying a tray of kuchen.*)
LISA: The coffee is on the stove. (*Zoltan has seated himself at the piano. He is improvising softly.*)
ZOLTAN: (*Has a sudden idea.*) Rosa, in the second act, where they are sitting around the campfire, and it is moonlight and the chef is serving the—the—chuck from the chuck wagon, maybe it would be nice a western song—*tres doucement*—(*Plays a chord or two and sings a line of the well known song of the cowboy.*) "Git along, little dogie, git along—" (*There is heard the ring of the front doorbell. As Lisa vanishes into the kitchen Rosa turns toward the hall.*)
ROSA: It must be Jeffrey. (*Rosa goes to the door. From the door comes the sound of Rosa's voice and Jeffrey's in gay greeting. Off.*) Jeffrey! Hello! How brown you are!
JEFFREY: (*Off.*) Rosa, my pet! Lovelier than ever! (*Jeffrey Crandall enters. An imposing figure, a bit on the heavy side. He is deeply tanned, rather annoyingly healthy looking.*) Zoltan, my boy! (*The two men embrace Continental fashion.*) You're looking wonderful! Wonderful! (*By this time he has turned away and is headed in the direction of the cake tray.*) Ah! Dobosche Torte! (*As he picks up a piece and takes a huge bite.*) I wish I weren't dieting!
ZOLTAN: At this time of the year it is not hard to tell the playwrights from the producers. The playwrights are white. (*A gesture to indicate a long sallow face.*)
JEFFREY: This? Oh, just a month or so in Palm Springs.
ROSA: I thought it was Palm Beach.
JEFFREY: But all those places—Palm this and Palm that—they're all right, but—in the old days you'd get on a boat—everybody you knew on board—get to London, see all the plays—find out what Noel and Charley Cochran and Gerald were up to. Hop over to Paris and have a look at Guitry. And I always saved the best for last. Budapest and Vienna! You and Rosa. The Schloss and the *cafe melange*, the caviar and the Tzigane music . . .

ROSA: Yes, yes, Jeffrey. But the schloss is now a handful of ashes, and we are in Sixty-second Street, New York. And you have read Zoltan's play and that is the important thing. (*There is a pause. Zoltan is standing with a rather painfully expectant smile.*)

JEFFREY: Oh, yes. I was coming to that. Uh— (*A false start, a slight clearing of the throat.*) uh—the—uh—

ZOLTAN: You do not like it.

JEFFREY: (*Too heartily.*) No, no! I like a lot of it! That scene where the cowgirl comes in and—uh—lots of things. And the whole idea—this thing of your writing a play about America—I think it's great! Great! But this particular play— (*Refreshes his memory with a look at the cover.*) Mustang. I'm afraid you haven't perhaps traveled around enough. You know, the West is another world. The way they talk and everything. (*He pages through the manuscript briefly. His eyes on the manuscript, he mumbles a line to himself and then, aloud, comes up with an example to illustrate his meaning.*) Here. He says to the girl, "I love you, little podner. Your hair is as silky as cactus." (*Zoltan taps Jeffrey gently on the arm, takes the manuscript slowly out of his hand, crosses the room and drops it quietly into the wastebasket.*) Now, now! (*Deeply pained.*) I could be wrong, you know. (*Zoltan looks at him quizzically with a shake of the head.*)

ZOLTAN: You are not talking to a student with his first play. Here is Zoltan Lazko.

ROSA: (*Goes to Zoltan, links her arm through his as she speaks to Jeffrey.*) He kicks and screams if the coffee is not hot, but a real blow he takes like a hero.

JEFFREY: (*Unhappily.*) This was a good try, Zoltan—but if you'd take something you know more about—something nearer home.

ZOLTAN: Nearer home! Let me ask you, Jeffrey, just for example. Something happens to this country—it could be—something terrible. And suddenly you must run for your life. So you go—where? Let us say South America. Here in this country you are a successful business man. You are used to doing things in the American way. Now you find yourself no longer Jeffrey Crandall, the famous producer. You are a stranger, with one suit of clothes and no money, in a foreign country. No one cares whether you live or die. But you must live somehow. You are a producer of plays, that is all you know how to do. You do not know the language, the customs, the methods of business. The food, the tempo, the manners—all are strange to you. How do you begin? You must learn the language, you must read plays in the language, you must find money, a theatre, actors, designers—and everything is not done *your* way—it is their way. So you say to yourself, do not be frightened. But you are frightened. And every day time is passing, and you are a little older. It could happen, Jeffrey, even to you. It could happen today to any man.

JEFFREY: (*Coughs, rather uncomfortably.*) Well—yes—let's hope not. . . . Listen, darlings, I'm with you. I don't know where the world's heading. I don't even know where the theatre's heading. I have to run like hell myself to keep up. Why, I'm going into rehearsal next week with a play, I'm not sure I even know what it's about. It's a kind of tough hard-bitten thing. Who knows? It may be what they want. It's called *The Pig Is Dead*.

ZOLTAN: A romantic play.

ROSA: You said—rehearsal next week?
JEFFREY: Monday, hot or cold.
ROSA: I am an actress out of a job.
JEFFREY: Oh! Well, I'm afraid there's nothing in it for you, Rosa.
ROSA: Nothing at all?
JEFFREY: Everything's cast except one little bit. . . .
ROSA: I would play a bit.
JEFFREY: (*Somewhat embarrassed.*) Oh, darling, you're Rosa Rucker! This is *really* a bit. A drunken bum. Comes into this saloon, her fellow's with her, they get into a brawl—no, no, this wouldn't be your dish.
ROSA: My dish has not been exactly caviar lately. Sitting under those palm trees you perhaps did not hear about a work of art entitled *The Corpse Said No*, in which Rosa Rucker played the hysterical maid. Four lines and seven screams. We went on the road. Erie—Hershey, Pa.—and Baltimore, where they open oysters and close plays. After that—anything is my dish.
JEFFREY: (*Trying to be tactful.*) Yes, but this thing, Rosa—uh—the girl's—uh—she's just a kid. The author wants somebody that's just a kid. *You* know. You wouldn't want to— Say! (*A look at his watch.*) I've got to be—uh— (*Lisa comes in with the coffee on a tray.*)
LISA: I am so sorry. The coffee is late. Nothing happened. I am just slow.
ROSA: Lisa, you have heard us talk of Jeffrey Crandall. Jeffrey, this is Lisa Kemper.
JEFFREY: Kemper?
ZOLTAN: Friedrich Kemper's daughter.
JEFFREY: Friedrich Kemper's daughter! But when did you . . . why wasn't I told!
ROSA: It's only a short time.
ZOLTAN: You were making that sunburn.
JEFFREY: Dear child, your father and I— I *know* you. You were about six years old, I was having dinner with your father, and you were brought downstairs to say good night.
LISA: Oh, dear, I hope I didn't recite!
JEFFREY: But you did.
LISA: (*Her eyes closed in mock pain.*) Was it a little verse? And did I do it in three different languages?
JEFFREY: French, German and English.
LISA: I was afraid of that.
"I stand before you dressed in white,
To wish you all a sweet good night."
Do you want it in French?
JEFFREY: No.
ROSA: (*Suddenly she comes to Lisa, tenderly her arm goes around her shoulder.*) Jeffrey, here is your drunken bum.
JEFFREY: Huh? (*Lisa, puzzled, looks at Jeffrey.*)
ROSA: We know this child. She is an actress.
ZOLTAN: At the moment, it happens, she is playing a waitress.
JEFFREY: Really! What in?
LISA: In any house where a waitress is required. Dinners, luncheons, parties.

JEFFREY: (*He looks at her, an appraising stare.*) Well, that's miscasting if I ever . . . (*To Rosa and Zoltan.*) Why not! Friedrich Kemper's daughter ought to be able to . . . It's a little bit of a part, but it's a beginning. We go into rehearsal Monday. Want to try it?

LISA: (*An anguished pause.*) I'm . . . not . . . quite . . . sure . . . if I (*She stops.*)

ROSA: (*An urgent half whisper.*) Lisa!

LISA: (*She stands another moment, silent. Then she gathers herself together in decision. It is almost a physical effort.*) Yes!

JEFFREY: Fine! Come down to my office tomorrow morning at eleven. Know where it is?

ROSA: She'll find it.

ZOLTAN: Good, good!

JEFFREY: (*Gathering himself for departure.*) Well! . . . Rosa dear, be seeing you soon. . . . Lisa! In the morning! (*Goes to Zoltan, a warm grasp of the hand, a pat on the shoulder.*) Look, Zoltan, I—I've got an idea. Of course you're going to do another play. But while you're thinking about it how would you like to help me out by coming down to the office a few days a week? A lot of the time I'm not there—it'd be wonderful if you'd do it—sort of read plays and one thing and another. What do you say? It'd be a big help to me.

ZOLTAN: (*With a great deal of manner.*) You are very kind, Jeffrey. But I am afraid my temperament is not suited to office work.

JEFFREY: Well, I just thought—uh— Sorry— (*A glance at his watch, he is bustling into his coat.*) Good Lord! (*A quick dash over for another piece of cake.*) I'm late for my massage! (*He is almost gone.*) And don't worry, Zoltan. You're as good as you ever were! (*He is gone. There is a brief pause, the three face each other.*)

LISA: You are angels, both of you! I must tell Kurt! (*She goes. Zoltan and Rosa look at each other.*)

ZOLTAN: So. I wrote an American play— Rosa, I tell you something. For the first time I am really frightened.

ROSA: Zoltan, I have seen you at the height of your success. But never was I prouder of you than just now.

ZOLTAN: But out of it came anyway something. Lisa now has her chance. And that is as it should be. The young people.

(*Within the room at the sound of the chattering voice Zoltan sends an inquiring glance toward Rosa. Almost soundlessly her lips form the words Sophie Marelle. He tries to bolt to his little room, but he is caught in mid-flight.*)

STEPHANIE: (*Entering from hall.*) Oh, I'm so glad you are both in. I've brought Sophie Marelle. She just happened to drop into the shop at closing time. (*A look which says "worse luck." Marelle enters. She is practically hidden behind the massive modern jewelry which bedecks her. Her fur wrap, her hat, her gown are tomorrow's fashions and would pay her country's national debt.*)

MARELLE: (*Who speaks only in italics.*) *My pets! I've been longing to see you! Where have you been all this time! I don't see you any*where! *Where have you been hiding, you bad things!* . . . *Zoltan, you dazzling genius you, are you cook-*

ing up something wonderful for us next season?

ZOLTAN: (*As his eyes go to the manuscript in the wastebasket.*) Thank you. It is already cooked. . . . If you ladies will excuse me . . . I have some work . . . (*He edges toward his little workroom. He goes.*)

MARELLE: I used to *love* Zoltan's plays. Always so gay, and about such charming people. He hasn't written anything lately, has he? I haven't seen any. I don't even see you and Zoltan at openings.

ROSA: We live very quietly, Sophie. We have to. We were not as fortunate as you. We were able to bring nothing with us.

SOPHIE: Oh, I did manage to get a few paintings out—and a little jewelry. And I had a few pennies tucked away over here against a rainy day. Really nothing.

ROSA: How clever of you.

STEPHANIE: (*Moving to tray.*) Sophie, a cup of coffee? . . . Oh, it's cold.

MARELLE: Never mind. I don't dare! I'm in agony half the time. This American food simply . . . my dears! There isn't a decent restaurant in town. . . . You can't buy anything fit to eat, you can't buy anything fit to wear. . . . Stephanie, I'm not going to order a rag this spring until you open your shop.

STEPHANIE: You wouldn't like the clothes I'm going to make, Sophie. They're going to be so sly and simple. No bunches, no lumps, nothing dangling from them at all. Just line and fabric—and figure.

MARELLE: Oh! . . . I'd be willing even to invest. Surely you haven't all your backing yet.

STEPHANIE: I have. And my virtue is still intact.

MARELLE: Oh, dear, I'm beginning to feel so frustrated here! I'm blocked at every turn. You can't buy *this!* You can't buy *that!* You can't buy *anything!* (*Anna, a glass of milk in her hand, comes into the room from the kitchen.*) Try to buy a car! Do you realize what you have to go through to get a Cadillac?

ROSA: Sophie, this is Anna Zinsser, of whom you may have heard. Anna, Madame Henri Marelle.

MARELLE: (*Mystified, but rising to the occasion.*) Yes, indeed! How delightful, Miss—uh—

ANNA: Tell me, what happens if you do *not* get a Cadillac?

MARELLE: I beg your pardon?

ANNA: If you do not get a Cadillac, what do you do?

MARELLE: (*A little uncomfortable laugh as she looks from one to the other for support.*) Why—really—I—I never heard quite—I use the old one, of course.

ANNA: I merely wondered. (*She goes quietly toward the stairway and up. Marelle's eyes follow her in bewilderment.*)

MARELLE: Why, that was one of the oddest— What a silly question! Who is she?

ROSA: She is one of our friends who lives here.

MARELLE: How cosy! All of you together!

ROSA: We're very comfortable. (*Zoltan strolls back into the room.*)

MARELLE: Don't you ever miss the old days?—I do.—Here I am, stuck in those six dreary rooms at the Waldorf. When I think of the way you and Zoltan used to— You're really heroic not to complain. My little house in Paris was sweet and of course the place in Cannes—but you, with your schlosses and villas and palaces!—Oh, well, we're all in America *now*, aren't we? That has changed things.

ZOLTAN: It has not changed you. You are still the same woman.

MARELLE: Oh, thank you. How sweet of you! I must skip along, it's getting to be . . . (*Stephanie hands her bag.*) Oh, by the way, Rosa. I almost forgot. I'm having a little thing on the eighteenth—not too little, really—about sixty—Waldorf. There'll be a lot of people who'll remember you. And I wondered if you'd want to come and—uh—act a little bit for us. Some little Viennese character things . . . and make us cry into our champagne. It might be awfully good for you, and of course, I wouldn't expect you to perform without—uh—a fee of some sort.

ZOLTAN: You want Rosa Rucker to sing for her supper.

MARELLE: Well—uh—

ROSA: Wait, Zoltan. (*Turning to Marelle.*) What would the fee be for such an appearance?

ZOLTAN: Rosa!

MARELLE: (*With a somewhat uncertain glance to Rosa.*) Why, I hardly know— I don't know what it would be—would you think about—a hundred? (*Rosa merely looks at her.*) Two hundred! (*Hastily.*)

ROSA: I will come for five hundred dollars and I will perform for you and your guests.

MARELLE: Oh, that will be enchanting! My secretary will send you the details. Dinner is at eight—suppose you—ah—come at ten-thirty. Au 'voir. (*And she is gone.*)

STEPHANIE: (*Getting pocketbook from piano bench.*) Rosa, I didn't mean to bring her, she just came with me.

ROSA: It's all right, Stephanie. I'm very glad she came.

STEPHANIE: (*Under her breath as she goes up the stairs.*) That unspeakable rat! Coming here and daring to . . .

ZOLTAN: Rosa, how can you! Marelle, that *schmutz-frau*. Lower than this we will not come. That fish-knife she wore up here. (*He indicates his shoulder.*)

ROSA: She is not important, Marelle. But *we* are important. Five hundred dollars will buy food and heat and rent. For five hundred dollars I would juggle cigar boxes.

ZOLTAN: But you would not let me give my play to those two Rustle Bustle boys.

ROSA: That was different. That was you. And you are a great playwright.

ZOLTAN: (*A glance toward the door through which Jeffrey has vanished a short while ago.*) I am a great *garnichts*. But I would rather be me, here with the cockroaches, than Sophie Marelle at the Waldorf with all that loot she sneaked out with. Who told her, I wonder, to be so farsighted! It would be interesting to know.

(*Enter Kurt and Lisa from the kitchen. In their manner there is an effect of quiet resolve and understanding.*)

KURT: We thought Madame Magnifique would never get out of here. Look, what are you people doing Saturday afternoon?

ZOLTAN: Saturday after— I have a little dressmaker coming in.

KURT: Because we'll need a couple of flower girls.
ROSA: (*As she embraces them both.*) Lisa!
KURT: The bridegroom is a well-known taxi-man about town.
ZOLTAN: Kurt, my boy!
ROSA: You must be married here, in this room!
LISA: Yes, yes, I would love that!
ZOLTAN: My dear children. (*He kisses Lisa.*) At last we hear some really good news. It is like the happy ending of a play, it is right, it is what should be. (*Suddenly he takes complete charge.*) We will have a real wedding. The bride comes down those stairs, I am playing the wedding march, then I get up and give the bride away. (*All this in pantomime.*)
ROSA: You are going to play all the parts, Zoltan?
LISA: All but two.
ZOLTAN: (*Stunned by a sudden recollection.*) Rosa! (*He strikes his brow with a clenched fist.*) Now it comes to me!
ROSA: What is it, Zoltan?
ZOLTAN: We forgot to get married!
ROSA: (*Dismissing it.*) Oh, Zoltan!
ZOLTAN: We go down to the place tomorrow, we— I have an idea! (*He faces them all, beaming.*) But kolossal! A double wedding! First I walk in with Lisa, then . . .
ROSA: Zoltan!
ZOLTAN: (*From his heights.*) H'm?
ROSA: In all the years that we have—not been married, I have listened to many of your ideas. Some were wonderful, some were so-so. But this one! Only a genius could think of anything so bloodcurdling.
LISA: Or so dramatic.
ROSA: Lisa! The wedding dress! What do you think? Your blue? Could we manage a new one?
LISA: Rosa dear, please don't think I am being silly or fanciful. But I would love to look really like a bride. A bride with a long white dress even if I have to use a tablecloth, and a veil if it's only my serving apron. (*A gesture to her head.*) And a father and a mother and friends . . .
KURT: And a bridegroom.
LISA: (*With deep feeling.*) Oh, yes! A bridegroom.
ROSA: I will make a wedding dress for you with my own hands!
ZOLTAN: Lisa, if Rosa is to be the seamstress, better the tablecloth with a hole for the head. (*A smiling Vilna comes into the room.*)
VILNA: I hope you don't mind. I couldn't help hearing. May I offer my congratulations?
LISA: Thank you, Vilna.
VILNA: (*To Kurt.*) So you are settling down, Kurt. After being such a lad with the ladies.
KURT: Mm. Going to be rough on them.
ZOLTAN: (*The baffled playwright.*) Vilna, you are always making entrances and exits.
VILNA: (*As she goes toward the kitchen.*) Maybe we will all be making exits pret-

ty soon. They have been surveying all afternoon on this block—men with those instruments. And the man next door must be dying. There is now another nurse. That makes three. (*Pleased with what she has accomplished, she flounces off.*)
ZOLTAN: Ah! She likes to imagine trouble.
ROSA: No, Zoltan, I saw them, too, measuring.
KURT: Don't let her panic you. (*Turning to Lisa, he takes her face gently in his hands.*) After what we've seen, you and I, it takes more than a man with a tripod to scare us, doesn't it, dearest?
LISA: (*With a new serenity.*) I am not afraid any more. I'm not afraid of anything. Suddenly I am a new person. I have *you*—and the theatre—and my friends! I have everything! I don't care if we live in the subway.
KURT: Good, let's celebrate! Let's have dinner at some place we can't afford. Nothing schnitzely.
ROSA: Chinese food! (*The doorbell rings. It rings again immediately and insistently.*)
KURT: That's the idea! (*He crosses to door.*)
ROSA: That's the way I like to hear you talk, Lisa.
ZOLTAN: Now all those fears are behind you. (*A man's voice in low even tones at outer door.*)
MAN'S VOICE (WALLACE): (*Off.*) Miss Lisa Kemper?
KURT: (*Off.*) Yes, what is it?
MAN'S VOICE (WALLACE): (*Off and low.*) Immigration and Naturalization.
ROSA: (*Very low.*) What did he say? (*Kurt apprehensively precedes the two men into the room. The two men who enter are quiet, bland, poker-faced. Though there is nothing sinister about them, they carry with them an air of portent. Dark suits, dark coats, soft hats. Their manner is courteous. The older man is the spokesman. The younger looks as though he were present in the event of trouble. The older man is named Tim Wallace. The other is simply known as Black.*)
WALLACE: (*As he surveys them.*) Good afternoon. (*Rosa and Zoltan nod their heads.*) Is one of you Lisa Kemper?
LISA: (*When first she speaks she has, to her own surprise, no voice at all. She tries again.*) I am Lisa Kemper.
WALLACE: (*He produces his identification folder, and shows it. His assistant does the same.*) Department of Immigration and Naturalization.
LISA: (*Hardly to be heard.*) No!
KURT: What's this all about?
WALLACE: (*Turns to regard Kurt with a long appraising scrutiny.*) What's *your* name?
KURT: Kurt Heger. Here's my hack license. (*Kurt holds it for Wallace's inspection. Black is taking notes.*)
WALLACE: (*A quick keen look at license. Then his gaze carries slowly around to Zoltan.*) Your name is—?
ZOLTAN: Zoltan Lazko!
WALLACE: Oh, yes. (*The eye, like a searchlight, passes on to Rosa.*) You're Mrs.—uh—?
ROSA: I am Rosa Rucker.

BLACK: *(Pencil poised.)* Miss?
ROSA: *(With a gesture that obliterates titles or classifications.)* Rosa Rucker.
WALLACE: There are just a few questions, Miss Kemper—do you mind if I sit down?
ROSA: Oh. Please. I'm sorry. *(Wallace sits. He settles himself to business. Zoltan and Rosa seat themselves uneasily. Lisa and Kurt remain standing. As Wallace is leisurely assorting his papers Lisa looks fearfully at Kurt; he tries to reassure her with a smile. Rosa sends a glance toward Zoltan and he too tries with a gesture to make little of the situation.)*
WALLACE: *(Mumbling his essential facts to himself, as he thumbs through the papers.)* Uh . . . Kemper . . . Lisa . . . born Vienna, Austria . . . age—uh . . . England June third nineteen . . . uh . . . arrived U. S. . . . port of Boston, Mass., January seventeen . . .
LISA: But I have done nothing! I don't understand!
KURT: *(Very low.)* Quiet.
ZOLTAN: *(Never a patient man.)* Look, my good man! Here we are in America! What do you want with this girl? Tell us.
WALLACE: *(Drones on to himself, unheeding.)* Affidavit for entry . . . agreeing support and maintain Lisa Kemper . . . "I guarantee that she will not become a public charge . . . Signed, Zoltan Lazko." *(He gives Zoltan a searching look.)*
KURT: I'll support her. We're getting married Saturday.
WALLACE: Got your license?
KURT: We're getting it tomorrow.
WALLACE: *(Sceptically.)* Uh-huh.
KURT: *(Infuriated.)* Look here! If you're trying to— *(He takes a step or two toward Wallace, but Black quietly insinuates himself in a manner to block him.)*
WALLACE: "Released from Displaced Persons Camp. Went to England . . ." How long were you in England?
LISA: I—I—
ZOLTAN: You see the condition she is in. I will answer for her. She is our own child!
WALLACE: Your child! Says her your father was— *(His pronunciation is strictly American.)* Frydrich Kemper.
ROSA: Friedrich!
ZOLTAN: Naturally Friedrich Kemper was her father.
WALLACE: *(A look from Zoltan to Rosa.)* And the mother was Helena Kemper.
ROSA: Of course she was Helena Kemper.
WALLACE: I don't get this?
ROSA: Ach! She is not really our child. We have known her from the day she was born. Her father was our dearest friend—the famous Friedrich Kemper.
ZOLTAN: The greatest King Lear that Europe has ever known.
WALLACE: *(Drily.)* That so?
ZOLTAN: *(Despairs of ever making this man understand.)* Auch recht. . . . Would you please . . . what is it you are here for? What is wrong?
WALLACE: It's a matter of illegal entry.
LISA: It's not true! Everything was in order.
KURT: In what way was it illegal?

WALLACE: (*To Lisa.*) Did you spend a good deal of time in a hospital in England? Nursing homes, they call 'em over there?
KURT: What if she did! (*Wallace disregards this, looks at Lisa.*)
WALLACE: Did you or didn't you?
LISA: Yes.
WALLACE: How long?
LISA: It was a year. Maybe a little more.
WALLACE: Don't you know? Whether it was a year—or more?
LISA: It was—more.
WALLACE: What was the matter with you?
LISA: I was ill.
WALLACE: Were you ill, or were you—? (*He taps his head with a finger meaningly.*)
LISA: I had—I had been through a great deal—I was—but I am well now.
WALLACE: Nervous breakdown, would you call it?
KURT: I'm damned if I'll stand any more of this! Come to the point!
ROSA: Suppose she *was* ill? Then what?
WALLACE: (*Keeping his calm even tone.*) Well, if the illness was of the kind we've been led to believe, she could be deported.
LISA: Oh, no!
ROSA: Lisa, child!
ZOLTAN: This cannot be!
KURT: (*Who has been doing some thinking.*) Just what do you mean by "led to believe?"
WALLACE: We act on information supplied to us from various sources.
KURT: What kind of sources?
WALLACE: (*A vague gesture.*) Well—uh—
KURT: You mean to say if any screwball phones in, or writes a letter, you put people through a thing like this! (*A realization of what Kurt means now dawns on Zoltan and Rosa.*)
WALLACE: The rules of the Department—
KURT: Department! Hah! Stick around! (*Exits.*)
ROSA: (*Her face wreathed in smiles of triumph. She flashes a look at Zoltan, who, too, is beaming.*) There is an old saying in Hungarian—Aki masnak vermet as maga esik bele es ez bele is fog esni!
ZOLTAN: (*To Wallace.*) Remember that! (*Vilna's voice, high and shrill, is heard from the kitchen.*)
VILNA: (*Off.*) You let me alone. Take your hand off my arm! I don't know anything about it!
KURT: (*Off.*) Anything about what?
VILNA: (*Off.*) Whatever it is, I don't know anything about it! (*Kurt and Vilna appear. Kurt is propelling Vilna from kitchen.*)
KURT: (*Bringing Vilna down to face Wallace.*) Here's your "source of information."
VILNA: It's a lie!
WALLACE: Who's she?
ROSA: She is Vilna Prager. She is in love with this boy. He is going to marry Lisa

Kemper. It is as simple as that.

ZOLTAN: If you are looking for somebody *crazy*—

WALLACE: (*Slipping a letter out of the dossier.*) Did you write this letter?

VILNA: No.

KURT: (*Between his teeth.*) Oh, yes you did!

WALLACE: (*Puts pencil and paper in her hand.*) Here. Print what I tell you . . . "in a nursing home in England." (*Vilna makes as though to put the pencil to paper.*)

VILNA: So! I wrote it! I believe it! She should not be here!

(*Wallace calmly begins to pack up his papers. A nod to Black.*)

WALLACE: I figure jealous women cost this Department a million dollars a year. (*To Vilna.*) If I were you, my girl, I'd get myself another boy friend and stop writing letters.

KURT: (*To Vilna.*) I pulled you in here, and now, by God, I'm kicking you out.

VILNA: Don't worry. I'm already packed. I've made my plans. Some day you'll brag that you ever knew me—you greasy hack driver! You and your loony bride! (*As Kurt starts furiously toward her.*) Don't you touch me! (*She runs upstairs and disappears. Kurt goes swiftly to Lisa.*)

ZOLTAN: (*With a great sigh of relief.*) So! What do you think of such a monster? . . . Now, gentlemen, can we offer you, perhaps, some refreshment?

ROSA: A glass of wine? A cup of coffee?

WALLACE: (*Has now replaced all the documents in his briefcase except one which he is now studying. He speaks in the same level emotionless voice.*) I have here the affidavit, signed by Zoltan Lazko— (*He levels a finger at Zoltan.*) that's you—made out by you in behalf of Lisa Kemper. (*He shows Zoltan the document.*) You wrote this?

ZOLTAN: (*Adjusts his monocle, glances at paper.*) It is in order.

WALLACE: It says here you have in excess of six thousand dollars in the bank. Have you?

ZOLTAN: At the moment—no.

WALLACE: Did you have when you signed this affidavit?

ZOLTAN: I had written a play which was about to be produced. A play can make hundreds of thousands.

WALLACE: Did it?

ZOLTAN: No.

WALLACE: How much did it make?

ZOLTAN: Nothing.

WALLACE: So you didn't have six thousand dollars.

ZOLTAN: With a play you cannot tell. I *hoped* it would make a million.

WALLACE: Oh, you hoped.

ROSA: But you do not understand. He did not mean to— (*Wallace silences her with an impatient gesture. He takes a moment to look further through the affidavit.*)

WALLACE: Also, it says here you are the "greatest playwright in the world." Are you?

ZOLTAN: Perhaps I am not the one to say—

WALLACE: Well, you say so here. Sworn statement.
ZOLTAN: (*Cornered.*) All right. I *am!*
WALLACE: You're the greatest playwright in the world, but your play didn't make a red cent.
ZOLTAN: But that is the theatre! In the theatre you can be the greatest genius living, and still you will have failures. You cannot write a success every time.
ROSA: Hauptmann—Sudermann—Schnitzler!
WALLACE: Who?
ROSA: (*In desperation.*) Never mind.
WALLACE: (*Quietly, to Black.*) Nest of cuckoos.
ROSA: Look, Mr. Lazko has written maybe fifty plays. Sometimes they are successful, sometimes they are not successful.
WALLACE: Mm, h'm. Then why doesn't he get a job he knows something about?
ZOLTAN: My work, it is not for you to say what I do. In two weeks I am an American citizen. I was today in your courtroom for citizens.
WALLACE: Yes, I know. So was I.
ZOLTAN: What?
WALLACE: I was there, too.
ZOLTAN: You were there!
WALLACE: (*Takes a small notebook from his pocket. Looks at notes.*) Who is this Reinhardt that you said ought to be running this country?
ZOLTAN: The country! I did not say he should be—
WALLACE: (*Looks at notes.*) You also criticized Federal Judge Marcus J. Hazlitt in his conduct of the proceedings.
ROSA: Mr. Lazko was speaking only of the dramatic effect.
WALLACE: (*His attention drawn to Rosa.*) You live here?
ROSA: Yes.
WALLACE: (*Looks at each.*) You two married?
ROSA: No.
ZOLTAN: (*To Rosa.*) You see!
WALLACE: (*Writing in his little book.*) Moral turpitude . . . False affidavit . . . (*Gets hat and briefcase.*) Thank you all very much for your cooperation!
ZOLTAN: (*Stopping Wallace.*) But wait! The affidavit. Is that why I was today not made a citizen?
WALLACE: I wouldn't know about that.
ZOLTAN: But what is to come of this? What do you do?
WALLACE: I just get the facts and turn them over to my superior. . . . You'll hear from us. Good evening. (*Wallace and Black exit. For a moment all stand motionless. There is a brief period of readjustment. Zoltan and Rosa exchange glances.*)
LISA: And now I bring trouble to you. You who have been so good to me! You should never have brought me here.
ROSA: But here is where you belong, Lisa dear.
LISA: (*A shake of the head.*) I thought when I came here it would be over. But now it is the same thing, again and again and again. When did I come here, when did I go there, when did I do this, when did I do that? (*She rises.*) I don't know, I don't know, I don't know—you heard what that girl said. She thinks I am—

(*She pauses, her eyes go with fear toward the stairs as she recalls what Vilna has shouted.*)

KURT: (*Crosses to Lisa and holds her.*) You're not worrying about *her!* She's just sick and twisted.

LISA: I don't know. I don't know. (*Lisa goes up the stairs.*)

ROSA: I must go to her.

KURT: No. Leave her alone for a while. I'll go up later. (*Deep in thought, he goes off to kitchen. A despairing look. Rosa and Zoltan stand a moment looking into each other's eyes. From the hallway above stairs come the blithe sounds of a gaily whistled tune. It is interrupted by Vilna's harsh high voice.*)

VILNA: (*Off. A snarl as she apparently bumps into Rudy.*) Ahhh! Can't you see where you're going, you over-dressed store dummy!

RUDY: (*Off.*) Sorry, Cinderella. (*A door slams. Rudy descends the stairs. He is in dinner clothes, a white silk scarf hangs from his shoulders, a soft black hat is worn at a rakish angle, his dark topcoat is over his arm. He comes jauntily into the room and, standing before the mirror, begins to adjust his scarf.*) What's the matter with little Miss Venom! She bumped into me, snarled like a wildcat. I thought she was going to knife me.

ROSA: The girl is a demon. She is leaving, thank God!

RUDY: You mean she's out! Good! (*A final touch to the scarf.*) How do I look?

ROSA: What? Oh. Uh—you look dazzling, Rudy. Doesn't he, Zoltan?

ZOLTAN: (*Dully, not looking up.*) Dazzling.

RUDY: Well, I'm off to battle for my honor. If I'm not home by six A. M., call the police. (*He is gone.*)

ZOLTAN: (*Desperately.*) Why did they not make me a citizen? Rosa, what could they do? God knows I meant no harm. But those men—the way they— Rosa! If I am to be sent away from here, back again over there . . .

ROSA: If that happens, Zoltan, I would go with you.

ZOLTAN: To what! They have vanished, all of them, the friends that we knew. They were the first to be exterminated—the thinkers, the artists, the scientists. We would stumble through the streets like ghosts, you and I. Here we are failures, Rosa, but we are at least huddled here together for comfort and understanding—Anna, Martin, Stephanie, Rudy—all of us with our troubles and our bewilderment. And so we make a life.

MARTIN: (*Appears in the doorway, his air is one of amused jauntiness.*) Caveat emptor! I am now a captain of industry.

ROSA: Martin! What happened?

ZOLTAN: You have good news?

MARTIN: I have a job. But every week the pay envelope. No more chocolate drops, peddling from door to door.

ROSA: Martin, I am so happy for you. Tell us!

MARTIN: Wholesale! Wholesale ladies' garments. All day long the clothes must go from the work room to other buildings to sell or something. They are put on hangers, very orderly, in a little hand truck. (*As he talks he is illustrating the business of hanging the clothes and the square shape of the hand truck.*) And I push the truck through the streets to the other buildings. Everybody is running, I run too. "Heads up!" I am supposed to say. "Heads up!" and they do!

ROSA: (*Aghast but trying to hide her feelings.*) Why, Martin, how—how interesting.
MARTIN: I think I go up to my room a little bit. With the pushing it is at first a little bit— (*He pushes back his shoulders to indicate the strain he has been under.*) It is only because it is the first day. I lie down a little.
ROSA: Would you like something, Martin? A hot bowl of soup?
MARTIN: I think I just lie down. (*He goes up the stairs slowly. Rosa turns slowly to Zoltan.*)
ZOLTAN: So! Judge Martin Link. Six months from now will that be Zoltan Lazko?
ROSA: Zoltan! No! (*A swift purposeful step is heard on the stairs. It is Vilna dressed up for departure, suitcase in hand. A spiteful figure, she stands framed in the archway.*)
VILNA: Well, love and kisses! I can't tell you how it breaks my heart to leave this charming household.
ZOLTAN: Please. No speeches. Only go.
VILNA: (*Low and venomous.*) With pleasure! This place, full of broken-down failures! (*Her voice rises shrilly.*) Why don't you get wise to yourselves! You with your drooling old plays that nobody wants to see—and that silly old hag who thinks she's an ingenue! (*Rosa's hands cover her ears, as though to shut out these dreadful words.*)
ZOLTAN: Get out!
VILNA: (*Her voice rising still higher.*) You make me sick! All of you! What are you doing here anyway! They don't want you here! Nobody wants you—anywhere! Go bury yourselves! (*With a cackle of contempt she stamps out. The outer door bangs. Rosa's hands come down, one hand covers her mouth as though to stifle a scream. Her eyes stare in horror. Zoltan stands for a moment avoiding Rosa's eyes. He now makes a bravado attempt to belittle Vilna's outburst.*)
ZOLTAN: We—we take into the house an alley cat, it spits at us—that is all.
ROSA: (*Without much conviction.*) It has been a horrible day. We must not let this—disturb us, Zoltan.
ZOLTAN: (*Stands silent a moment.*) But it is true. We are finished, Rosa. The girl spoke truth.
ROSA: Do not say that, Zoltan.
ZOLTAN: The plays—everything. Zoltan Lazko is finished. Never again will I hear from an audience that glorious shout, "Bravo!" Finished! Our good friend Stefan Zweig knew what to do. And so do I.
ROSA: Zoltan, what are you saying!
ZOLTAN: The dramatist knows when to ring down the curtain. (*Rosa buries her head in her arms. She is weeping.*) Rosa! Rosa! Don't, my *liebchen*.
ROSA: What has happened to us, Zoltan? There we were, the most famous pair in Europe. And now suddenly—
ZOLTAN: It is not us, it is the world.
ROSA: Then I am sick of the world, I am sick of life.
ZOLTAN: (*A sudden outburst.*) What is it with this country! What has happened! All right, I am old, I do not matter. But Lisa—she brings here youth and talent and life—and they want to send her away. Always who has come here? Young people. The courageous—the ambitious—the strong. Then suddenly they close

the doors. So what happens! The old blood marries the old blood, like in Europe, and there is no fresh. I tell you a closed country is a dying country, just as a closed mind is a dying mind.

ROSA: You are right, Zoltan. Life is too much for us—the whole world. We are finished, both of us.

ZOLTAN: (*Stares at her with a full realization of her despair.*) Rosa! You say this! For the first time—you! (*Zoltan paces a brief moment, gathers himself together with a mighty resolve.*) No! We do *not* give up! The government says I go back. I will show the government. The plays are finished—all right, I do something else. I will shovel coal. I will dig ditches, I will drive a taxicab like Kurt! *I* belong here, and *you* belong here, just as the Pilgrim Fathers, and ham and eggs and Toscanini belong here! Here we are and here we will go on! My coffee! I want my coffee!

CURTAIN

ACT III

SCENE: *There is a gala look about the room, what with a few spring flowers and a side table laden with folded napkins, glassware, bottles. Apparently a festivity is in the offing. On the hall rack hang Zoltan's black cape, satin lined, his top hat. His ebony stick with the gold head stands there. A pair of white evening gloves—Rosa's—hang over the back of a chair.*

TIME: *April, two months later. It is about six o'clock.*

At rise: *Rosa Rucker comes in from the kitchen carrying a small pile of plates which she places on the table. Though she is wearing a practical and enveloping housecoat it is evident that evening finery is hidden beneath it. Her hair is formally dressed, a glittering ornament sets it off, her high-heeled evening slippers show beneath the apron. In the midst of this an agitated Kurt dashes into the room from outdoors. Even as he runs he is stripping off his coat sweater. He is grimy and unshaven. He is carrying a newspaper which he tosses onto a chair.*

KURT: I'm late! I'm on my way home, Thirty-Six and Broadway, and a big lunk gets into my cab and says Long Island City! I dump him out there and another one gets in, says the Bronx. (*By now, as he leaps up the stairs, he is stripped to the waist.*) How's Lisa?

ROSA: (*Calls after the disappearing figure.*) She is fine. She is sleeping. (*A quick appraising glance around the room and she is off again. From the kitchen regions, you can hear another fragment of the song, very accented. The sound of the street door closing. Zoltan appears in the doorway. The flowing cape, the broad-brimmed black hat, the monocle, the cane, all are still part of his outdoor costume. He is wearing spats, too, in deference to the cool spring air. But in his manner there is lacking a certain sprightliness. The buoyancy is gone. He removes his cape and tosses on it a bag of peanuts and a package of cigarettes, both of which he takes from his pocket. His glance goes towards the kitchen.*)

Rosa enters briskly. She is carrying a stack of napkins which she places on the laden table. Rosa, bustling.) Zoltan, just tonight you come home late. You should be dressing.

ZOLTAN: (*Lighting his cigarette.*) Plenty of time. Always it takes you longer than it does me.

ROSA: (*As she darts back to the kitchen.*) I am all finished, except for my dress. Anyhow, it takes you hours.

ZOLTAN: (*Calling after her.*) Just because you are now married, please do not talk like a married woman. (*He fumes a little at the injustice of it.*)

ROSA: (*As she enters Zoltan cracks another peanut.*) And peanuts! Making love to the squirrels in Central Park again!

ZOLTAN: I am very popular with them. They are now my public.

ROSA: (*Peers into the bag.*) Nothing but shells left. (*She is about to drop the bag into the wastebasket when he stops her.*)

ZOLTAN: Ah—ah—ah—ah! (*He tenderly rescues the bag, tears off a bit of the top.*) I wrote down here a telephone number. A man sitting next to me on the bench—but wonderful!

ROSA: Was he as wonderful as that man down on the Battery who stole the three dollars from you?

ZOLTAN: This is an altogether different *mensch*. A great man!

ROSA: He told you this!

ZOLTAN: He tells me nothing. But we sit there in the sun, and the tree are just beginning green, and he feeds the squirrels and I feed the squirrels, and the pigeons walk at our feet. And the whole world seems to know that this man sits here, because there comes by, you would not believe it, maybe a dozen people. One wants to know should the government pass a new bill about houses, and he tells him. (*He rises.*) And the next one says something about Wall Street, should it be twenty million or thirty million, and he tells him, too; and another one says, how much longer do you think the oil will last in this country, and he tells him, exact to the quart. To one he says, "Good-bye, Senator," and to another one, "Tomorrow in Washington I will take it up with the President." In another country such a fellow would be surrounded by soldiers standing with guns. Here he sits on a park bench and feeds the squirrels. *Unmoglich!*

ROSA: What is his name—this man who is so important?

ZOLTAN: I did not ask him, maybe he thought I knew. *My* name he knew—when I told him. He has seen my plays for years. He knows Budapest, Brussels, Paris, Rome. The world. Then suddenly, he looks at his watch, very politely he shakes hands, he stands up—six and a half feet he is, straight like a boy, and white hair, thick; the way he looks at you it comes out the other side. And he says, "I am proud to have met you, I hope to see you again," he gives me his telephone number, I write it down on this paper. (*He puts the bit of paper on the table, smooths it out contemplatively.*)

ROSA: (*Rises.*) A man who cannot afford an office cannot be very much.

ZOLTAN: We all sit there and arrange the world. What else have I got to do? All my life a playwright, now I am nothing. I do nothing. I am nothing.

ROSA: But, Zoltan, you have been working at several interesting things. And dignified. Just because there have been unfortunate contretemps . . .

ZOLTAN: Contretemps! First, I read plays for Jeffrey. Comes along a manuscript, a boat full of men in the Pacific Ocean, nothing happens, they sit and look through a telescope at girls, someone pulls up a palm tree, no love story, nothing. I do not even speak of it to Jeffrey. So I am no longer a play reader. (*He picks up his work: cards, pencil, etc.*)

ROSA: Anyone can make a mistake in the theatre.

ZOLTAN: So a lecture fellow says I should make talks to clubs of women. The theatre, myself—they are both subjects I am very fond of. So I try it. I go to a place, Passaic, New Jersey. I make my talk, there is a very nice applause, a woman stands up in the front row and asks me a question. "Do you write the words in the plays, or do the actors make them up?" So there on the table is a pitcher of water . . . (*He makes the appropriate gesture. He places his work on the table: picks up a pencil, pulls the pad toward him as though preparing to write.*)

ROSA: Zoltan, you are not going to work now! At this hour!

ZOLTAN: Just one little verse I have to write. Mother's Day. I took down today to the man the rest. But this one he did not like. I must do another.

ROSA: (*Picking up a card and reading.*) "Mother dear . . ."

ZOLTAN: (*Taking the card from her.*) No, no, no. (*The ring of the telephone has cut through his speech.*)

ROSA: (*Answering the phone.*) Hello! . . . Yes, this is Mrs. Lazko . . . Yes, he's here. . . .

ZOLTAN: Who is talking?

ROSA: But he must go to the theatre tonight. . . . Who is talking? . . . He will be home after the theatre, but we have some friends . . . Who is this?

ZOLTAN: What do they want?

ROSA: Immigration and Natural . . . Hello! . . . Hello! (*Quietly she hangs up the receiver, her gaze on Zoltan.*)

ZOLTAN: So. It has come. Those men again. That is why, each time I go to become a citizen, there is something wrong with the papers. (*He shakes his head, undeceived. A sigh.*) Perhaps Martin is the lucky one. When you are dead there are no more fears.

ROSA: Stop such talk, Zoltan! Tonight belongs to Lisa. It is her opening night. For her sake we have got to be happy—or at least pretend to be happy. Gay! Gay!

ZOLTAN: (*In a voice of fury.*) All right! Gay! No money! No future! Perhaps to be deported! Gay! (*Sits.*) Where is the child? Already at the theatre?

ROSA: She is taking a nap. A real actress can always sleep before an opening.

ZOLTAN: How can I sit there in that theatre tonight! (*The doorbell rings.*)

ROSA: (*As she goes to answer the ring.*) If only after this she can be sure of herself, and go on with her work, and marry Kurt. (*She is now out of sight in the hallway, her voice is raised.*) He has behaved beautifully about it—Kurt. (*The sound of the door opening. Her voice is heard in a high and happy tone of surprise. Off.*) Rudy! How in the world!

RUDY: (*Off.*) Rosa! My wonderful Rosa! (*Rosa, Rudy and a Third Figure come into the room. The unknown person is Jane Velvet, the motion picture star. Jane Velvet's fur wrap, her gown, her jewels, her evening bag all are meant to register in that photograph flash intended for tomorrow morning's tabloids.*)

Their cost would represent the average man's comfortable annual salary. Rudy, in his way, is no less resplendent. A dashing figure in tails, top hat.)
ROSA: Zoltan! Look!
ZOLTAN: *(Arms outstretched.)* The bride and bridegroom!
RUDY: Jane—the two most wonderful people in the world! They are my father, mother, sister, dearest friends—they are everything I have—except you. This is Jane Velvet, my wife.
ZOLTAN: Loveliest of ladies, like a dazzling creature from another sphere, wafted through the clouds to make radiant our sordid little world. *(He bows low as he kisses her hand in formal Continental fashion.)*
JANE: *(Right to the point.)* And did we bust a gut to get here!
ROSA: Tell us, when did you arrive? Why didn't you let us know? Lisa is opening tonight. You know that? We are so excited! And now, you! *(She calls up the stairway.)* Stephanie! Anna! Rudy is here! Rudy and Jane! *(Stephanie's voice from upstairs: "Wonderful!")*
ZOLTAN: Sit down, sit down! Here, let me take your wrap. *(As Jane's sumptuous wrap is removed there is revealed such a dazzling expanse of bare white shoulders and bosom, such jewels and color and fabric as to make a production in itself.)*
RUDY: Jane finished her picture yesterday. We grabbed the first plane out. We just popped in here for a minute. I had to see you people first of all. And have Jane meet you. We're going to the opening, of course. I called Jeffrey.
ROSA: This is really your honeymoon! Zoltan! Some sherry! Something!
RUDY: No. No, we have to go to a dinner at the Colony. Much rather stay here, Rosa, and talk to all of you.
ROSA: We are having our dinner after the theatre. A little party for Lisa. Jeffrey is coming up. Can you join us then?
RUDY: What about it, darling? Can't we ditch those people at 21?
JANE: Sure we can. It's only Rank and Schenck and Schmank and Schmenk— *(Stephanie and Anna come down the stairs.)*
STEPHANIE: *(Calls from stairway.)* Rudy, dear boy! Hello!
RUDY: Stephanie darling! Anna! This is Janie. Janie—Stephanie and Anna!
ANNA: How do you do.
JANE: Hello. *(Anna wears that same plain dark dress. Stephanie is beautifully dressed in a quiet dark theatre dinner gown. She is a figure of elegance and distinction. Kurt comes down the stairs.)*
STEPHANIE: Even without Rudy, we know you so well from your pictures.
KURT: Hello, old man!
RUDY: And here is Kurt. *(Kurt is in dinner clothes that are correct, but a little shabby.)*
KURT: Well! A princess who really looks like a princess!
JANE: Say, I know I'm not an honest-to-God princess; but I fell in love with a sure-enough prince, didn't I, Sexy? *(She runs a hand up the back of his leg, intimately. He stops her.)*
RUDY: *(Complacently.)* At first sight, just the way they do in the movies.
JANE: And maybe you think it hasn't got those Hollywood belles biting their nails! The best they can marry is bandleaders.

RUDY: Say, where is Lisa? Lisa is missing. Where is the future star?
KURT: Rosa, shouldn't I call her?
ROSA: No, let the child rest.
ANNA: (*Who has been appraising Jane Velvet with a scientifically observant eye.*) You know, you are very pretty. You do not need all those clothes.
JANE: Say, if I could just leave 'em off. But you know the Johnston office.
RUDY: Don't you see why I am crazy about this girl? She's as wholesome as bread. Doesn't try to read Proust, never heard of Cesar Franck, doesn't collect paintings or anything. Just a great girl.
JANE: And he's a great guy. Doesn't try to educate me. You know—like white wine with fish, stuff like that. Hell, I don't need to tell you folks. You know him.
ROSA: For a prince he is a fine sweet fellow.
JANE: Only thing is, he's as stubborn as a frozen pump. Won't let me pay for anything, says he's going to make plenty out of his new ski place. But I get even. (*She turns back his coat sleeve, his lapel, his other cuff with deft quick movements.*) Emerald cuff links, pearl dress studs, jeweled cigarette case, platinum wrist watch. Pull up your trousers, honey. (*Rudy does so, revealing a magnificent garter.*) Gold garters. . . . Melted down as he stands he'd bring a hundred thousand dollars.
RUDY: (*Glances at his watch.*) Heh! We ought to be off.
JANE: Let 'em wait. Can't we just relax here in New York? I think I *will* have a glass of sherry.
KURT: I'll get it.
JANE: I'm so tired of punching the clock every day. Up at five, in bed at nine. When I was a kid back in Altoona, and my old man had to get up at five and go to the mines, it meant he was just a poor mugg. I'll bet Hollywood is the only town in the world where, if you have to get up at five to go to work and get to bed at nine to catch your sleep, it means you're a hell of a success. (*As Kurt proffers the sherry.*) Thanks, bub.
ZOLTAN: Tell me, do the writers in Hollywood also get up at five?
JANE: Writers! They never get up. Get to the studio at one, lunch till three-thirty, look at a picture and go home.
ZOLTAN: I could accustom myself to such a life. I am just now not so busy.
JANE: Oh, yes! Rudy told me! *You're* a writer, aren't you?
ZOLTAN: I am so considered.
JANE: I know. You write plays. You wrote the *Doll House*, or something. (*A bright little nod to Rudy, as though to say, "See how smart I am!"*)
RUDY: (*Fondly.*) Listen, my dumb bride, you are talking to the greatest Hungarian playwright who ever lived.
JANE: No kidding! Say, there's a lot of you goulash boys in Hollywood. I can't pronounce their names.
ZOLTAN: When first I came here a few years ago I was hounded—but hounded by the Hollywood impresarios, but I was of course busy with my own work. Now, however, I happen to have a moment of leisure; perhaps when you return to Hollywood . . .
ROSA: (*Quickly.*) Rudy, are you and Jane staying in New York? What are your plans?

RUDY: Our plans right now are twenty minutes late. Come on, brainless. Can we drop anyone? We have a car. (*The group is on its feet. There is a moment of rather aimless chatter, during which bits of talk overlap. They are all moving vaguely toward the doorway.*)
ANNA: Au 'voir. I must go to my work. (*She goes upstairs.*)
KURT: I better wake Lisa. I'll pound on her door.
ZOLTAN: We meet at the theatre, everyone. Backstage after the play.
RUDY: See you later, you people.
JANE: Come on, Ski Pants!
KURT: So long. Excuse me if I beat it. (*He goes.*)
STEPHANIE: I have never been to Hollywood. Is it really as fantastic as it sounds?
JANE: It's a monkey house all right. . . . Say, that dress of yours is just beginning to sneak up on me. At first it looks kind of plain, but— Where'd you get it?
STEPHANIE: I made it.
JANE: You made it!
ROSA: This is Stephanie, Incorporated.
RUDY: Remember, honey?
JANE: Sure enough! Ye-e-es! (*Self-doubt comes into her mind.*) Say, this is kinda noisy, isn't it? (*Her own dress.*)
STEPHANIE: Not at all. After all, you are a public figure. They demand glamor from you.
JANE: Oh, this is an old one. I never wear my best to an opening. They grab at you—anything's likely to happen.
ROSA: In my day they took the horses out of the carriage, now they take the clothes off the actress. (*Zoltan, at the piano, is now really attacking the waltz time of "Zwei Herzen Im Drei Viertel Takt," his head is wagging, he is humming, the music mounts louder and louder as the following scene progresses. While Rudy stands patiently by, hat in hand, the three women—Jane, Rosa, Stephanie—plunge into an animated discussion of clothes. Gradually their words are drowned by the music, so that we only see a pantomimic scene in which shoulder lines, hem lines, sleeves, neck lines are outlined in air.*)
JANE: Anyhow, I'd love to come around and see your things. I need everything. You know how it is, you can't wear the same things twice among the same people.
STEPHANIE: I wish all my clients felt that way. It would be wonderful for business.
JANE: I can't get used to this year's clothes. Too covered up.
ROSA: I like any style that emphasizes the womanly figure.
JANE: I hate the long skirt. What's the use of having good legs!
STEPHANIE: Ah, but what you put on the bottom you take off the top.
JANE: If you keep that up long enough we'll be falling all over ourselves—but Holy God! (*Her gestures indicate a neckline that begins at the waistline. Meanwhile the doorbell has rung. It is Jeffrey Crandall who now enters. He is in dinner clothes, noticeably pale in comparison to his former Florida tan, and he is, at the moment, in a state of agitation.*)
JEFFREY: Yacketty, yacketty, yacketty! What is this! A mob scene!
ROSA: (*Turning in surprise.*) But, Jeffrey! On an opening night!
JANE: Hello, Mr. Crandall!

JEFFREY: Hello, Janie. Swell! Swell! You're just leaving, huh?
RUDY: (*Indicating his position against the doorway.*) I got this far.
JANE: Mr. Crandall, is this play any good for pictures? God, the stinkers they've been handing me!
JEFFREY: H'm? No. (*Indicates her costume.*) Nobody wears anything like that in it.
JANE: I get you. Everybody spitting through their teeth. I like a play with jokes, and they all wear beautiful clothes—they make love—not at the same time, of course. . . . See you later, everybody! (*A farewell gesture from Rudy. They are gone.*)
STEPHANIE: A somewhat informal princess—but I like her.
JEFFREY: Refreshing! An interesting end to the House of Hapsburg.
ZOLTAN: Jeffrey, why are you home—this hour, before an opening?
STEPHANIE: Are you coming up, Rosa? I'm dying to see my dress on you.
JEFFREY: No, no! I'd like Rosa to stay a minute. If you'll excuse us . . .
STEPHANIE: Of course. Call me when you come up, Rosa. (*She goes up the stairway.*)
ZOLTAN: Jeffrey, what is wrong?
JEFFREY: Where's Lisa? Can she hear us?
ROSA: (*A shake of the head.*) What is it, Jeffrey?
JEFFREY: (*His voice low.*) It's those men from the Immigration Department.
ZOLTAN: I knew it. The telephone. Ten minutes ago.
ROSA: Zoltan! Calm. Now, Jeffrey?
JEFFREY: They came into my office at four o'clock this afternoon. Same men you saw. I've been wrestling with them ever since.
ZOLTAN: They want *me!*
JEFFREY: Don't get excited. It's you and Lisa both. (*A gesture from Zoltan meaning, "I can stand it. Only tell me."*)
ROSA: Lisa! But that was all settled.
JEFFREY: (*Shakes his head.*) Once they put their machinery in motion it goes right on. They'd put their man in England on it, and he'd started investigating. They dug out all the hospital records, statements from some doctor. They don't believe it was just illness. On the papers it says mental case. (*To Zoltan.*) And you're the one who brought her here.
ZOLTAN: I did only what I thought was good.
JEFFREY: That money you dreamed up—that six thousand dollars—why didn't you come to me?
ZOLTAN: You were in—I should know! Jamaica!
ROSA: Jeffrey, be more— What is it they want?
JEFFREY: Now don't let this upset you too much. They're supposed to take you both to Ellis Island. You and Lisa.
ROSA: Ellis Island! Zoltan—that means they are sending you back! (*Sits.*)
JEFFREY: No, no. Not necessarily. I got my lawyers on it. We'll work out something. But don't let on to Lisa. (*A glance up the stairs.*) She mustn't know about this until after the performance. I had a hell of a time getting them to wait. She had just left the theatre and they wanted to come up here. I offered them everything except a piece of the show. Cigars and Scotch and dough and a trip

to Havana. They didn't even hear me. Then, in desperation, I tried the simple truth. I said, "This kid is a wonderful actress. She's going to make a hit tonight. Will you give her a chance to make it?" I didn't think they'd know what I was talking about, but they said yes.

ROSA: Where are they now?

JEFFREY: They're waiting down at the theatre. They're going to sit in a box, and as soon as the curtain falls, they're going to arrest her.

ZOLTAN: And me.

JEFFREY: I'm afraid so.

ZOLTAN: I may never see this room again. Suddenly it looks beautiful to me.

ROSA: (*Almost hysterically.*) Tonight! (*Jeffrey stops her with a warning gesture as Lisa's and Kurt's voices are heard from the stairs.*)

KURT: (*Off.*) We'd better hurry.

LISA: (*Descending the stairs.*) Just remember not even to blink or you'll miss my whole scene. (*The three on stage quickly assume a composure they are far from feeling. Lisa and Kurt are gay and excited.*) Why, Jeffrey! What are you doing here!

KURT: Is she fired?

JEFFREY: I was up—uh—near here, and I thought I'd—uh—

LISA: Shouldn't you two be dressed or something?

ZOLTAN: We were just starting.

ROSA: It takes me only a minute.

LISA: I'm sorry I missed Rudy and the bride. Kurt says she's wonderful.

ZOLTAN: (*Abstractedly.*) Quite so. Yes.

LISA: Oh, well, I'll see her here tonight, Kurt says.—How darling of you, Rosa, to give me a party. I warn you, I shall eat a lot.—I suppose I should feel terrified and shaky, but I don't. I feel gay and exhilarated and sure of myself.

KURT: The kid's *ausgelassen*.

LISA: (*Linking her arm through Kurt's.*) I'm going to be a great actress, and Kurt's going to be a great novelist and we'll live happily ever after—if only he'll get to work and finish his book.

KURT: Maybe I will—now that you've stopped squirming.

LISA: Oh, when I think of how badly I behaved that day. But I was so frightened. You don't know anything about this, Jeffrey, but I almost didn't go into the play at all. Two government men came here and there was a terrible girl here who did such frightful things—

KURT: Heh, I knew I had something to tell you! She got into my cab today.

ROSA: Not Vilna!

KURT: Vilna, with four other gals. In front of the Roseland Ballroom. La Ballerina is now a dime a dance.

ZOLTAN: Inflation.

ROSA: Zoltan, we must dress. (*Realizes the situation.*) Jeffrey, you will wait for us?

KURT: No, you don't. You promised. In my cab. I'm coming back for you two.

ROSA: Yes, yes. We promised Kurt. In his taxi. But—why don't you wait a while, Jeffrey?

LISA: Oh, come down with us. I'd feel so important riding with the producer.

JEFFREY: Yes. My car is waiting. I'll stay a minute or two. There's something I

want to—uh—
KURT: (*His attention caught by an item in the paper.*) Heh! What's the name of that guy next door? The old man that owns the house here and was always dying?
ROSA: Trowbridge. He is not dead!
KURT: Not exactly. (*Reads.*) "Aged Recluse Marries Nurse." (*Rosa rushes to Kurt, peers at paper. Reads, mumbling.*)
ROSA: Let me see!—"a quiet ceremony" . . . I should hope so—"Will continue to reside—" Zoltan, that means we are safe here. We can stay.
ZOLTAN: (*Ironically.*) Safe!
KURT: What do you think of the old boy! He must be seventy-five if he's an inch!
JEFFREY: What is all this?
ROSA: He owns this house. . . . I will tell you later . . . I must dress. Zoltan! Zoltan! (*Zoltan follows Rosa.*)
KURT: (*To Zoltan and Rosa, who are now on the stairs.*) Be right back for you. I'll blow the horn three times. Honk! Honk! Honk!
ZOLTAN: I will try to remember. Honk-honk-honk. (*They are up the stairs.*)
LISA: (*Poised for departure.*) Jeffrey dear, you know—at the bar—where I pick up the glass—I think it's the third drink—yes—and I put it down like this. Suppose I put it down before I speak instead of afterward?
JEFFREY: Please, on an opening night, don't try to change anything. Play it as you've been playing it.
LISA: Tomorrow night may I try it?
JEFFREY: (*Avoiding her gaze.*) Tomorrow night.
KURT: (*Becomes the haughty butler.*) The taxi waits, milady.
LISA: Good-bye, dear Jeffrey, and thank you, Jeffrey, for the lovely flowers. Thank you for everything. Thank you, and thank you, and thank you. (*They are gone. Alone, Jeffrey paces a bit. Dials on the telephone, gets no answer, hangs up in annoyance. Picks up the newspaper, opens it, throws it aside. Stands staring a moment. Glances impatiently up the stairs. Anna comes down the stairs on her way out. Certainly this is not a figure in gala attire. The plain dark dress.*)
ANNA: My good wishes, Mr. Crandall, for Lisa's play tonight.
JEFFREY: (*Coming out of deep thought.*) What? Oh—uh—thank you very much, Miss Zinsser. You're not going?
ANNA: I cannot tonight. I am hoping to see it another night.
JEFFREY: (*A trifle grimly.*) Don't wait too long. (*Anna jams her hat on her head with one careless movement. She reaches for her coat, plunges one arm into a sleeve. Proffering his help.*) Here—let me!
ANNA: Let you what?
JEFFREY: Help you with your coat.
ANNA: (*Pleased with this novelty. Glows a little.*) Oh! Thank you. In the laboratory this does not happen to me. It is very pleasant. (*The donning of the shabby coat becomes quite a ceremony.*) I would have so liked to go tonight, because of Lisa. But it happens in the laboratory tonight, we are conducting a very important experiment.
JEFFREY: (*Politely disinterested.*) Something new?
ANNA: No, no. We have been working on this for a long time, hoping to find the

right formula. We never know when we will hit upon it. We try this, we try that, sometimes we think—ah, this is it! We fail—and we try again.
JEFFREY: Say! We're in the same business!
ANNA: Suddenly—success! We do not even know why.
JEFFREY: Neither do we!
ANNA: It is very exciting!
JEFFREY: Right! (*Extends his hand and takes hers.*) Hope you have a hit tonight! (*Anna smiles and exits. Immediately Zoltan descends the stairs. He is in full evening dress.*)
ZOLTAN: I have jumped into my clothes. Rosa comes at once. Jeffrey, what do we do?—Think! Think!
JEFFREY: I've been tearing my brains out. If we can get Lisa out of this thing—maybe they won't hold it against you—the affidavit.
ZOLTAN: We are not criminals. There must be someone we can go to.
JEFFREY: How do you go to anybody? Who's there to go to on a thing like this? (*Rosa comes swiftly down the stairs. In the beautiful evening gown supplied by Stephanie, Inc., we see for the first time what a handsome and distinguished woman this is. Over one arm she carries a wrap.*)
ROSA: We must not waste time. We must go down to the theatre and talk to these men. Come!
JEFFREY: Talk! I've talked to them for hours. This is the government. They've got their orders. They are going to arrest both of you tonight and take you to Ellis Island. You and Lisa.
ROSA: Ellis Island!
ZOLTAN: Who gives these orders? That is the man to find!
JEFFREY: How do you find a man like that at twenty minutes to eight at night! We don't even know who he is.
ROSA: (*Puts cape on piano.*) Ellis Island. Who is the head of Ellis Island?
JEFFREY: He couldn't do anything. Now listen. Here's what my lawyers tell me. You come up for a hearing on the Island. Tomorrow—next year—I don't know when. If we lose that, it gets appealed. Some board or other in Philadelphia. If we lose that, then the only chance is the Attorney General of the United States. He's final.
ZOLTAN: Then he's the man we want. Call him up!
JEFFREY: What!
ROSA: Yes, do we bother with Philadelphia and boards!
JEFFREY: Call up the Attorney General!
ZOLTAN: Why not?
JEFFREY: He won't be there at this hour, a man like— He's a cabinet officer. How can a person go to a phone and expect to get— He's one of the most important men in the— (*Zoltan has pushed the phone into Jeffrey's hand.*) Oh—uh—I want the Attorney General in Washington— Why—Department of Justice, I suppose.—Yes.—What? (*He looks at the dial number on the phone.*) Endicott 2-1342— (*Covers transmitter with hand, turns to Zoltan and Rosa.*) This is damned foolishness. I can't even remember his name. I think I met him once at a Gridiron dinner.
ZOLTAN: Good, good—there you are!

ROSA: Is he a sympathetic man?
JEFFREY: The Attorney General! Christ, I don't know!—Hello! Is this the Department of Justice? (*He covers the transmitter, turns to Zoltan and Rosa.*) They're open!—I want to speak to the Attorney General. Is he still there?—My name is Crandall—Jeffrey Crandall, of New York. He knows me.—Oh! Well, what's his home number?—But I know him very, very well. What's his name? (*He listens, there is no sound. The connection is broken. With a growl, he hands the receiver to Zoltan, who listens a moment, then hangs up.*) I told you it's no use! You can't do things that way. The Attorney General.
ROSA: The President! The President is above the Attorney General!
JEFFREY: Oh, no! No, you don't! I am not going to let you make complete jackasses out of yourselves.
ZOLTAN: (*Recalling his Naturalization home work.*) "The Citizen shall have the right to petition the President for a redress of grievances." It says.
ROSA: Yes! After all, Abraham Lincoln saved the boy who was going to be shot. These are people you can talk to. Please!
JEFFREY: You can't *do* such a thing!
ZOLTAN: But here is a Democracy . . . isn't it?
JEFFREY: Democracy! But suppose a hundred and fifty million people all try to call up the President every time they were in trouble. What would happen?
ZOLTAN: It would be a busy line.
ROSA: (*To Jeffrey.*) But this is Zoltan and Lisa— Let us at least try. This will be the end of them— This will be the end of all of us.
JEFFREY: Look, you've got to face it, you people. You can't just pick up a telephone— (*By way of illustration, he picks up the bit of paper on which Zoltan had written the telephone number of his park acquaintance.*) and change the laws of the country. It's idiotic! You can't do it! (*He crushes the paper into a wad in his hand. Zoltan sees this. He takes it from Jeffrey, smooths it, reads it, is at telephone dialing.*)
ROSA: What! What are you—! Zoltan, are you crazy!
ZOLTAN: I tell you this was a real fellow.
JEFFREY: Who? Who's he calling?
ROSA: He doesn't even know.
ZOLTAN: I met today a man in the park . . .
JEFFREY: A man in the park! Look, it's ten minutes to eight, we've got to get down there—
ROSA: Zoltan! This is nonsense!
ZOLTAN: Hello! Hello! Here is Zoltan Lazko. Would you be so kind, it is very important, I would like to speak to this number, the man who is feeding the squirrels in the park today.
JEFFREY: Squirrels! (*Looks at Rosa, she at him.*)
ZOLTAN: . . . It is *you*! Excuse me I call you like this. But you seemed in the park a fine big man. It is a terrible thing we have here . . . a wonderful young girl—I told you about her a little . . . tonight she opens in a play . . . a talented actress and this is her chance . . . but they are taking her, the Immigration people, Ellis Island. And because I made for her the affidavit they are coming also for me. . . . No, no, I did a good thing, but they make it out wrong. . . . Please, can we

come tonight and talk to you? . . . No, no, after the play, we must go now to the play, it is her opening night in America, this child. . . . (*Hopelessly.*) You go to bed at ten o'clock every night. . . . Then tomorrow, please? (*Listens, turns to others.*) He goes eight o'clock in the morning to Washington. (*It begins to dawn on Jeffrey that perhaps this is really a person of consequence. Slowly with a look of intense concentration, he advances on Zoltan at the telephone.*) . . . You have a first appointment at seven in the morning! (*His hopelessness deepens.*) We come at half-past six.

JEFFREY: (*Grabs phone.*) My God, it's Bernie! Bernie Baruch! Is this you? Bernie! Bernie! This is Jeffrey Crandall. . . . Yes, I'm here at Lazko's. I know all about it. I needn't tell you who Lazko is, you know all about that. The girl is in my play. She's a wonderful girl. It's a deportation case. An absolute outrage, one of those technical damn things. . . . Bernie, would I have her in the play if there was any doubt about this thing? I give you my word this is a gross miscarriage of justice. . . . If you'll let us put it up to you— . . . Bernie, you've known me for twenty-five years— have I ever— Look, Bernie, what are you doing right now? . . . But this is international *too!* in a way. It's just one girl, but she stands for all of the— Will you come down to the theatre and talk to her? Will you let me pick you up in five minutes and come down to the theatre?—Great!—What?—If it *is* a miscarriage of justice you'll help them; if it is not, you won't. Well, believe me, it is! Thanks, Bernie! (*He hangs up.*) The one person in the world who can start the wheels turning! Zoltan, you are the greatest man of our times!

ROSA: My wonderful Zoltan! You see what can happen from only a bag of peanuts in the park!

ZOLTAN: And who wanted to throw out the peanuts! (*Stephanie, in evening gown and wrap, comes down the stairs.*)

STEPHANIE: Shouldn't we be going? Isn't it time to go?

JEFFREY: (*Crossing up hall to get coat.*) It is for me. I've got a stop to make.

ROSA: Stephanie, what do you think! Zoltan went in the park today and met a wonderful man, and this man is going to make everything right! A magic thing!

STEPHANIE: (*To Zoltan.*) Zoltan, how romantic!

ZOLTAN: It *is* romantic. This is a romantic country. In such a country anything could happen! Anything!

JEFFREY: That's right.—Stephanie, I've got to go across the park, but will you drive down with me? My car's outside.

STEPHANIE: I'd love to. (*She crosses to Rosa.*) Perfect—the dress is perfect, even if I do say so. You look very distinguished, Rosa.

JEFFREY: That *is* a wonderful dress, Rosa. You look like the old Rosa—I mean, the young Rosa.

ROSA: It's all Stephanie. She made it and gave it to me. Stephanie's the girl to do the clothes for your next play, Jeffrey. She can convey a whole character with a ruffle.

JEFFREY: Well, I'd like a lot of ruffles in my next play. I'm sick of these skirt and sweater jobs, like this one tonight. Tough—hard-bitten.

STEPHANIE: I'm ready for a play with star dust in it. A play with magic, romance and illusion.

ZOLTAN: Oh, so romance is back again, eh! Love is once more permitted! And who

is the master of romance and love in the theatre! Lazko!
JEFFREY: Nothing would make me happier.
ZOLTAN: After all, the greatest plays in the world—what are they about? Love.
JEFFREY: Suits me! I think there's money in it. Come on, Stephanie. Don't be late, you two!
STEPHANIE: See you at the theatre.
JEFFREY: And don't worry about Ellis Island. We've got Superman on our side. (*Jeffrey and Stephanie exit to hall.*)
ZOLTAN: Tomorrow morning—Act One. Already I have an idea—if only I can do it.
ROSA: You will see! There are lovers at Coney Island just as there were in the Prater in Vienna. And the chocolate sodas at Liggett's are for them sweeter than the Maiwein of Budapest. Suddenly you look yourself again, now you are the Zoltan I used to know.
ZOLTAN: I need a new dress suit—a man in my position.
ROSA: (*Picking up cape from piano, puts it on.*) Yes, Zoltan.
ZOLTAN: Rosa, I feel this will be my greatest play. In the end, the real artist rises above his environment. Look at Shakespeare! In England there was war and pestilence and the Spanish Armada was knocking at the gates, and in the middle of it all, what does he write! He writes *Romeo and Juliet*! (*From the street comes the sound of a taxi horn. HONK, HONK, HONK.*)
ROSA: It is Kurt. We must go.
ZOLTAN: (*Puts on cape.*) And today who remembers what that war was about! But everybody remembers Shakespeare.
ROSA: Yes, Zoltan, and do not think I have missed the comparison.
ZOLTAN: All right. I am not Shakespeare, but I have as good a chance as he had. Better! The world today is even *worse* than it was in his time.
ROSA: What a bit of luck, Zoltan.
ZOLTAN: Yes, sir! This time I write a masterpiece. A *real* American play. But Wunderbar! . . . How do they say on the radio? Zoltan Lazko writes again! (*The honk of the horn is heard again as the CURTAIN falls.*)

END

THE LATE GEORGE APLEY

John P. Marquand
&
George S. Kaufman

[1944]

The Late George Apley was first produced at the Lyceum Theatre, New York, on November 21st, 1944, with the following cast:

Margaret	*Mrs. Priestley Morrison*
George Apley	*Leo G. Carroll*
Catherine Apley	*Janet Beecher*
John Apley	*David McKay*
Eleanor Apley	*Joan Chandler*
Wilson	*Byron Russell*
Amelia Newcombe	*Margaret Dale*
Roger Newcombe	*Percy Waram*
Horatio Willing	*Reynolds Evans*
Jane Willing	*Catherine Proctor*
Agnes Willing	*Margaret Phillips*
Howard Boulder	*John Conway*
Lydia Leyton	*Ivy Troutman*
Emily Southworth	*Mabel Acker*
Julian H. Dole	*Howard St. John*
Henry	*Sayre Crawley*

Staged by George S. Kaufman

THE SCENES

ACT I
George Apley's house in Beacon Street, Boston. Thanksgiving Day, 1912.

ACT II
The same a week later.

ACT III
The same the following morning.

EPILOGUE
A corner of the Berkeley Club, 1942. (Small set in corner of the stage.)

ACT I

SCENE 1: *Mr. George Apley's living room on Beacon Street.*

TIME: *Thanksgiving Day, 1912.*

AT RISE: *The curtain rises on a large room which, like many rooms in Boston, is half sumptuously and half carelessly furnished, without any unity of decoration, and yet this very lack of unity gives a comfortable sense of continuity, showing that the place has been occupied for many years by a family in comfortable circumstances. Margaret, the Apleys' maid, a grim, austere woman of about seventy, in a meticulously starched uniform, is seen near the bay window, engaged in a curious horticultural pursuit. She is holding an insecticide sprayer and as the curtain rises she crosses to the ivy and starts sprayer here and there. She does not turn her head when the front door in the outer hall slams.*

Mr. George Apley enters presently, in black overcoat and high silk hat. He has a morning paper under his arm, and as he is taking off his gloves, he sees Margaret, squares his shoulders to meet a new emergency.

APLEY: (*He speaks in the calm, suppressed tone of a man who wishes to face the worst, and can stand it.*) What is it now, Margaret? (*As he speaks Wilson, an elderly butler, comes in and crosses to Apley, taking his hat and coat.*)

MARGARET: It's the green bugs on the ivy, Mr. Apley. They're back again. The leaves are crawling with them. You can see for yourself.

APLEY: I don't see why it is that something like this invariably happens on Thanksgiving. (*Wilson has taken coat and crosses out to hall, puts coat there and exits. Apley puts on his glasses.*) Last year there was a blizzard, and the year before that the mince pies fermented . . . (*He sits, picks up paper.*) Let me see, Mrs. Apley bought that ivy in 1890—or was it in '92? At any rate, it's down in the plant book. (*He opens his newspaper and starts to read.*)

MARGARET: We had some trouble with it about the time of the Spanish War, but never anything like this.

APLEY: Well, we can't do anything about it now, Margaret, just before Thanksgiving dinner. It's just another of those little things, Margaret—little things that interfere with our lives.

MARGARET: Yes, sir.

APLEY: (*He thinks—rises with newspaper, puts paper on sofa.*) Let me see, Emerson has something capital to say about that. (*Margaret, at the mention of Emerson, thus warned, tries to escape.*) Wait a minute, Margaret! (*She is caught. Apley, meanwhile, is searching the bookshelves.*) Margaret!

MARGARET: Yes?

APLEY: (*With the air of a Supreme Court justice handing down a decision.*) Where—is Emerson?

MARGARET: The brown book, isn't it?

APLEY: Emerson's Essays, Margaret. You know it very well. It ought to be right here beside Thoreau . . . (*He finds it at the very end of bookshelf.*) Oh, here it is, next to Hawthorne. (*Severely.*) You've put it next to "The Scarlet Letter," by Hawthorne.

MARGARET: Well, it belongs there with the other brown books, doesn't it?

APLEY: It certainly does not belong there. (*He is paging through it.*) Ah, here we are. Listen to this, Margaret.

MARGARET: Yes, sir.

APLEY: (*He reads.*) "God appears with all His Parts in every moss and every cobweb. If the good is there, so is the evil; if the affinity, so the repulsion." There you have it.

MARGARET: (*She nods.*) Yes, sir! (*Margaret escapes. Apley affectionately turns a page and is replacing it in the bookcase as Mrs. Apley enters. Catherine Apley is in her middle years, and still quite lovely.*)

CATHERINE: (*Crosses to dresser, puts snapdragons in vase.*) I've just spent a whole hour in the conservatory with the snapdragon. The snapdragon are beautiful. And I've put some on the dining-room table—a great mound of them, between the pumpkins.

APLEY: (*Crosses to sofa, picks up paper, sits.*) Snapdragon and pumpkins? You've never done that before.

CATHERINE: Yes, I know. It just came over me.

APLEY: Sounds rather radical. . . . Where's John? Isn't he here yet?

CATHERINE: He'll be here. You know how slow the trolleys are from Cambridge.

APLEY: (*Annoyed.*) He ought to be here now, with Agnes coming for dinner.

CATHERINE: (*Sits next to Apley.*) That reminds me, George. Don't forget Agnes is having her coming-out party a week from tonight.

APLEY: Agnes coming out already? John will be a married man before we know it.

CATHERINE: Not too soon, I hope.

APLEY: Oh, not right away, of course. Still, everyone seems to think—

CATHERINE: Nothing's ever been said.

APLEY: Little Agnes! I suppose it's seeing her grow up, right next door— What about Eleanor? Where is she?

CATHERINE: Upstairs changing her dress.
APLEY: Does it seem to you, Catherine, that Eleanor has not been quite her own self, these last few weeks?
CATHERINE: I have noticed something. But a young girl, George—it's to be expected. (*The sound of the outer door slamming.*) There's John now. (*John, the son of the house, appears in the doorway. A good-looking lad of twenty.*)
JOHN: (*Going up the stairs.*) Hello, everybody!
APLEY: Are you ready for dinner?
JOHN: (*Disappearing up the stairs.*) Just going up to wash!
APLEY: (*Rises. Calling after him.*) Can't you wash at Harvard?
CATHERINE: Hurry up, dear. And see what Eleanor is doing. . . . (*As Apley reseats himself.*) George, will you hand me the Phillips Brooks calendar? (*He rises, crosses to desk, with paper.*) Agnes' coming out party is going to give us a very complicated week. . . . (*Apley returns to sofa, gives Catherine calendar, sits.*) Thank you. . . . Now, tomorrow there's the Symphony. We must go to that—we're sitting in the new seats.
APLEY: (*Who has been looking at paper, stops.*) Oh, yes. . . . I don't know why we ever changed.
CATHERINE: But you've been waiting for years, dear, till Mrs. Warren died, so we could move forward.
APLEY: I never knew it would put us next to the Hopkinses.
CATHERINE: The Bradley Hopkinses?
APLEY: Yes. Don't you think, Catherine, that if we're sitting next to them, people may think that our tastes verge on the radical?
CATHERINE: Why, George?
APLEY: You know what Bradley Hopkins said about that unfortunate Debussy selection, "Afternoon of a Faun." (*He lowers his voice.*) He said—he enjoyed it very much, and a great many people heard him say it. And if we're sitting next to them—
CATHERINE: I'm sure it'll be all right. (*Returning to calendar.*) Now, Saturday night is dinner at Major Higginson's, and Sunday we'll have to be at King's Chapel. I think, George, we ought to take the automobile. We never seem to use it. (*Apley looks at folded paper a bit.*)
APLEY: I wouldn't do that, Catherine. You know Patrick doesn't drive it well. He's much more used to horses.
CATHERINE: I really don't see any use having an automobile—
APLEY: Catherine, Patrick has driven the family for forty years. He drove for Father. I won't have anything done to hurt his feelings. We'll take the carriage.
CATHERINE: Of course, George.
APLEY: (*Looking at calendar over Catherine's shoulder.*) Now—on Monday afternoon there is a trustees' meeting of the Sailors' Home, and Monday night is the Monday Night Club. Tuesday— Oh, yes! The Save Boston Society. It's about allowing an electric sign on the edge of the Common.
CATHERINE: Must you go to that, too, George?
APLEY: (*Rises, leaves paper on sofa.*) Dear me! Tuesday—I completely forgot. The Blue Hill Bird Watchers' Society is meeting.
CATHERINE: Is that more important, George?

APLEY: This particular meeting—I think it is, my dear. There has to be another President of the Bird Watchers—you remember old Dr. Beech died last week. And I have every reason to believe— (*He lets her guess his secret.*)
CATHERINE: (*Rises.*) Why, George, that's splendid.
APLEY: Mind you, I don't say I'm worthy of it. But—I've never missed a Sunday bird walk.
CATHERINE: Yes, I know, George.
APLEY: What really tipped the scales in my favor, I think, was last Sunday, when I saw the yellow-throated linnet. I told you about that, didn't I?
CATHERINE: I—think so.
APLEY: A yellow-throated linnet, in November. I think I'm the only living Bostonian who has seen one in November. I wish I could get you to take more interest in birds, Catherine.
CATHERINE: I'll try, George, if you're the president. (*Crosses to sofa, sits, picks up calendar.*)
APLEY: It would look better from the general point of view.
CATHERINE: (*Her attention back on the calendar.*) Tuesday night is the Tuesday Night Club. (*She looks up.*) George.
APLEY: (*He stops.*) What is it, my dear?
CATHERINE: We seem to be doing so many little things always—
APLEY: Little things? You don't mean the Tuesday Club?
CATHERINE: Not exactly. It's just everything.
APLEY: (*A look at calendar.*) Wednesday afternoon is the Boston Waifs' Society. I must go to that—I'm a trustee.
CATHERINE: (*Puts calendar down.*) Ye-es.
APLEY: Then what could I give up, Catherine?
CATHERINE: (*Rises. Hesitantly.*) I don't know. But if you were active in the management of the mills . . . if we were more like other people. . . .
APLEY: My dear, that would not excuse us from our obligations. (*Catherine turns to Apley.*) Someone has to be a trustee of the Boston Waifs; someone has to look after the Sailors' Home. My grandfather . . . my father . . . These are things that have come down to me, Catherine. Last week alone, Catherine, I attended twelve meetings of different organizations—charitable, civic. Father was on most of them. (*He picks up calendar, then puts it on table, and sits.*)
CATHERINE: (*Sits next to Apley.*) I forget how much time you give to others— how little you think of yourself.
APLEY: I have to think that I am paying back something for what I have.
CATHERINE: (*Picks up calendar.*) Of course, George.
APLEY: I suppose I have been poured into a mould, Catherine, but it is not such a bad mould after all. (*Eleanor comes down the stairs. A nice-looking girl, unblemished by cosmetics. Shirtwaist, low heels.*)
ELEANOR: (*As she comes down stairs.*) Good morning, Father.
APLEY: (*Rises, crosses to Eleanor.*) Well, here is my little girl. Is she going to give her father a kiss? (*Catherine rises, takes calendar to desk.*)
ELEANOR: (*As she kisses him.*) Of course, Father.
APLEY: But what are you wearing, my dear? You look as though you were going for a walk.

ELEANOR: I am going for a walk.
CATHERINE: A walk, dear?
ELEANOR: Yes!
APLEY: You can't very well go for a walk before dinner, Elly. They're all coming at any minute.
ELEANOR: I'm not going before dinner, Father. Afterwards, when dinner is over.
APLEY: Then don't you think you might run upstairs and change, dear? It's only that they may think you're being a little rude and careless.
ELEANOR: Oh, Father! Do you really mind so much?
CATHERINE: Are you going for a walk *with* someone, dear?
ELEANOR: Yes, I am.
CATHERINE: A young man, perhaps?
ELEANOR: Yes.
CATHERINE: Well, if it's a young man, George—
APLEY: (*Crosses to Eleanor a bit.*) Yes, of course. Er—who is he, Elly?
ELEANOR: (*Bracing herself.*) His name is—Howard Boulder.
APLEY: Who?
ELEANOR: Howard Boulder. You'll like him, Father.
APLEY: Boulder . . . (*A mute questioning look at Catherine, who answers with a blank shake of the head.*) It certainly isn't Boston. (*In a strained voice.*) Where does he come from, Elly?
ELEANOR: Oh dear!
CATHERINE: You know where he comes from, don't you?
ELEANOR: Yes.
APLEY: Well, where?
ELEANOR: (*A deep breath.*) New York.
APLEY: New York? (*Looks at Catherine.*)
ELEANOR: (*As Apley turns back to her.*) Now come, Father. Don't be prejudiced.
APLEY: (*He puts a brave face on the situation.*) Well, as a matter of fact, I know some people from New York. Several—people. New York is—it's not Boston, but—er—
CATHERINE: Where did you meet him, dear?
ELEANOR: At the Brattle Hall dance last Saturday. An usher introduced us. I was sitting in the dump.
APLEY: The dump? What under the sun is the dump?
ELEANOR: (*With some impatience.*) You know, the place where the girls sit after a dance. And then the ushers bring people up, Father.
APLEY: What is this young man doing in Boston, dear?
ELEANOR: He's giving lectures at Harvard, at Emerson Hall. He's very brilliant, Father.
CATHERINE: Lectures? Why didn't you tell us sooner, dear? How nice.
APLEY: What sort of lectures does he give?
CATHERINE: Here they come, George. (*She takes a step toward door.*)
APLEY: (*Ignoring the interruption.*) What sort of lectures, Elly?
ELEANOR: American Literature. It's one of those fellowships that are paid for out of somebody's will. And he's done so well he's coming back in February.
APLEY: Why, that would be the Jonathyn Smythe Fellowship! (*Wilson crosses*

hall.) That changes everything! Well, well! Catherine, Buzzy Loring is the chairman of the Jonathyn Smythe Fellowship!
CATHERINE: Really!
APLEY: Well, no wonder he got to Brattle Hall!
AMELIA: (*Off.*) Well, Wilson, and how are you?
APLEY: (*As he hears Amelia.*) It's Amelia! (*He takes paper from sofa and puts it on desk.*)
WILSON: (*Off.*) Good morning, Mrs. Newcombe! Mr. Newcombe! (*Catherine crosses to door.*)
ROGER: (*Off.*) Wilson! (*Amelia Newcombe sweeps in aggressively.*)
CATHERINE: (*Shaking Amelia's hand.*) Well, Amelia, how good of you to come!
AMELIA: (*Crossing to Apley.*) Where else should we go on Thanksgiving, Catherine? My own brother!

(*Enter Roger.*)

APLEY: Amelia, how are you?
CATHERINE: Roger!
ROGER: (*Shaking Amelia's hand.*) Catherine!
AMELIA: (*As she embraces him and pats him on the shoulder none too gently.*) George, you need a haircut!
APLEY: Really, Amelia!
ROGER: George . . . Eleanor . . . (*He sits.*)
ELEANOR: Uncle Roger. Aunt Amelia!
AMELIA: (*Suddenly surveying Eleanor.*) What's that you've got on, Eleanor? It looks terrible!
ELEANOR: I'm sorry!
APLEY: (*Proudly.*) Eleanor has a young man calling for her. They're going to take a walk.
CATHERINE: Yes!
AMELIA: (*Sits.*) What young man? When I was a young girl no one ever called on me on Thanksgiving.
ROGER: Too late now!
APLEY: He's quite an intelligent young man who gives lectures. The Jonathyn Symthe Fellowship at Harvard. You know the Jonathyn Smythe Fellowship, Roger. Buzzy Loring is the trustee for it.
ROGER: Oh, yes. . . . You know, I've worked out a way of remembering everything that Buzzy Loring is the trustee for?
APLEY: Is that so? How do you do it?
ROGER: Whatever it is, if you're not the trustee for it, he is. (*Wilson appears from hall with sherry on tray.*) Ah, here's the old Saint Bernard!
AMELIA: (*Refusing with a wave of the hand.*) Well, Wilson. Are you having a happy Thanksgiving?
WILSON: Yes, thank you, Mrs. Newcombe.
ROGER: Of course he is. Doesn't he *look* happy?
AMELIA: Where's John? I don't see John.
APLEY: He'll be down in a minute.

AMELIA: And our talkative Cousin Jane?
APLEY: They're all coming! Horatio, Jane and Agnes. (*Wilson offers tray to Apley . . . he takes a glass.*)
AMELIA: Well, why aren't they here? It's just next door. (*Wilson offers Roger sherry. He takes it.*)
ROGER: Thank you, Wilson.
AMELIA: (*Rises.*) Roger! Roger! You promised me— (*Wilson exits.*)
ROGER: Thanksgiving, dear.
AMELIA: Thanksgiving or not, Roger—
ROGER: (*Indicates portraits on wall.*) Look at your ancestors on the walls. They have a port complexion.
AMELIA: (*As she looks at portraits.*) Our ancestors had high color because they lived— George!
APLEY: Yes, Amelia?
AMELIA: The Gilbert Stuart portrait of great-grandmother has a new crack in it. Right there—across the nose.
APLEY: (*Looking at portrait.*) That crack? Why, that's always been there, Amelia.
AMELIA: It's a new crack, and it ruins the Apley nose.
APLEY: But I remember that crack in the old dining room when I was ten years old.
AMELIA: If Father had left me those portraits, and I think he always intended to—
APLEY: You got the silver tankards with the whistles, Amelia. I got the portraits.
AMELIA: I can only say that if they were hanging in my parlor—

(*Horatio Willing has come into the room.*)

HORATIO: Well, well! There's wine in the air today! Catherine! (*He shakes her hand.*)
CATHERINE: Horatio!
HORATIO: (*Shakes Apley's hand.*) George!
APLEY: Horatio!
HORATIO: Eleanor, my dear! What was it Harriet Prescott Spofford said: "Dear the people coming home, all the glad and happy play! Dear the thanks too, that we give, for all of this Thanksgiving Day!"
ROGER: Once more, please! (*Jane, Horatio's wife, enters. Jane is a subdued woman, and you gather that it may have been Horatio who subdued her.*)
APLEY: Ah, Jane! (*She shakes Apley's hand.*)
JANE: Good afternoon, Cousin George. Catherine! (*She shakes Catherine's hand.*)
CATHERINE: Jane!
JANE: Roger! Eleanor! Amelia!
AMELIA: Sloppy Jane! That's what they used to call you at Miss Hendricks' School. You've forgotten to take off your galoshes again. (*Jane lifts her skirts a bit.*)
HORATIO: (*Severely.*) Jane!
JANE: Oh, I'm sorry. (*She makes a quick exit.*)
CATHERINE: Where's Agnes? Didn't you bring Agnes?
HORATIO: (*Calling.*) Agnes, dear.
AGNES: (*Off-stage.*) Yes, Papa!
HORATIO: Your Cousin Catherine is asking for you.

AGNES: (*Off-stage.*) I'm coming, Papa! (*There is a moment's pause, and then Agnes enters. She is a rather pallid girl with a large bow in her hair, and she clutches a small package done up in tissue paper. She crosses to Apley as he comes to her and puts his arm around her shoulder.*) Hello, Cousin George!
APLEY: How are you, my dear?
AGNES: Hello, Cousin Catherine!
CATHERINE: How do you do, Agnes?
AGNES: Hello, Cousin Roger!
ROGER: Agnes!
AGNES: Eleanor!
ELEANOR: Hello!
AGNES: Hello, Cousin Amelia!
AMELIA: What are you so pale for? Nothing to be scared about—just the family.
AGNES: I'm—not scared, Cousin Amelia. (*Jane enters and Catherine takes her to a chair.*)
CATHERINE: Sit here, Jane. (*She sits. Wilson enters same time as Jane, with sherry, goes to Jane. She takes a glass.*)
AMELIA: Well, where's John? Agnes is here and not John. (*Agnes blushes a little at this.*)
APLEY: (*Calling.*) John! (*Wilson crosses to Horatio, gives him sherry.*)
JOHN: (*On stairway.*) I'm here, Father! (*He comes into the room.*) I'm sorry. Hello, everybody!
ROGER: Hello, John.
JOHN: Aunt Amelia.
AMELIA: John.
APLEY: A bit late, aren't you, John?
JOHN: I'm sorry, Father. (*Wilson exits.*)
CATHERINE: (*Puts sherry on table. Motioning to John.*) Here's your cousin Agnes, dear. Aren't you going to speak to her? (*It is obvious, from the polite ripple of expectancy, that everyone has been waiting for this encounter.*)
JOHN: Oh! Hello, Agnes.
AGNES: Hello, John.
HORATIO: (*Beaming, patting her arm.*) Well, Agnes?
AGNES: Yes, Papa?
HORATIO: Aren't you going to give John his present?
AGNES: (*Clutching package.*) Oh, Papa! Not right now.
HORATIO: But why not now as well as any time?
JANE: (*Rises.*) Horatio, if she doesn't want to give it to him now—
HORATIO: Of course she wants to give it to him now. Why shouldn't she—? (*Pushes Agnes a bit.*)
AGNES: (*Embarrassed, crosses to John.*) It—isn't anything. Just—something I made for you.
CATHERINE: Something you made? How sweet!
AGNES: It's—a necktie.
HORATIO: A knitted necktie. She's been knitting it for two weeks. Give it to him, Agnes.
AGNES: It isn't as good as it ought to be.

AMELIA: Well, give it to him anyhow. (*Agnes thrusts package at him.*)
JOHN: Thanks, Agnes. Thanks very much. (*He starts to put package in his pocket.*)
CATHERINE: John, aren't you going to open it? Everybody wants to see.
APLEY: Yes, John. Open it. When a pretty girl gives you a present—
ELEANOR: He's blushing.
JOHN: I'm not. (*Slowly opens the package. The necktie within is obviously homemade.*) Well, thanks. It was nice of you to make it, Agnes. Thanks.
CATHERINE: John, isn't it beautiful? Why don't you put it on right now?
HORATIO: Oh, he doesn't have to do that, Catherine.
AGNES: (*Hoping he won't.*) Oh, no. I'm going to make him another one with a lot more stripes in it. (*There is an awkward silence. Then John silently stuffs package into his pocket and backs slowly away from Agnes. Jane sits. Catherine sits.*)
HORATIO: (*Putting glass on table.*) Oh, I knew I had something to tell you. This morning on Park Street, just outside the Union Club, I ran into Walter Noble. He told me about the Bird Watchers, George. George is going to be the next president of the Bird Watchers. (*There is a little chorus of congratulations.*)
AMELIA: Well.
ROGER: Really!
APLEY: No, no, no! It's not definite at all yet.
HORATIO: He implied it very strongly.
APLEY: It isn't decided yet—you really mustn't say anything about it. It's rather interesting, though, how it came about.
ROGER: Do tell us!
APLEY: At least, it helped a great deal. (*Eleanor crosses to fireplace chair. Apley takes everyone in. John crosses to piano, strolling.*) It was in the Lawrences' pasture, last Sunday—just where the path forks toward the brook. Not the big brook, the little brook. (*Big gesture, small gesture.*) Anyhow, I don't know what first caught my attention. There was no sound. (*Just then John picks at the piano. Apley turns and gives him a reproving look.*) Merely a flash of color in the junipers—(*Wilson enters, crosses to Catherine, whispers to her, then exits again*)—a bright flash of yellow, but I had time to raise my glasses and there on the lower limb of that big shag-bark hickory by the stone wall—
CATHERINE: (*Rises. She has received word of dinner from Wilson, and now tries gently to interrupt.*) George.
APLEY: Sitting there quietly, just as though it were midsummer—
CATHERINE: (*A little louder.*) George.
APLEY: Not making a sound, mind you— What, my dear?
CATHERINE: Dinner is ready. (*She gestures to Amelia.*)
APLEY: Oh. . . . Well, we'll go in. . . . Amelia. (*Amelia rises. Jane rises.*)
ROGER: (*A man desperate.*) But WHAT was sitting there? You can't leave us dangling!
APLEY: A yellow-throated linnet!
HORATIO: No!
APLEY: Yes!
ROGER: No!
APLEY: Yes!

AMELIA: Well, I don't understand all this nonsense about birds. A bird is all right in its place, but why pry into its private life?
APLEY: Did you ever read Emerson on birds?
AMELIA: No!
APLEY: Well, you should! Horatio? And John, suppose you give Agnes your arm.

(*John offers Agnes his arm.*)

AMELIA: (*Surveying the picture with pleasure.*) Ah . . . (*As John and Agnes start crossing they exit in the following order: Catherine, Jane, Amelia, Horatio, Eleanor, John and Agnes.*)
APLEY: It was right there on the lower limb, and as I looked it burst into song. Like this . . .

(*Roger has started out after everyone else has gone in and as he passes into dining-room door, Apley takes a small whistle out of his pocket and blows it as . . .*)

THE CURTAIN FALLS

SCENE 2: The return of the family after dinner.

The women come in first. Slowly, heavily, all giving evidence of that unwelcome repletion which so often follows a Thanksgiving dinner.

Amelia, Jane, then Catherine. Amelia goes to sofa, sits. Jane sits on the opposite end of the sofa. Catherine crosses to desk, picks up fans, gives one to Jane and one to Amelia, then sits between them. Amelia has started fanning herself, the other two join in and they fan themselves two or three times in unison. . . .

CATHERINE: The men will be coming in to smoke. I wish they didn't smoke those cigars. (*She addresses Jane.*) Horatio never smokes, does he?
JANE: Horatio never does anything. (*The men now enter. Horatio comes in and sits heavily in a chair. After he is settled, Roger enters holding a snifter brandy glass, with a large portion of brandy in it. He is about to sit when . . .*)
AMELIA: Isn't that your second brandy, Roger?
ROGER: (*Puts glass on table.*) Third. (*He sits. He gives a big groan, then opens his vest, undoing the buttons. He pats his stomach, loudly, several times.*)

(*Apley enters with a box of cigars and offers Roger the box.*)

APLEY: Roger?
ROGER: (*Taking cigar.*) Thank you, George. (*He clips his cigar from watch chain clipper.*) Remember the first time you and I ever tried a cigar, George? We couldn't have been more than seven—we stole them out of your father's desk. (*He lights his cigar.*)
APLEY: (*Who has lit his cigar.*) Father saw us take them and made us smoke them to the end.

ROGER: I don't think we smoked again until we finished rowing on the Harvard crew.
APLEY: That's right, at New London after the race. We've had some good times together, Roger.
AMELIA: Roger was always a very bad influence on you, George.
ROGER: I wish I still were. (*John and Agnes enter.*)
APLEY: (*Motioning them to settee.*) Why don't you children sit there? (*They have crossed to settee and sit, John at the right end, Agnes at the left.*)
ROGER: (*Looking at Apley and rising.*) Have I . . . Have I your chair, George?
APLEY: No, no . . . Well! (*Apley sits. Horatio takes desk chair, turns it and sits in it. Apley notices the children.*) Move over, John, don't be shy! (*He gestures with his hand. John moves a bit closer to Agnes.*) John is going to get a gold watch if he doesn't smoke before he's twenty-one. We have a little agreement.
HORATIO: What a beautiful relationship you and John have always had. I can't imagine anything ever coming between you. (*Eleanor comes in. Apley motions her to a chair and she sits.*)
APLEY: Elly, dear. (*Horatio sighs. Roger sits and groans. There is a long silence.*)
JANE: (*As though to herself.*) We've sat in these same seats for eighteen Thanksgivings.
HORATIO: Why, what a peculiar thing to say, Jane. Why shouldn't we?
APLEY: What would Thanksgiving be without a family?
HORATIO: It's very good of you, George, to include Jane and me. After all, Jane is only your third cousin.
APLEY: It is possible to be very fond of a cousin, Horatio.

(*Horatio beams. Then he turns to his wife.*)

HORATIO: (*With a meaning look.*) Jane, dear.
JANE: Thank you, Cousin George.
APLEY: And your little Agnes is quite like our own daughter.
AGNES: (*Rises.*) Thank you, Cousin George. (*John rises.*)
CATHERINE: Are you ready for your coming-out party, Agnes?
AGNES: I hope so, Cousin Catherine.
APLEY: First Eleanor and now Agnes. Two big grown-up girls. Everyone is flying from the nest—eh, Horatio?
HORATIO: (*Ever in agreement.*) Flying from the nest.
CATHERINE: Is Agnes' dress finished yet, Jane? (*Jane is apparently absorbed. Horatio makes a move towards her.*) Jane.
JANE: (*Coming to.*) What was that? Excuse me, Catherine.
CATHERINE: Is Agnes' dress finished for the party?
JANE: Oh, yes. Almost.
AMELIA: That little woman cuts dresses very low, Jane. You must be sure it isn't too low.
JANE: Yes, I will.
CATHERINE: It can always be filled in with tulle.
ROGER: H'm? What can be filled in?
AMELIA: Never mind, Roger.

ELEANOR: Thank goodness my party's all over. I don't know anything more scaley than coming out.
CATHERINE: Scaley? Where did you hear that word, dear?
ELEANOR: I don't know. I just—heard it.
CATHERINE: Did you ever hear the word scaley, George?
APLEY: No, I never did.
ELEANOR: (*Quickly.*) I just happened to hear it. (*She rises. Quickly changing the subject.*) Are you excited about coming out, Agnes?
AGNES: Oh, yes. I think coming out must be wonderful, except I'm a little bit afraid I'll be afraid.
ELEANOR: There's nothing to be afraid of. You just see the same old faces. No Yale boys, no Princeton boys. Just Harvard boys.
APLEY: And what is the matter with Harvard boys?
ELEANOR: (*To Apley.*) Nothing, Father; they just go to Harvard. (*To Agnes.*) And they've all got to dance with you whether they want to or not, because it's your party.
AGNES: Oh, dear.
CATHERINE: Eleanor, you mustn't frighten your cousin.
ELEANOR: It's just that I think coming-out parties are an outmoded folk custom. It's the old idea of introducing the virgin to the tribes.
CATHERINE: Really, Eleanor!
APLEY: Why, Eleanor, there are some things that we simply don't mention!
ELEANOR: Why shouldn't we mention them?
APLEY: Well, dear! Savage tribes!
ELEANOR: Really, Father, if things exist I don't see why we shouldn't face them.
APLEY: Because we do not face virginity in the drawing room after a Thanksgiving dinner.
ELEANOR: (*Hotly.*) Well, I think—
APLEY: (*Sharply.*) Eleanor!
ELEANOR: (*Getting control of herself.*) I'm sorry, Father . . . Would you mind excusing me? I think I'll get my coat. (*She runs up the stairs shaking her head in disgust. There is an embarrassed pause.*)
APLEY: John, why don't you take Agnes out to the conservatory and show her the rubber tree?
JOHN: She saw it last week.
APLEY: (*Firmly.*) It's grown since then.
JOHN: (*Reluctantly.*) Well—(*Turns to Agnes.*)—do you want to see the rubber tree?
AGNES: (*Starts walking.*) I'd love to, John.
JOHN: (*None too graciously.*) Come on, then. (*They both exit quickly. The elders are now alone.*)
AMELIA: (*Gesturing toward stairs. Bluntly.*) How old is Eleanor?
CATHERINE: She's nineteen.
ROGER: That's about the right time.
AMELIA: That will be about enough from you this afternoon, Roger.
HORATIO: I must say she's getting some very peculiar ideas.
APLEY: The girl is just young. We were all young. (*There is a snort from Amelia.*)

Except Amelia. . . . Well now that the children are gone, (*rises*) there is a little family matter that I might take up. . . . It's about Cousin Hattie.
HORATIO: Cousin Hattie?
AMELIA: Cousin Hattie is dead. She's been dead for a month.
APLEY: That's just the point. So long as she was alive she gave us very little trouble. A check now and then, and I made it my business to call on her once a year, although it meant driving almost out to Dorchester.
AMELIA: What else have you got to do besides driving out to Dorchester?
APLEY: I did not mind the drive, Amelia. But the Henry Apleys are a very distant branch of the family—they are barely Apleys at all.
CATHERINE: (*Rises.*) George, do you really think you should go into this? I'm not sure you did the right thing.
APLEY: I am convinced that I did, Catherine.
AMELIA: What is all this about?
APLEY: It's about Cousin Hattie's burial.
ROGER: Good God, haven't they buried her yet?
APLEY: (*To Roger.*) They buried her at Mt. Auburn, and to that I have no general objection. The family plot at Mt. Auburn is completely democratic—any Apley connection, no matter how remote, is welcome to rest there if he chooses. Even you, Horatio.
HORATIO: (*Delighted.*) By Jove! Thank you, George. (*Apley bows an acknowledgement.*)
ROGER: Well, you're all fixed now, Horatio.
APLEY: The question, however, is one of Cousin Hattie's location on the lot. I always try to be present at every family interment, but in the case of Cousin Hattie I was unavoidably absent.
ROGER: Well, so long as Cousin Hattie was there . . .
APLEY: Please, Roger. . . . Last week, when Catherine and I were motoring to Concord, we stopped for a moment at Mt. Auburn. I was particularly anxious to see how the arborvitae border was doing back of Father's stone. Suddenly, to my astonishment, I saw a new headstone of pink granite with a recumbent figure upon it. There in our part of the lot was Cousin Hattie, large as life—
AMELIA: Well, there's nothing you can do about it now. She's there.
APLEY: (*Firmly.*) On the contrary. I have written Henry Apley a letter explaining that he must move his mother somewhere else—say, down to the bottom of the slope.
HORATIO: I think George is right. It was very pushing of the Henry Apleys, putting their mother right where George might want to go.
APLEY: That is hardly the point, Horatio.
HORATIO: The only thing is, people will take sides. It will create unwelcome talk.
ROGER: It won't create any talk at all. Who gives a damn where the Apleys are buried?
APLEY: (*To Roger, bristling.*) Don't think that I enjoy this. I find it very unpleasant and painful, but—

(*Agnes has suddenly entered. John stands behind her.*)

CATHERINE: (*After a pause.*) Why, children! Back so soon?
AGNES: We saw all the flowers.
APLEY: Obviously you haven't been very entertaining, John.
JOHN: We just thought we'd come back.
CATHERINE: (*Easing the situation.*) Why don't you play something for us on the piano, my dear? Have you learned any new pieces?
AGNES: Oh, no! I'd rather not.
HORATIO: (*Rising.*) Of course, Agnes. . . . She *has* learned a new piece.
AGNES: But not now, Papa.
APLEY: We would all like to hear it very much, Agnes.
AGNES: (*Looks around reluctantly.*) Well . . . (*Crosses to piano. Horatio crosses to crook of piano.*)
CATHERINE: What kind of piece is it, my dear?
AGNES: (*Sits.*) It's—it's a waltz.
CATHERINE: A waltz . . .
APLEY: I am very fond of waltzes. And so is John. Aren't you, John?
JOHN: Yes. (*Apley motions him to sit. He does.*)
AGNES: It's a new one. It's from "The Quaker Girl," and it's called "Come to the Ball." (*Horatio starts her off, beating out the time by waving his hands. She starts hesitantly at the beginning, and with increasing confidence, she plays and sings a verse and a chorus of "Come to the Ball." Roger sits contemplating his glass, and as the first chorus is almost three-quarters through, on "you all" he drains his brandy glass, for support to carry him through the ordeal of listening. Horatio hums the difficult parts of the song to give Agnes support.*)
CATHERINE: (*At end of first chorus.*) How nice!
AMELIA: (*At end of first chorus.*) Charming! (*Horatio tells Agnes to play again, everyone joins in singing.*)
APLEY: (*As they start singing.*) Sing, John! (*On second line of second chorus Eleanor comes down the stair. As she is halfway down she nods towards the hall, as though to let Wilson know that she is answering the door. She disappears. On fourth line she re-enters.*)
ELEANOR: Father—(*She comes down more.*) Father! It's Mr. Boulder! (*All the voices fade out, Horatio trailing off last.*)
APLEY: (*Rising.*) Well, ask him to come in, Eleanor.
CATHERINE: (*Rises.*) Of course, Eleanor. (*Roger and John rise. Eleanor beckons to the unseen guest. He comes in—young and perhaps a little carelessly dressed. He is not the least embarrassed. . . . He throws his coat over the post on the stairway and enters with Eleanor on his right.*)
ELEANOR: This is Howard Boulder, everyone.
APLEY: How do you do, Mr. Boulder?
BOULDER: How do you do, Mr. Apley.
APLEY: (*Shakes Boulder's hand.*) Eleanor's been telling us about you. This is Mrs. Apley.
BOULDER: How do you do, Mrs Apley?
CATHERINE: Mr. Boulder. (*She crosses to the sofa and sits down.*)
APLEY: And this is Mr. Boulder, everyone. (*A chorus of greetings.*) Won't you stay for a while?

BOULDER: (*Sits after the ladies are seated.*) Why, thank you, Mr. Apley. (*Horatio sits at desk chair. Roger sits.*)
APLEY: (*Offers cigars.*) Just a family party. . . . Will you have a cigar, Mr. Boulder?
BOULDER: No, thanks, but if you have a cigarette . . .
APLEY: (*Looks at Catherine.*) I'm sorry. I've never gone quite so far as cigarettes. (*He puts box down again.*)
BOULDER: (*Bringing out his own.*) That's all right—if you don't mind?
APLEY: Not at all. (*Boulder lights up. Roger rises and watches Boulder. Every eye, of course, is on him, but he is seemingly quite unaware of it.*) Mr. Boulder is giving the Jonathan Smythe lectures at Emerson Hall. That's quite an achievement at your age, Mr. Boulder.
BOULDER: I'm probably a year or two older than I look. Besides, I'm pretty used to it.
ELEANOR: He's been lecturing ever since he got his Ph.D.
APLEY: Indeed? And where was that, Mr. Boulder?
BOULDER: At Yale.
APLEY: (*Looks at Catherine, then to Roger.*) Yale!
ROGER: (*Nodding.*) That's what he said!
APLEY: What do you lecture on, Mr. Boulder?
BOULDER: It's a course on American Literature. Particularly the Concord group.
APLEY: (*With approval.*) The Concord group! (*To the room.*) Why, that would be all the great figures. Emerson, Thoreau, Alcott.
BOULDER: (*A smile.*) You should hear me read "Little Women."
APLEY: You must come to dinner some time, Mr. Boulder, so we can have a long talk about them. As a young man my father once met Thoreau. Emerson once came to breakfast with Dr. Oliver Wendell Holmes.
AMELIA: (*Clarifying the whole thing for Boulder.*) That was in our grandfather's house on Louisburg Square.
BOULDER: I see.
APLEY: You make me anxious to hear your lecture, Mr. Boulder. What is it called?
BOULDER: The Concord Myth.
APLEY: (*Slowly.*) The Concord Myth? (*Roger clears his throat loudly, as though to say "Well, well, well," indistinguishable. Apley, slowly.*) I can't very well picture Emerson as being a myth.
BOULDER: Oh, Emerson's all right as far as he goes, sir. But there was a good deal of scaley writing up there in Concord.

(*The Apleys exchange looks—they have recognized the word. Eleanor, of course, also realizes what has happened.*)

ELEANOR: Perhaps we'd better be starting. If we're going to walk all the way to Cambridge . . . (*Eleanor rises on this speech, Boulder rises, putting out cigarette as he does so.*)
CATHERINE: (*Rising.*) Walk to Cambridge? But why, dear?
ELEANOR: Just for the walk. We're going to have tea at a friend of Howard's—Mr. Boulder's.

APLEY: You didn't tell us about that, dear. What friend?
ELEANOR: It's a Mr. Frankfurter. Mr. Felix Frankfurter.
APLEY: Frankfurter?
ELEANOR: He teaches at the Harvard Law School.
APLEY: (*Reluctantly.*) Oh! Well, if he's on the Law School faculty—
CATHERINE: (*Smoothing it over.*) Of course, George.
APLEY: Of course . . . Frankfurter . . . I must say, though, Mr. Boulder, that I don't quite understand your attitude on Emerson. I can't recall that he ever wrote anything "scaley," as you put it.
BOULDER: Well, take some of his poetry. "Burling, dozing bumblebee" or "The Mountain and the Squirrel had a quarrel." (*He burlesques this as he reads it.*) Now, if Emerson hadn't written that, you know what you'd say. That's the point I make in my lecture.
APLEY: (*Chilly.*) I can't imagine that the hall is very crowded.
ELEANOR: Oh, but it is, Father. They're asking him to come back in February. Nobody else has ever been asked twice.
APLEY: And what are you going to lecture on in February, Mr. Boulder?
BOULDER: "The Dead Hand of Emerson on American Creative Thought." (*Looks at Eleanor.*) Well, it's been awfully nice to meet Eleanor's family, sir.
ELEANOR: (*Following him up.*) Good-bye.
BOULDER: And don't forget about dinner. Good-bye. Good-bye, Mrs. Apley.
ELEANOR: Good-bye, everyone. (*Boulder ushers Eleanor out. Agnes rises.*)
ROGER: (*Rising, crosses to console, puts brandy on it.*) Well, that was quite a breezy boy.
APLEY: (*Sits.*) I don't understand it. What can be the matter with the Harvard Corporation to allow anyone, in Emerson Hall, mind you, in Emerson Hall— (*He stops, appealing to the group in silence.*)
HORATIO: It's shocking.
ROGER: What do you care? You're not a Harvard professor.
APLEY: I am a Harvard man. Emerson and I were both Harvard men. (*Thoughtfully.*) I wonder if Buzzy Loring ever heard those lectures.
HORATIO: I'm sure he never did. He couldn't have.
APLEY: He would not tolerate such nonsense for a minute.
HORATIO: Of course not!
CATHERINE: (*After a pause.*) Agnes, do play some more. (*To Apley.*) Wouldn't you like Agnes to play some more? George?
APLEY: What? Oh, yes. . . . Yes, of course.
JOHN: (*Unable to stand it any longer.*) I'm afraid I've got to go.
APLEY: What?
JOHN: I'm sorry, but—I've got some studying to catch up on, and—
CATHERINE: But surely, John, there's no reason to be in such a hurry. You can wait and hear Agnes play.
JOHN: I did hear her play. I mean—I wish I could, Mother—I'd love to, really, but—I'm pretty late already. (*To Apley.*)
APLEY: Late for what?
JOHN: Well, there's a great deal of reading and—a French examination.
CATHERINE: You're being very thoughtless, dear, to Agnes, to everyone.

JOHN: I'm sorry, Mother, please excuse me. Aunt Amelia . . . Cousin Jane . . . Agnes, you'll excuse me, won't you? (*He goes quickly up the stairs. Catherine gestures apology to all.*)
APLEY: (*Rises.*) I don't understand the children today.
CATHERINE: (*Weakly.*) I know that he *has* studies to do. (*There is a pause.*)
HORATIO: (*Stiffly, crosses to door.*) Well, as long as her cousins can't stay to entertain her, I think we may as well go, too, don't you, Agnes?
AGNES: (*Who sits stricken at the piano.*) Yes, Papa! (*Rises, crosses to Horatio.*)
HORATIO: Come, Jane. (*Jane rises and crosses to door.*)
APLEY: Oh, come now, really, Horatio.
HORATIO: After Agnes knitted that necktie, too. (*Exits, followed by Apley.*)
APLEY: (*As he exits.*) It isn't like John. He never could have intended to be rude. I can't understand it.
AMELIA: George can't even manage his own children. I should have been the boy. Father always said so.
ROGER: Oh, come now, Amelia. Don't always pick on George.
AMELIA: I'm not blaming you, Catherine. I feel very sorry for you.
CATHERINE: (*Flaring up.*) I don't feel sorry for myself, Amelia. I'm perfectly satisfied.
APLEY: (*Returning.*) Ah, well.
AMELIA: We'll be going, too, George. (*Rises.*)
APLEY: You're not leaving so early, Amelia?
AMELIA: What's there to stay for if everybody's gone? I did think we might have at least one Thanksgiving without a family quarrel. Good-bye, Catherine, good-bye, George! (*Exits.*)
ROGER: The Pilgrims had the Indians, George. We have Amelia. (*Exits.*)
CATHERINE: (*Looking after them.*) Amelia's manners are getting worse all the time. (*Crosses to desk, replaces desk chair.*)
APLEY: You know Amelia, Catherine.
CATHERINE: Indeed I do.
APLEY: (*Sighs.*) I was looking forward to a happy family party—John! (*As he sees John attempting to sneak by doorway.*) John, come in here! (*John does so and puts his books in a chair wearily.*) John, I can't believe, I won't believe, that you intended what you did just now. I've always been so proud of you, John. I don't think you understand how much you have hurt everyone's feelings. It isn't like you, John. Now come. Tell your mother and me—what's the matter?
CATHERINE: Aren't you feeling well, dear?
JOHN: Of course!
CATHERINE: Have you got yourself in some sort of scrape at college?
JOHN: No. Of course not.
APLEY: Then what is it?
JOHN: I don't see why I should stand here and be questioned! If Eleanor can go out, why can't I? (*Picks up books and papers, leaves envelope.*) Why can't I lead my own life, like everybody else! (*He bolts out the door.*)
APLEY: (*Calling.*) John! (*But there is only the door slam.*)
CATHERINE: Don't be too hard on him, George. When children are growing up— when we were his age—

APLEY: When we were his age we knew how to behave. (*Turns away.*)
CATHERINE: I'm not so sure, George.
APLEY: (*Sniffing the air.*) Catherine, are you using violet perfume?
CATHERINE: Certainly not. What a question!
APLEY: I smell perfume. Cheap violet perfume. (*Catherine also sniffs, then looks at Apley. She too has smelt it. Apley sniffing again, goes slowly to the envelope that John has left in the chair.*) It's this thing. It reeks of violets.
CATHERINE: What is it?
APLEY: It's an envelope. (*He smooths it out a little.*) Addressed to John. Addressed to John in a woman's handwriting.
CATHERINE: A woman's handwriting?
APLEY: This explains his whole behavior. (*Giving the envelope a closer look.*) Oh, my God!
CATHERINE: George, what is it?
APLEY: It's postmarked Worcester!
CATHERINE: Worcester—(*Apley lets hand drop.*)
APLEY: The girl—is a foreigner, Catherine. (*The envelope falls to the ground.*)

CURTAIN

ACT II

TIME: *It is about four-thirty in the afternoon a week after the Thanksgiving dinner.*

AT RISE: *Catherine Apley is entertaining one of those little groups of her contemporaries who meet in Boston at regular intervals. Her guests are Amelia, Jane, and two others, Lydia Leyton and Emily Southworth. Voluminous petit-points and knitting bags show that the afternoon has been spent in a useful pursuit. But now, sewing forgotten, the ladies are gathered cozily about a little tea table where Catherine presides before a heavy silver tea service.*

AMELIA: So there we were, living in the South End in a beautiful bow-front house. Tim, the coachman, had just come up with the victoria to take George and me to Miss Hendricks' primary school.
JANE: Oh, I remember. We used to sing "Fly Little Bird, Fly Round the Ring."
AMELIA: Well, George and I were on the front stoop, and just then Father came down. We happened to look at the brownstone steps across the square, and he gave an exclamation. It surprised me, because Father was usually very careful with his language.
LYDIA: What did he say?
AMELIA: He said "Thunderation!" And then he said, "There is a man in his shirt sleeves on those steps." And the very next day he sold the house and we moved to Beacon Street.
CATHERINE: Those South End houses had the most beautiful woodwork. You can see the dark walnut doors if you go there now.
LYDIA: It must have been lovely there before the Irish moved in.
EMILY: I wish I'd lived there in those days. Of course by the time I came here it was all so different.
LYDIA: I keep forgetting you're not really a Bostonian, Emily. I always think of

you as one of us.

EMILY: I suppose it's because I love Boston so.

CATHERINE: What's that queer little Western place you came from, Emily?

EMILY: Detroit.

CATHERINE: Oh, yes. Our automobile came from there.

LYDIA: You know, last summer Oswald and I were thinking of going to Yellowstone Park, but we found it easier to go to Europe. In London we stayed at Garland's Hotel, of course, and the very first day we must have run into at least six Boston people, who were staying there. We had a wonderful time—it was just as though we hadn't left Boston at all.

CATHERINE: It's a comfort to know the right place to stop. (*Margaret enters with teapot on tray, crosses to tea table and places pot on tray.*) Oh, thank you, Margaret.

AMELIA: How are your teeth, Margaret?

MARGARET: They're better, thank you, Mrs. Newcombe.

CATHERINE: George had her go to his dentist. It doesn't drop any more, does it, Margaret?

MARGARET: (*Stopping in the doorway, pushing her plate up with an almost imperceptible movement.*) No, ma'am. (*She exits.*)

EMILY: Who is George's dentist?

CATHERINE: His father's dentist on Bay State Road.

AMELIA: I gave him up years ago. He's so old he can't see cavities.

CATHERINE: No, but he's very good if you find your own cavities and point them out to him. (*She turns to Emily.*) Don't you want some fresh tea, Emily? (*Catherine takes cup, gives Emily fresh tea.*)

EMILY: Thank you, Catherine.

CATHERINE: Lydia?

LYDIA: No, I really ought to be flying. It's late. (*Putting sewing into bag.*)

CATHERINE: Oh, don't go yet, Lydia.

JANE: What number meeting is this?

CATHERINE: What number, dear?

JANE: I mean how many times have we all met at this embroidery group?

AMELIA: What else would you be doing if you weren't here?

JANE: Why, I don't know.

EMILY: I should think you'd be awfully busy, with Agnes coming out tonight. Has she a nice party dress?

JANE: Oh, yes. I think so.

AMELIA: (*Flatly.*) It's going to be too low in the bosom.

JANE: I have some tulle.

CATHERINE: Why don't you send her over before dinner, Jane, when she has her dress on? George and I might have some ideas.

JANE: Very well, Catherine.

LYDIA: (*To Jane.*) I suppose John has asked Agnes for the supper dance tonight?

JANE: John? Yes, he has.

CATHERINE: Do you remember how George used to fill out your dance program, Jane?

JANE: Yes, that was how I met Horatio. George wrote him in.

CATHERINE: With this new cutting in, I don't see how you can ever decide whom you like best. George and I danced and danced.
EMILY: Were you engaged then?
CATHERINE: Oh, no. It was—quite a while after that.
AMELIA: George was sent abroad for a year first. To forget.
JANE: To forget what?
AMELIA: Never mind, Jane.
JANE: I remember he went abroad, but I didn't know it was anything like that.
AMELIA: It wasn't. It doesn't matter now.
CATHERINE: It's all right, Amelia. I don't know two people in Boston who are happier than George and I.
EMILY: When did you get engaged? When he came back from abroad?
CATHERINE: (*Tight-lipped.*) Yes.
EMILY: Right away?
CATHERINE: Yes.
AMELIA: They were sitting in the parlor one night and her father came in and said, "When is the wedding going to be?"
CATHERINE: I can remember about you and Roger, too, Amelia. (*Warningly.*)
AMELIA: With Roger things went so far I told him he *had* to speak to Father.
JANE: (*Taking in the circle.*) Did any of your husbands—ever do anything—romantic?
EMILY: Romantic?
LYDIA: Husbands don't do romantic things. They're not supposed to.
CATHERINE: George has always been thoughtful, and kind. And a wonderful companion.
JANE: But wasn't he ever—you know what I mean? Even on your honeymoon?
CATHERINE: We had a perfect honeymoon. We went to Rye Beach—the Farragut House. We rode every day, and in the evening we read Emerson.
LYDIA: I think Boston men make the best husbands, don't you? I mean, when you consider everything.
AMELIA: Boston men are emotionally dependable—they're trained that way. But every once in a while something very strange does happen.
EMILY: How do you mean?
AMELIA: Do you remember Sonny Walker?
LYDIA: Oh, yes.
EMILY: What about him?
AMELIA: He used to lead every cotillion, but now his name is never mentioned.
EMILY: But why?
CATHERINE: He shot a squirrel.
EMILY: What?
CATHERINE: A tame squirrel. It used to come to his window for crumbs, and one day something just happened to him, and he shot it.
LYDIA: He had to resign from the Bird Watchers.
CATHERINE: And the Berkeley Club, too. It never was straightened out. He just left Boston and never was heard of again.
EMILY: My!
CATHERINE: (*Slowly.*) It's funny, isn't it?

LYDIA: What?
CATHERINE: Boston. I mean when you come to think about it. (*She still speaks slowly, a little surprised at her own heresy.*) Growing up in it, the way we did, we just didn't think about it at all. I know I didn't.
LYDIA: What are you talking about?
AMELIA: (*Rises.*) I never heard you say a thing like that before in your life, Catherine. What's there to think about?
JANE: I know what Catherine means.
LYDIA: Well, I don't.
AMELIA: I do, and it's all nonsense. There are certain *facts* in Boston, but there's nothing to think about. (*Sits on sofa.*)
CATHERINE: (*Thoughtfully.*) I'm probably wrong. It's the children, I suppose. Realizing that they're growing up, and that they're at a point where . . .
AMELIA: Children don't know what they're doing, and they have to be told. It's very simple—you just tell them.
CATHERINE: You haven't any children, Amelia.
JANE: (*As the outer door is heard, rises, goes to desk, picking up gloves.*) Here's George. (*Emily rises after putting cup on tea tray, picks up sewing bag.*)
EMILY: Already? What time is it?
CATHERINE: (*Pulling herself together.*) Is that you, dear? (*Apley enters.*)
APLEY: Oh, good afternoon, everybody!
LYDIA: Hello, George!
EMILY: Hello, George!
CATHERINE: A cup of tea, dear?
APLEY: No, thank you, it's a little late for tea.
AMELIA: George always puts his guests at ease. (*Jane crosses to door.*)
LYDIA: (*Rises, picks up sewing.*) George is right. We really must be flying.
APLEY: No, no. I didn't mean that, Lydia.
EMILY: Remember, everybody! My house next week.
CATHERINE: (*Rises.*) I wish you wouldn't all go right away.
LYDIA: Oh, but we must. Good-bye, George.
APLEY: Good-bye, Lydia. (*They have exited, first Jane, then Emily, then Catherine, and finally Lydia, after her last line to George. There is a pause. George looks at Amelia.*) Aren't you going, too, Amelia?
AMELIA: (*Putting away sewing things, then.*) George, do you know that at ten o'clock at night Eleanor and that young Boulder were seen standing on Commonwealth Avenue, laughing at William Lloyd Garrison's statue!
APLEY: (*Crosses to desk, puts chair to desk.*) Oh, never mind about Eleanor and Boulder, Amelia! (*Catherine re-enters.*)
AMELIA: (*Rises, looking sharply at Apley as she crosses.*) I'm going up to the attic.
APLEY: (*Turns.*) What for?
AMELIA: I want Mother's old cuckoo clock! (*She picks up her skirts and stalks up the stairs.*)
APLEY: That's not fair, Amelia. You've already taken the brass finger bowls. (*He crosses to Catherine.*) I ought to go with her.
CATHERINE: We're never going to use it, George.
APLEY: That's not the point. Amelia's whole attitude—(*He breaks off.*) Oh! The

committee hasn't been here?
CATHERINE: Committee?
APLEY: The committee from the Bird Watchers. They're voting this afternoon. The formal notification. (*Enter Wilson.*)
CATHERINE: They haven't come yet, George.
APLEY: (*Looking at watch.*) It's after five. . . . Oh, good evening, Wilson.
WILSON: (*Picking up table.*) Good evening, sir. (*He starts to door.*)
APLEY: I'll wear the pearl studs this evening, Wilson, not the moonstones.
CATHERINE: The moonstones look better, George.
APLEY: Not in a gathering of your girls. The pearl studs, Wilson.
WILSON: Yes, sir. (*He exits with tea things.*)
APLEY: How long have we had Wilson, Catherine?
CATHERINE: Eighteen years, George.
APLEY: Eighteen years. He is due for a raise. (*Letter in hand.*) Here is a letter from Henry Apley, Catherine. Cousin Hattie has been moved. (*Looks at letter.*)
CATHERINE: I hope you didn't hurt his feelings.
APLEY: He has taken her out of Mt. Auburn entirely. He need hardly have done that. "In view of your astonishing attitude"—I don't think my attitude was astonishing—"it is my present plan to have her buried at sea. I trust you have no prior rights in the ocean." That seems an unnecessary remark.
CATHERINE: (*Taking letter from him and placing it on table.*) George, I wish you'd think about the children! Somehow I wish you hadn't gone quite so far as to send Horatio to Worcester. Do you think he was quite the person?
APLEY: Please, my dear. He's simply making some casual inquiries. He has a classmate in the Worcester Antiquarian Society.
CATHERINE: But so far as we know, John and this girl may not even be—really serious.
APLEY: My dear, I think I know the signs of infatuation when I see them. I've been out to Harvard and asked some questions. And I find John has overdrawn his account at the Cambridge Trust Company, and now he is beginning to sell his clothes.
CATHERINE: His clothes? Oh, George!
APLEY: To a second-hand dealer named Max Keezer. I saw this myself. John's new blue serge is hanging in Mr. Keezer's window.
CATHERINE: His best suit?
APLEY: Mr. Keezer purchased it for a dollar ninety-seven cents.
CATHERINE: Why, what does John need a dollar and ninety-seven cents for?
APLEY: To buy flowers, Catherine. I stopped in at the florist and inquired.
CATHERINE: I didn't know it had gone so far.
APLEY: Oh, not so far that it can't be managed, my dear. Has Eleanor come in yet?
CATHERINE: (*Crosses to sofa, sits next to Apley.*) Not yet. Now, please don't be upset, George. I told her she could go to tea with Mr. Boulder.
APLEY: Why under the sun should that upset me, dear? Mr. Boulder is leaving for New York tomorrow.
CATHERINE: (*Watching him.*) But he's coming back in February.
APLEY: (*Rises.*) Oh, yes, yes.

CATHERINE: (*Rises.*) George, I think we may as well face it. I think that he and Eleanor are interested in each other.
APLEY: (*Unruffled.*) These things will all adjust themselves, given time, Catherine. You remember what Emerson said, "The mind—" (*The voice of Eleanor in the hall pitched a little high:* "Hello, is anyone at home?" *Turning to door.*) There she is.
CATHERINE: (*Rising.*) Here we are, Eleanor.
BOULDER: (*Off.*) Well, we got this far!
ELEANOR: (*Off.*) Do you think you ought to come in?
APLEY: That doesn't sound like Eleanor. (*Eleanor appears in the doorway. It is true that she is not quite herself. Boulder enters behind her.*)
ELEANOR: Hello, you two sweet old things. (*Boulder comes behind her.*)
APLEY: Why, Eleanor!
ELEANOR: (*Waving a playful finger at them.*) I know what you've been doing, you two sweet old things. You've been talking about me! And if you weren't talking about me you were talking about John, weren't you?
APLEY: (*Ignoring her.*) How do you do, Mr. Boulder.
BOULDER: Good afternoon, sir. Mrs. Apley?
CATHERINE: Mr. Boulder.
ELEANOR: Where do you think we've been? I'll give you three guesses.
APLEY: I'm sure I don't know.
ELEANOR: To the Copley Plaza.
APLEY: Really? I've never been there myself.
ELEANOR: And what do you think we did?
APLEY: I'm sure I don't know what anyone does at the Copley Plaza.
ELEANOR: We went to a tea dansant and we didn't have any tea.
CATHERINE: What did you have, dear? Little cakes? (*Boulder looks to Eleanor, then to Catherine, then back to Eleanor.*)
ELEANOR: (*Shaking head.*) We had cocktails. I had two, and so did Howard. (*Crosses to Boulder.*)
BOULDER: Well, that really sounds much worse than it was, sir.
ELEANOR: (*Putting arm on him.*) And what do you think Howard said each time? He said: "When duty whispers low, thou must, the youth replies I can." (*Boulder looks at Apley.*) Howard says it's one of Emerson's most nauseating lines. (*Boulder looks at Catherine, then at Apley.*)
APLEY: (*Icily.*) I don't think we should keep Mr. Boulder, Eleanor. I'm sure he has another engagement.
ELEANOR: No, he hasn't—have you, Howard. . . ? (*Eleanor takes Boulder's arm.*)
BOULDER: I really must pack—(*To the Apleys.*) I'm leaving for New York tomorrow.
APLEY: Oh, yes.
BOULDER: Then good-bye, sir.
ELEANOR: Good-bye, Howard.
BOULDER: Mrs. Apley. (*Turning to Eleanor.*) I'll see you in February—(*Making his exit.*)
ELEANOR: (*Hesitates, then follows him up.*) Good-bye. (*Boulder, low, off,* "I won't be back until February." *Apley crosses to Catherine, they look at each*

other.)
APLEY: What are they doing?

(*Giggle from Eleanor in the hall. Then Eleanor enters, carrying hat.*)

ELEANOR: Well.
CATHERINE: I think you'd better go upstairs and lie down for a few minutes, dear.
ELEANOR: Can't I ever see *anyone* without being criticized?
CATHERINE: Eleanor, please.
ELEANOR: I know what you'd like. You'd like to throw me at one of my cousins, like John. Well, I don't believe in inbreeding.
APLEY: My own little girl. I know it wasn't your fault, Eleanor . . .
ELEANOR: (*Giggling.*) I wish you could see yourselves. You act as though I'd sinned.
CATHERINE: Eleanor!
APLEY: Eleanor, it seemed to me that when you saw him to the door, there was a scuffling sound in the hall.
ELEANOR: You must have been listening.
APLEY: Eleanor, did that young man—?
ELEANOR: He tried to.
APLEY: Tried to what? Did he try to kiss you?
ELEANOR: Yes, he tried to, and I let him.
CATHERINE: Oh, Eleanor.
ELEANOR: And we aren't even engaged!
APLEY: I think we've heard enough for now.
ELEANOR: Didn't you ever kiss Mother before you were engaged?
APLEY: Will you please take her upstairs to her room?
CATHERINE: (*Crosses to Eleanor.*) Come, dear.
ELEANOR: (*Voice breaking a bit.*) You don't understand what I'm talking about because you haven't read Freud.
APLEY: Who?
ELEANOR: Dr. Sigmund Freud. If you had, you'd know that emotion is healthy, Father.
APLEY: Catherine, take her out of here and give her some black coffee.
CATHERINE: (*Crosses to Eleanor.*) Come, Eleanor.
ELEANOR: Oh, Father! Can't you see! (*She begins to cry.*)
APLEY: (*In a voice of thunder.*) Catherine! (*Catherine and Eleanor move toward stairs.*)
CATHERINE: You'll be better in a few minutes, dear.
ELEANOR: (*Catherine takes her upstairs.*) Just because he isn't in the Social Register, because he isn't exactly like everybody else . . . Just because he's a Yale man. (*Apley stands statuesque and grim, and the two mount the stairs to the tune of Eleanor's hysterical sobbing. He clinches his hands and unclinches them. Then, collecting himself a bit, he goes over to the bookcase and takes down Emerson. As he does so, the doorbell rings. He pulls himself together somewhat, remembering that this may be important. As Wilson passes him in the hallway, he stops him.*)

APLEY: Oh, Wilson. If some gentlemen are calling, bring them right in. I'm expecting them. (*Crosses back to desk stand waiting in front of it. Wilson bows and goes to door. But it is Horatio's voice we hear.* "Mr. Apley home, Wilson?" "Yes, sir, he is." *Horatio enters. He bears himself importantly.*)
HORATIO: Well, I'm back, George.
APLEY: Ah! Sit down, Horatio, and tell me everything. Everything. (*Sitting middle of sofa.*)
HORATIO: (*Sensing something in Apley's manner.*) Is something the matter?
APLEY: (*Shaking his head.*) Nothing . . . please—(*Gestures Horatio to sit. Horatio takes off coat, puts it on back of chair, sits down.*)
HORATIO: (*Settling himself, and starting in.*) Well—their name—is Dole.
APLEY: Dole?
HORATIO: Julian H. Dole.
APLEY: And the girl?
HORATIO: Myrtle.
APLEY: (*In a voice of doom.*) Myrtle Dole!
HORATIO: Mr. Dole is the president of the Dole Tool and Die Company.
APLEY: What is a tool and die company?
HORATIO: I don't know.
APLEY: Does he belong to any clubs?
HORATIO: I hadn't thought of there being any clubs in Worcester.
APLEY: Did you see the house?
HORATIO: Yes—it's a yellowish brown house, with a lot of ginger-bread on it—scrolls and twists and things— (*He outlines these strange curves with his fingers.*) There was an iron door on the lawn. (*Apley shuts his eyes—the pain is too great.*) And two iron dogs and a fountain. Of course the fountain wasn't working at this time of year.
APLEY: (*With finality. Rises.*) John cannot have seen their house.
HORATIO: He's been there, George.
APLEY: How do you know?
HORATIO: The maid told me. I was—inside—the house.
APLEY: Inside. How in the world did you get there? (*Margaret enters and goes up the stairs, carrying a tray with coffeepot, and a hot water bottle.*) Wait a minute.
HORATIO: What is it?
APLEY: (*Dismissing his question with a wave of the hand.*) It's all right. You didn't just ring the doorbell?
HORATIO: Not until I had a plan. I thought at first I would say I was the man to read the gas meter, but I decided I was hardly the type. So I said I was a friend of John's, that I happened to be passing through Worcester, and he had asked me to stop and inquire if he had left his umbrella. (*He leans back, vastly pleased with himself.*)
APLEY: By Jove, I wouldn't have thought of that.
HORATIO: (*Generously.*) Of course you would, George, if you'd put your mind to it. Anyway the maid said he hadn't left his umbrella.
APLEY: But then you had to leave.
HORATIO: No! I happened to look down at her feet and saw she was wearing one

shoe and one slipper, and it started me thinking. I asked her if she had a bunion.
APLEY: By Jove! And did she have?
HORATIO: No. But she'd turned her ankle. I got her to tell me about it, and from that we fell into pleasant and easy conversation. As you know, I have a way with women.
APLEY: (*Impatiently.*) Yes, Horatio. What did you find out?
HORATIO: (*Lowering his voice, rises, crosses to Apley, looking around.*) John has been there several times. She said John was a nice young man, and it was cute to see him so sweet on Miss Myrtle when Miss Myrtle was so sweet on him. Those are her words, not mine.
APLEY: Obviously.
HORATIO: Also, he telephones her every night from Harvard. The conversations are very lengthy. In addition, there are two letters daily. And flowers. All the time.
APLEY: (*Thinking.*) The whole thing, of course, is nothing but sex. (*Horatio nods, in full agreement.*) Personally, Horatio, it has always seemed to me that sex is largely nonsense.
HORATIO: I know what you mean. I never heard it put quite that way.
APLEY: I want to be broad-minded about this. These people, these Julian H. Doles, (*Catherine starts coming downstairs*) are probably very nice people in their way, and from their point of view—(*He stops as he sees Catherine.*) Ah! Here is Horatio, my dear.
HORATIO: Good evening, Catherine.
CATHERINE: You've been to Worcester? What happened?
APLEY: It's about what we expected, Catherine—I'll tell you later. How is Eleanor?
CATHERINE: She's better. Margaret is with her.
HORATIO: Is Eleanor ill?
APLEY: No, no. She's quite all right.
HORATIO: I felt sure something was the matter.
APLEY: (*Annoyed.*) There's nothing the matter at all. She had tea with that young Boulder at the Copley Plaza.
HORATIO: Boulder? Well, if that's all—
APLEY: (*Ill at ease, and anxious to stop Horatio's revelation.*) It's nothing, Horatio. He kissed her and she's resting.
HORATIO: What?
CATHERINE: (*Sits on sofa.*) It's quite all right, Horatio.
APLEY: Yes—thank you, Horatio. You've been a true friend, a friend in need. Good-bye. (*Pushes Horatio to door, handing him hat and coat.*)
HORATIO: Anything further I can do?
APLEY: No, no. Thank you.
HORATIO: I'm sure there's a way of handling this, George, and that you'll find it. Look how well you handled the Boulder matter. *He* won't be coming back again—See you at dinner. (*He goes.*)
APLEY: (*Catherine rises. Uneasily.*) Yes, yes.
CATHERINE: (*Puzzled.*) Did he say Mr. Boulder won't be coming back again?
APLEY: (*Pacing it.*) No, he won't, Catherine. I felt it wise to write a letter about

him to Buzzy Loring. I simply asked him if he knew what Boulder was saying about the late Ralph Waldo Emerson. He didn't and he was deeply shocked. *(Enter Amelia downstairs, carrying cuckoo clock. Catherine turns away a bit.)*
CATHERINE: *(Sitting on sofa.)* I hope it was the right thing to do, George.
AMELIA: What is the matter with Eleanor?
APLEY: *(Quickly.)* Nothing at all, Amelia.
AMELIA: Don't tell me nothing at all! I know better!
CATHERINE: She isn't feeling well, Amelia!
AMELIA: She's intoxicated!
APLEY: Amelia!
AMELIA: I don't know how else to account for it. She came out into the hall with her hair flying, looked right at me, and said, "Freud would certainly like to get at you!" What does she mean by that? *(She exits.)*

(Agnes appears suddenly from hall. She is extremely self-conscious, and with some reason. She is dressed in a rather dowdy white ball gown, clearly constructed by a local seamstress. She carries long white gloves and a handful of tulle, and has obviously come at her mother's orders.)

AGNES: Oh, I didn't realize . . . I came in the back way, I wanted to show Margaret—but she wasn't . . .
APLEY: *(Pulling himself together.)* That's quite all right, my dear. Come in.
CATHERINE: *(Rising.)* Of course, Agnes. You look charming, my dear.
AGNES: Thank you, Cousin Catherine.
CATHERINE: *(Trying to adjust the tulle.)* Your dress is lovely, my dear. Lovely. Perhaps just an inch of tulle. Is your mother coming over?
AGNES: No, she's busy about the dinner.
CATHERINE: Well, Hannah can sew it upstairs. *(Fitting her.)*
APLEY: Somehow it doesn't look much like a ball gown, does it?
CATHERINE: Of course it does, George. When she has her gloves on . . . put on your gloves, darling.
AGNES: *(Trying to struggle into the gloves.)* They take quite a while.
APLEY: Do you like those frills?
CATHERINE: Everyone has them, George.
AGNES: Don't you like it at all, Cousin George?
APLEY: Who said I didn't like it, dear? I've no doubt we'll all like it very much once we get accustomed to it. *(Apley crosses up to console to get pearls.)*
AGNES: *(To Catherine.)* Accustomed to it?
APLEY: And now I have something for you. *(He takes a jewel box from the console drawer and draws forth a lustrous string of pearls. Crosses to Agnes, puts the box on the table.)* My grandmother's pearls!
CATHERINE: *(Trying to cheer Agnes.)* George! You didn't tell me!
APLEY: I want you to wear them tonight, my dear. Because we all hope that some day . . . *(Agnes shyly looks away.)* There! *(Apley drapes them around her neck.)* They're just what you needed.
AGNES: *(Low-voiced.)* Yes, Cousin George.
CATHERINE: They look lovely on you, my dear. *(Encouraged, Agnes takes a ten-*

tative step to the mirror, parades back. She is beginning to feel a little better, but Apley promptly sees to that.)
APLEY: Splendid. . . . Now no one will notice the dress at all!

(*The sound of the door slamming and John bursts into the room.*)

JOHN: (*Quickly.*) Father, I've got to speak to you!
CATHERINE: Why, John dear, what's happened?
JOHN: (*Not hearing her.*) I want to see you alone, Father!
APLEY: Don't you see your mother? Don't you see Agnes?
JOHN: (*His voice rising.*) I want to see *you!* (*A second's pause. Apley and Catherine exchange looks. Apley nods.*)
CATHERINE: (*To Agnes.*) Suppose we go up to the sewing-room, Agnes.
AGNES: (*Looking bewildered at John.*) Yes . . . Cousin Catherine. (*They exit up stairs. John paces to sofa, takes off hat and coat and throws them on sofa.*)
JOHN: Father, Myrtle just called me up in Cambridge! I've been spied upon, and I won't stand it!
APLEY: This is not a barroom, John. It is not necessary to shout. You'll be twenty-one your next birthday.
JOHN: Then why don't you treat me as though I'd grown up, instead of sending Cousin Horatio sneaking up to Worcester!
APLEY: I had reasons for acting as I did.
JOHN: Reasons! You always have reasons! What are they? Can't you talk to me the way you would to someone else?
APLEY: Not very easily, John. Because you are my son.
JOHN: (*Turning away.*) Oh—
APLEY: I know a great deal more than you think, John. I know why you are so upset. You are in love, John.
JOHN: Yes! I'm in love and I'm proud of it.
APLEY: Of course you are. Of course you are. So was I at your age.
JOHN: What?
APLEY: More in love than you, I guess.
JOHN: How do you mean, more than I?
APLEY: Does that surprise you, John? I think I was, a little more.
JOHN: I don't know what you're—
APLEY: Quite drunk, quite mad with love. (*He sits.*) It was the most beautiful, the most impossible illusion that I've ever known.
JOHN: It isn't an illusion for me. It's the only thing that's real—the only time I've ever lived.
APLEY: Strange how life repeats itself. Strange and a little sad. I said those very words to my father, thirty years ago. It isn't an illusion, it's the only thing that's real.
JOHN: But it isn't the same! He listened to you! You and Mother got married!
APLEY: Yes. Your mother and I got married—later. (*John looks at him.*) I was in love with quite a different girl, John.
JOHN: You were? You?
APLEY: Yes, John.

JOHN: Who was it?
APLEY: It makes no difference now. Her father was quite high up on the police force.
JOHN: Why didn't you marry her?
APLEY: Because it was impossible. (*Rises.*) She never could have lived on Beacon Street and I couldn't have lived in the South End.
JOHN: The South End? Was she Irish?
APLEY: That shocks you, doesn't it, John? That shows we're really a great deal alike. You can call it snobbish, if you want to use a snobbish term. We didn't have the same tastes, the same inclinations. It never would have worked, John.
JOHN: It's not like that with Myrtle and me. It'll last forever!
APLEY: No, John. You and I can't do this sort of thing. We can't escape what we are. Other people may be able to, but we can't.
JOHN: Why can't we?
APLEY: You may as well face it, John. You were born in Boston.
JOHN: What's that got to do with it?
APLEY: Boston is not just a city—it's an environment. And you and I are what we are because of what our environment has made us. We have a certain position, John, and you will inherit it just as I did. There is such a thing as duty, and you'll never be happy running away from it.
JOHN: If you call marrying Myrtle running away from it, I'll be happy.
APLEY: Happiness is a very rare commodity, John—(*Sits.*) Especially in New England.
JOHN: All I know is I'm in love with Myrtle, and that's all that matters.
APLEY: No, John. Love is not all that matters. The little likes and dislikes that two people share in common, the small duties and activities that make up a day—these in the end are love. It's the little things that make for a satisfactory life. (*He brightens perceptibly—a definite change of mood.*) Now, for example: When I came back from abroad, that was when I started my collection of Chinese bronzes. They made a new man out of me. It might be a good idea if you started some sort of collection, John, Oriental daggers, or shaving mugs. It doesn't really matter what.
JOHN: Father!
APLEY: Frankly, I don't know why anyone likes Chinese bronzes, but I have one of the finest collections in the country. And I have to leave *something* to the Art Museum.
JOHN: Father, if you only knew what I was going through!
APLEY: (*Rises.*) But I do, John. Don't you see I do? I've been franker with you, my boy, than I've been with anyone else in my life. And now I am going to leave you for a minute, and there's something I want you to do for me.
JOHN: What?
APLEY: You've been very unkind to your Cousin Agnes lately. I want you to stay in this room for just a minute and say something agreeable to her. She's upstairs.
JOHN: What for? If you think—
APLEY: No, no. I have no such idea, John. But tonight is her coming-out party, and it is the least you can do. (*Crossing to door.*) I'll send her down. (*Stops.*) We have to go on living, John. (*John waits until his father is up the stairs, then picks*

up coat and hat from sofa, takes a few steps to the door. Then he stops for a second, and puts coat on chair. As he does this, Agnes starts downstairs. John crosses to a chair and sits. Agnes comes hesitantly down the stairs. Finding that John does not see her, she decides on her plan of campaign. She tiptoes gently to the piano and begins softly to play and sing the chorus of "Come to the Ball.")

JOHN: Oh! (*Pause while another eight bars of music plays.*) Hello, Agnes.
AGNES: (*At piano.*) You didn't mind my coming in, did you?
JOHN: No, I don't mind.
AGNES: Or playing the piano?
JOHN: No.
AGNES: I'm glad, John. (*She rises, exhibiting herself.*) Do you notice anything?
JOHN: No. What?
AGNES: Well, look!
JOHN: You're dressed for the party. It looks all right.
AGNES: That's not what I mean, silly. What else?
JOHN: You've got your hair done in a different way.
AGNES: But what else? What else?
JOHN: (*Snapping a trifle, turning away.*) I don't know.
AGNES: You're mad at me.
JOHN: No, I'm not, Agnes. I'm sorry. What is it?
AGNES: It's the pearls, John. Don't you see them?
JOHN: Oh, yes. They look—beautiful.
AGNES: Cousin George is letting me wear them, just for tonight. You don't mind, do you?
JOHN: Why, no, of course not.
AGNES: Oh, John, I'm awfully glad. From the way you've acted lately I was afraid you would mind. I'm awfully glad.
JOHN: (*Realizing the implication, becomes gentle, turns to her.*) Agnes, I've got something I want to tell you. Let's sit here for a minute—(*Agnes crosses to sofa and sits.*)
AGNES: Oh. . . . Yes, John. (*Her knight has come riding.*)
JOHN: (*Sitting next to Agnes.*) Agnes, if I've been rude to you lately, or thoughtless, I'm awfully sorry.
AGNES: Oh, John. You haven't been.
JOHN: We've known each other for a long while. Ever since we were children.
AGNES: Yes, John. I think I know you better than anyone else in the world.
JOHN: We've always played together in the summer, and in the winter we've always gone to dancing school together—for years and years. We've seen so much of each other that sometimes I've almost thought—
AGNES: (*Leaning a little closer toward him.*) Thought what, John? Oh, go ahead.
JOHN: Sometimes I've wondered if we don't know each other too well.
AGNES: Why—why—I don't see how two people—that is, a boy and a girl—*can* know each other too well, if—(*She stops in confusion and looks at her folded hands.*)—if—*you* ought to say it, John.
JOHN: Agnes,—you don't understand. I don't love you. I'm in love with someone else. (*John keeps watching her. Agnes takes a moment, but weathering it bravely.*)

AGNES: Who is it?
JOHN: (*Rises.*) It's no one you know, Agnes, but I'm in love with her. (*Turning to Agnes.*) I just couldn't help it. The minute I saw her.
AGNES: (*Again taking her time, and speaking calmly.*) All right, John.
JOHN: You're not—you don't mind, Agnes?
AGNES: (*Her voice strange.*) Of course I mind, John. I'm not going to pretend I don't. Of course I mind. But you can't help it.
JOHN: You're wonderful, Agnes.
AGNES: (*Rises.*) We can't help falling in love. Nobody can.
JOHN: I know you'll like her when you meet her. I hope we can all be friends.
AGNES: (*Looking at John, then out front.*) Everybody thinks—I'm going to have a rotten time at the party tonight. (*Her voice rises a little.*) But I'm not. I'm going to have a wonderful time. A wonderful time. (*She starts to walk out about three steps, then runs into the hallway and out. John stands looking after her, a little taken aback by the suddenness of her departure. Catherine comes down the stairs. John watches her as she slowly descends.*)
JOHN: I suppose Father told you?
CATHERINE: Yes—
JOHN: I don't expect you to understand. You and Father.
CATHERINE: Are you sure that you love her, John?
JOHN: Yes, and nothing you can say will change me.
CATHERINE: I'm not going to try to change you, John. If it will make you happy, marry her. (*John turns and stares at Catherine.*)
JOHN: What?
CATHERINE: Marry her if she loves you. Have you asked her?
JOHN: No! I was afraid that everyone—(*He looks at his mother anew.*) You mean it? What will Father say?
CATHERINE: I don't know—but I'll speak to him.
JOHN: (*He rushes to Catherine, kisses her impulsively.*) Mother, I love you! (*He moves to chair, picks up hat and coat.*) I'm going right up there! (*He starts to move toward door.*) I'm going to ask her tonight! (*He dashes out, we hear his voice at the front door gaily.*) Hello, Uncle Roger!
ROGER: (*Off.*) Good evening, John. (*Roger comes into the room.*) Hello, Catherine. John was in a hurry. (*Margaret starts coming down the stairs.*)
CATHERINE: (*Slightly dazed.*) Hello, Roger.
ROGER: Just thought I'd drop in for a minute. Is George in?
CATHERINE: Yes, he is. Oh, Margaret, will you ask Mr. Apley to come down? (*Picking up embroidery and jewel box from table.*) Mr. Newcombe is here. (*Margaret goes back up the stairs.*)
ROGER: Do you mind if I ring for Wilson?
CATHERINE: It's right there. (*Pulling a bell cord.*) If you don't mind, I'll leave you to Wilson, Roger.
ROGER: Yes, of course. (*Roger goes to the sofa and sits down. Catherine goes into conservatory. Wilson enters, bringing a tray of drinks.*) Ah, Wilson. How did you know?
WILSON: (*Putting tray on table, starts picking up decanter. Roger stops him.*) I saw you come in, sir.

ROGER: Don't bother. I'll pour them.
WILSON: Mr. Apley never takes anything stronger than a glass of sherry before dinner, sir.
ROGER: He will this time.
WILSON: (*Respectfully.*) Yes, sir. (*Exits. Roger pours out two Scotches, puts soda in one, and places it on table. He returns to sofa, sits, and puts soda in his own drink, as Apley enters.*)
APLEY: Roger—
ROGER: Hello, George. I asked Wilson to bring a drink for us. Hope you don't mind.
APLEY: What would you say, Roger, if I were to tell you that I haven't touched a Scotch and soda since you and I used to spend our afternoons at the club?
ROGER: I'd say you'd better touch one now. (*Apley looks at him.*) I don't know how to say this, George. Let me start this way. I was just coming out of the club when I ran into that old Mr. Jenks—you know, the one who always wears a muffler in the house. He'd been to a meeting of that Nature Club of yours—the Bird Watchers.
APLEY: (*All ears.*) Yes?
ROGER: They didn't elect you, George. They asked the committee for another name.
APLEY: (*Rises.*) Another name? Why? *Why*, Roger?
ROGER: (*Rising. With some reluctance.*) Because, George, they think you've been making a damned fool of yourself.
APLEY: (*Controlling himself with an effort.*) No one has called me a damn fool since Father died. . . . What happened, Roger? Why did they do it?
ROGER: Well, that cemetery business, for one. Cousin Hattie. Henry Apley showed your letter around.
APLEY: (*Forced calmness.*) What else?
ROGER: And it seems you've made an ass of yourself about that friend of Eleanor's—young Boulder. They say you pushed him out of his job because he was seeing too much of Elly. Did you?
APLEY: That is a barefaced lie, Roger.
ROGER: George, I wonder—I wonder if you see yourself the way other people see you. This Bird Watcher business—Cousin Hattie, Boulder—that's not important by itself, but it's—it's symptomatic of everything else you're doing.
APLEY: Don't you think it's too late, Roger, to reconstruct my habits?
ROGER: Not insofar as they affect other people, George. (*Places drink on table.*) I've seen Horatio, and that's why I'm really here. He told me he'd been to Worcester.
APLEY: Horatio always talks too much. What did he tell you?
ROGER: It wasn't so much what he told me as what I read between the lines. You're doing the same thing with John that you did with Cousin Hattie and Boulder. Raising objections about things that don't matter. Because you live in a narrow world, George.
APLEY: My world narrow?
ROGER: Yes! The man has an iron dog on his front lawn, so John can't marry his daughter. Is that being *broad*-minded, George?

APLEY: Have you realized what John will throw away if he married this girl? Everything that Boston has to offer is his for the asking. You can't say that is nothing, Roger.
ROGER: I've watched John grow up. It seems to me he has the makings of a man.
APLEY: He can't help it, Roger, with his ancestry.
ROGER: Well, George, he's in love now, isn't he?
APLEY: Who isn't when he's twenty?
ROGER: (*Slowly.*) Yes . . . You were in love yourself when you were twenty, George. Do you remember?
APLEY: (*Sitting.*) It is not kind of you to bring that up, Roger.
ROGER: Have you forgotten how you felt, George? The day your father found out about it, the last time you ever saw *her*, the night you walked up the gangplank?
APLEY: I am not so forgetful as all that, Roger.
ROGER: And then you came back and you married Catherine. And then John was born. Do you remember what you said to me, that day? You said, "I pray to God that he'll be happy."
APLEY: Yes. I remember, Roger. And then you and I went out and entered him for Groton.
ROGER: He isn't happy now, George. Think of how he must be feeling. Think of that, instead of worrying about iron dogs, and the Bird Watchers, and what people will say if you miss a meeting of the Tuesday Club. Be kind, George. You always have been to everyone in trouble. You've been generous. You've been understanding.
APLEY: Have I, Roger? I've always tried to understand.
ROGER: Then try—just once, George—to understand your children. Don't you want them to get just a little more out of life than you've had—somehow—somewhere?
APLEY: I'm not sure how much one has a right to expect of life, Roger. It has a strange way of escaping you. Before you know it, it has slipped out of your hands.
ROGER: Perhaps you've never stood up to it enough, George. God knows, I haven't either. All that you and I can do is to hope that others, those we love, do better. I guess that's all I'm trying to say.
APLEY: I have never meant to be unkind, Roger. I have never meant to be intolerant.
ROGER: I know you haven't, George. Why don't we leave it this way? We've had our chance, you and I. Let John and Eleanor have theirs. (*Stands looking at Apley a moment, then pats him on shoulder, and exits. Apley is left silent, thinking heavily. He looks after Roger, sits there, then he turns slowly, sees the Scotch glass on the table, but his mind rejects it. He rises, pours drink, puts it down and crosses to desk above sofa, takes down Emerson, crosses back to table, opens Emerson, picks up drink. He is standing there, glass in hand, as Catherine enters.*)
CATHERINE: Is Roger gone?
APLEY: Yes. He just left.
CATHERINE: What were you talking about?
APLEY: Oh, about when we were younger—about Eleanor—and John.

CATHERINE: *(Steps in a bit.)* George, I've done something that I must tell you.
APLEY: *(Abstracted.)* What, my dear? *(Looking at Catherine.)*
CATHERINE: George—John has gone to Worcester. He's gone to ask that girl to marry him. *(Apley's head turns slowly toward her.)* I told him to do it, George. I said that I would speak to you.
APLEY: We want him to be happy, Catherine. After all, he is in love.
CATHERINE: Have you been drinking, George?
APLEY: Perhaps I've been wrong about the children. Perhaps they have a right to fall in love. . . . Catherine?
CATHERINE: *(Very low.)* Yes, George?
APLEY: I've been thinking . . . Worcester isn't Boston, but it is in Massachusetts.
CATHERINE: Of course, George.

CURTAIN

ACT III

TIME: *The next morning about nine o'clock.*
SCENE: *Everything is on a sprightly, cheerful note. Fresh flowers on the tables, the brilliant sun of early winter streaming through the windows, if there were a canary by the window, and indeed there might be, he would be singing loudly out of sheer joy at the beauty of the day.*
AT RISE: *Apley is seen, busy at his desk, bright and spruce, each fibre of him tingling with a new sort of resolution which we have not observed in him hitherto. He has been busy writing letters, he has completed one, which is in its envelope, and now he is in the midst of a second. It is obviously an important document—he is judicially weighing and balancing each word. Finally he blots the page, picks it up, and holds it at arm's length, with the satisfaction of an artist who has achieved a masterpiece.*

APLEY: (*Calling into the next room, a resolute cheerfulness in his voice.*) Oh, Catherine! Have you finished breakfast?
CATHERINE: (*From the dining room.*) Yes, all finished, George.
APLEY: Then would you mind coming in for a minute? There is something I would like to read you. (*Hastily.*) Not out of a book, dear—something I have just written.

(*Catherine enters, bringing a white carnation.*)

CATHERINE: Here's a flower for your buttonhole. (*Crosses to Apley, puts flower in his lapel.*) Hold still! There! What is it, dear?
APLEY: It's a letter to Henry Apley, about Cousin Hattie.
CATHERINE: A nice letter?
APLEY: I hope you'll think so, dear. I don't want to let myself go too far, because

my position was basically just, but—well, this is just a rough beginning. (*Reading.*) "Dear Henry: It occurred to me, in thinking things over last evening, that we can all die only once. As it happens, I still have a little time to consider where I wish to be placed in the family plot, and Cousin Hattie hasn't. That is why I suggest that we both, this morning, adopt the motto 'forgive and forget,' and join our efforts in endeavoring to activate another little motto, which is peculiarly our own: 'Bring Cousin Hattie Back.' " I think that's rather neatly put, don't you, dear?

CATHERINE: (*Turning away a bit.*) Well—I see what you mean, George.

APLEY: And then I go on. (*He reads again.*) "I know that you are in delicate health, dear Henry, and that you will want to lie near her." . . . It's a hard letter to write.

CATHERINE: Yes—I think the idea is perfect, George, but there might be some other way of phrasing it. There'll be more time later. The children will be down any minute now.

APLEY: (*Putting letter in his pocket.*) Well, perhaps you're right.

CATHERINE: (*Impulsively.*) George, the children are so happy. When you saw their faces this morning, when you heard them joking and singing, didn't it make you feel how worth while it's been—what you said to them—your whole new attitude?

APLEY: My attitude is not new, Catherine. (*Eleanor starts down the stairs, humming "My Hero."*) I'm just the same as I always was.

CATHERINE: I know you are. (*Kissing him.*)

APLEY: (*Mollified.*) Well, then—(*Catherine picks up her sewing and sits on the sofa.*)

ELEANOR: Oh, Father! (*She impulsively gives Apley a great big kiss.*)

APLEY: Why, what's that for, dear?

ELEANOR: Nothing. Just a reflex.

APLEY: Oh, so that's what a reflex is.

ELEANOR: (*To Apley.*) Of course it is! When you're being such a sweet darling to John and me. (*To Catherine.*) And Howard just telephoned, too! He's coming over right away, and we're going to spend the day. It rhymes, doesn't it?

APLEY: What on earth are you going to do with a young man at nine o'clock in the morning?

CATHERINE: They could sit in the conservatory.

ELEANOR: I've thought out every minute of it. First we're going skating on the river, and then we're going down to Faneuil Hall Market. (*To Catherine.*) We're going to have lunch in that place where all the butchers go.

APLEY: Alone?

CATHERINE: George, no one will see them there.

APLEY: I don't agree with you, Catherine. Father's old butcher is still at Faneuil Hall. It will get around to every back door on Beacon Street.

ELEANOR: Well, we can hide if we see him.

CATHERINE: What about dinner, dear? Why don't you invite him here to dinner?

ELEANOR: I'd love to!

APLEY: Capital! And we'll each have a Martini cocktail. *One!* (*He sits down, picks up paper from table.*)

ELEANOR: (*Hugs Apley.*) Father, you're being such a darling! Isn't he?
APLEY: There are a lot of things about me that you don't know, dear. I'm quite famous for my Martini cocktails. You didn't know that, did you?
ELEANOR: Why, Father!
APLEY: The whole trick is chilling the glass first, resting it for five minutes in a bowl of finely pulverized ice. Then you lift the glass out very carefully, so as not to break it. (*He lifts an imaginary glass.*)
ELEANOR: (*Dutifully.*) You mustn't break it.
CATHERINE: You'd better have your breakfast, dear. You mustn't skate on an empty stomach.
ELEANOR: I'd forgotten all about breakfast. (*She exits.*)
CATHERINE: (*Fondly looking after Eleanor.*) Isn't it wonderful? Seeing her so happy?
APLEY: What's she so happy about? I didn't know she was so fond of skating.
CATHERINE: George, last night after Eleanor was asleep, I kept thinking about that book that she mentioned, by that man with the queer name—it begins with F.
APLEY: Oh, you mean Freud.
CATHERINE: Yes, that's the name. I thought it was only right, if Eleanor was interested in the book, that I should know something about it. But I couldn't find it in her room—she seems to have hidden it.
APLEY: (*Putting paper on table, rises, crosses to desk.*) Well, as a matter of fact, after what she said about the book, I thought perhaps I should glance at it myself—just to check up, of course. I think I dropped it back here somewhere. (*He reaches into the back of the bookcase, behind the other books.*)
CATHERINE: Is that why you didn't come to bed until two in the morning, George?
APLEY: (*Putting on glasses.*) Well, frankly, yes. It's really—quite interesting, if you face it tolerantly. It advances a theory that frankly never occurred to me.
CATHERINE: What's it about?
APLEY: (*Sits.*) Why—it's about the mind, really. The mind and the way human relationships affect the mind.
CATHERINE: What sort of relationships?
APLEY: Well—I don't know exactly how to put it, Catherine.
CATHERINE: Please say what you mean, George. If Eleanor has been reading it—
APLEY: Then I shall have to resort to a word that I have never used in your presence. It seems to be very largely a book about—sex.
CATHERINE: Oh!—But how can he write a whole book about—that?
APLEY: Dr. Freud does seem to pad it a little, here and there. For instance, he tells the story of a certain Mr. X. It seems that this Mr. X, when he was four years old, had an experience with his nurse that colored his entire life. Now I remember my own nurse very well. She was Hannah's sister, and I know that neither of us forgot ourselves even for a moment.
CATHERINE: But what happened between Mr. X and his nurse?
APLEY: That's what is so confusing. Nothing at all definite did happen, but after that he always dreamed of locomotives.
CATHERINE: George, the other night *I* had a strange dream, too.

APLEY: (*Rising.*) Perhaps you'd better not tell me about it until you've looked this over, Catherine. It seems to be Dr. Freud's idea that sex very largely governs the lives of people, in other parts of the country. Of course he comes from Vienna.
CATHERINE: I see. (*Apley is at desk, putting book back in its original place.*) There's no reason to hide the book, George.
APLEY: No . . . no. I'll put it right here, next to Emerson. Come to think of it, Catherine, they have more than a little in common. Freud is trying to do the same thing with sex that Emerson did without it. (*John comes clattering down the stairs and disappears into the hall.*) John! John, come in here a moment!
JOHN: (*From the hall.*) I've got to call up Myrtle!
APLEY: You've called her twice this morning! John! (*John reluctantly re-appears.*) You've told us nothing about last night—all we know is that you're going to be married. There are certain details that your mother and I ought to know.
CATHERINE: Yes, John. When are you going to bring Myrtle to see us?
JOHN: Mother, you'll be perfectly *crazy* about her. I wish you could have seen her when I—when I asked her. I think she looks prettiest when she's surprised—I've got to telephone her! (*Quickly exits.*)
APLEY: Find out when you can see her father! You must tell him your intentions today! You can't keep putting it off!
JOHN: (*Off-stage.*) Plenty of time! She's coming to town for dinner! (*Enter Amelia.*)
APLEY: Leave a message that you want to see Mr. Dole! (*Amelia has sailed into the room, just in time to hear this last remark of Apley's.*)
AMELIA: It must be true, what I hear, then! John is going to marry the daughter of a mechanic from Dorchester?
CATHERINE: Who told you that, Amelia?
AMELIA: My dear, it's all over Boston! Her father collects old iron in his front yard. (*Eleanor comes running across the room towards the front door.*)
ELEANOR: It's Howard! He's coming up the steps! Hello, Aunt Amelia!
AMELIA: (*Frigid.*) Who is coming up the steps?
APLEY: Mr. Boulder, Amelia. You know, the young man who lectures at Harvard.
AMELIA: Is he the one who has been plying Eleanor with liquor?
APLEY: I find Mr. Boulder both brilliant and charming.
CATHERINE: They're having lunch together at Faneuil Hall Market. (*Boulder and Eleanor enter.*)
BOULDER: Good morning, sir! Mrs. Apley! (*Eleanor sits on the sofa.*) It's a fine clear morning, isn't it?
CATHERINE: Good morning, Mr. Boulder.
APLEY: Mr. Boulder. Amelia, you remember Mr. Boulder?
BOULDER: How do you do!
AMELIA: Are you going to wear those clothes to lunch?
BOULDER: Sorry!
APLEY: They're quite all right for Faneuil Hall, Amelia.
AMELIA: Well, we might be able to explain Worcester, but this is the most terrible thing that has happened to the family since Uncle William married his trained nurse. (*She exits quickly. There is a rather awkward pause.*)
APLEY: Won't you sit down, Mr. Boulder? (*Apley sits.*)

BOULDER: Thank you, sir. (*Sits.*)
CATHERINE: Wouldn't you like a cup of coffee, Mr. Boulder?
BOULDER: Why, thanks, if it isn't too much trouble.
ELEANOR: (*Rising.*) I'll get it, Mummy. (*Exits.*)
CATHERINE: And don't mind us. If you care to smoke one of your cigarettes—
APLEY: (*Stiffly.*) Yes, do. By all means.
BOULDER: (*Opening his cigarette case.*) Will you have one, sir?
APLEY: (*After a flash from Catherine.*) Oh, thank you. (*He takes one with some curiosity, rather awkwardly.*)
CATHERINE: So you're leaving for New York tonight, Mr. Boulder?
BOULDER: (*Lighting match.*) On the midnight.
APLEY: It has always seemed to me quite a journey, Boston to New York.
BOULDER: (*Lighting Apley's cigarette.*) Oh, it isn't so far, sir.
APLEY: Sometimes most peculiar things happen on the journey.
BOULDER: (*Lighting his cigarette.*) Why, what sort of things, sir?
CATHERINE: Well, once Mr. Apley met a man in the smoking compartment who was drinking out of a bottle.
BOULDER: (*To Catherine, then turning to Apley.*) Indeed!
APLEY: He was a New Yorker, of course. Tell me, Mr. Boulder, where do you live in New York?
BOULDER: In Greenwich Village!
APLEY: Greenwich Village! Well, that sounds at least as though you were getting some fresh air. Have your parents always lived in New York?
BOULDER: No, sir. They came from Staten Island.
APLEY: Where?
BOULDER: Staten Island.
CATHERINE: It's in the harbor, George, behind the Statue of Liberty.
APLEY: (*Looking at Boulder, who returns look.*) Behind it? How peculiar! Your father is in business, I suppose?
BOULDER: (*A little nod.*) Canned goods.
APLEY: You don't mean retail?
BOULDER: Wholesale.
APLEY: Ahhh—(*Eleanor returns, carrying coffee cup and saucer, napkin.*)
ELEANOR: (*Placing cup on table.*) Here's your coffee, Howard.
BOULDER: Thank you.
APLEY: And get him an ash tray! Quickly, Eleanor! (*Eleanor quickly goes to table for ash tray. Boulder rises as Eleanor is about to give him the ash tray, and drops ash.*) No, it's too late. He moved.
BOULDER: I'm dreadfully sorry.
CATHERINE: Oh, it's nothing at all.
APLEY: (*As Boulder makes move to rub ash in rug with foot.*) The maid will sweep it up.
BOULDER: (*Taking ash tray with him, sits down, puts tray on table.*) I'll put it out.
APLEY: No, no! (*But Boulder has already done so.*) Well! (*Apley puts out his own cigarette too.*)
CATHERINE: George, wasn't there something else you were going to tell Mr. Boulder, about a letter? (*Eleanor sits down.*)

APLEY: Oh, yes. (*Taking letter out of his pocket. Rises. Horatio enters.*)
HORATIO: Good morning. (*Seeing Boulder.*) How do you do!
BOULDER: How do you do?
HORATIO: Am I interrupting?
APLEY: On the contrary, I'm very glad you came, Horatio. I want you to hear this, because what happened was entirely your fault.
HORATIO: My fault? What?
APLEY: (*Rising, giving letter to Boulder.*) I suggest you better take this to State Street right now, to Mr. Loring. I know his attitude will be quite different after he has read it.
BOULDER: Why, thank you ever so much, sir. I'll take it right over.
ELEANOR: (*Going out with him.*) Will you come back, Howard, just as soon as you can?
BOULDER: (*Catherine rises.*) Just as soon as I can. Thank you ever so much, sir.
CATHERINE: (*Following them.*) Won't you come back for dinner, Mr. Boulder?
BOULDER: Why, thank you. I'd be delighted. (*Eleanor and Catherine reappear in hall.*)
CATHERINE: (*As they start walking upstairs.*) You'll have to put on something warmer, darling, if you're going skating. (*They exit up the stairs.*)
APLEY: Well, Horatio! I suppose you are surprised.
HORATIO: But I don't understand. After what he said about Emerson—
APLEY: There are other writers beside Emerson, Horatio. (*Wilson enters and picks up coffee cup.*) It is time you learned that.
HORATIO: What?
APLEY: Wilson!
WILSON: Yes, sir?
APLEY: Mr. Willing would like a Scotch and soda, Wilson.
HORATIO: (*Softly.*) No, no.
APLEY: And bring me one, too.
WILSON: (*Puzzled.*) Yes, sir.—*Now*, sir?
APLEY: Now!
WILSON: (*As he exits.*) Yes, sir!
HORATIO: Are you ill, George? Your peculiar attitude at Agnes' dinner last night—
APLEY: (*Looking at Horatio, then crossing to desk.*) Horatio, have you ever heard of a man named Freud?
HORATIO: Why, no.
APLEY: (*Taking book out of desk.*) It has just occurred to me, Horatio, that it is probably *you* he is writing this whole book about!
HORATIO: (*Dazed, but flattered.*) No!
APLEY: You have always exerted a very bad influence on me—I may say an unhealthy influence.
HORATIO: Unhealthy! Why, George, I've followed you as Boswell once did Johnson.
APLEY: Who was it got me into the Bird Watchers? You did!
HORATIO: I never went as far as you with birds.
APLEY: (*Throwing book on sofa.*) Let's not argue over these trivia. What really matters, Horatio, is that you've interfered between me and my son!

HORATIO: You and John? I don't think I understand, George.
APLEY: You nearly ruined his life, Horatio!
HORATIO: (*Desperately.*) But how, George? What did I do?
APLEY: You went snooping up to Worcester, that's what you did! Bringing back all kinds of stories!
HORATIO: But you asked me to go to Worcester, George. Don't you remember?
APLEY: Let us not split hairs, Horatio. Thank God your intrigues were not successful. John is going to marry Myrtle Dole.
HORATIO: Myrtle Dole? But—what about Agnes?
APLEY: Agnes is a nice girl, Horatio. She has inherited a certain charm from her mother. But John is not in love with Agnes.
HORATIO: But, George, I've heard you say often that propinquity would lead to love.
APLEY: Propinquity! Damn propinquity. I'm speaking of love, real love, Horatio, something which I do not believe you have ever known in your sterile pedestrian life.
HORATIO: (*Now convinced that Apley has gone crazy, and bent only on escape, he starts for the door.*) Yes, George. . . . Well, I think I'd better go and talk to Agnes, she'll be very . . . yes . . . (*And he is gone. Wilson at this moment is entering with the tray of drinks.*)
WILSON: (*Seeing that Horatio is no longer there.*) Oh! I'm sorry, sir. Shall I leave this?
APLEY: No, never mind, Wilson.
ROGER: (*Enters, cheerily.*) Good morning! (*Wilson, without a word, puts tray down on table and exits.*)
APLEY: Oh—well—hello, Roger. It's nice you dropped in.
ROGER: What was the matter with Horatio? He was running down the steps. Left the front door wide open! (*Roger takes off his hat and coat and puts them on the sofa.*)
APLEY: Horatio is very narrow-minded. (*Pours scotch.*) Won't you join me, Roger?
ROGER: At half-past nine in the morning? I never thought I'd live to see the day.
APLEY: (*Roger crosses to Apley, takes drink.*) I have never done such a thing before, but this is in the nature of a celebration. John is engaged this morning, Roger. The girl from Worcester.
ROGER: George! I knew you'd do it.
APLEY: Wait till you see John, Roger. Just one look at him drives away any doubt I might possibly have had. (*Apley pours his own Scotch, using siphon.*)
ROGER: This has taken real courage on your part, George. Don't think I don't realize it—here's to John.
APLEY: Here's to John.
ROGER: (*Sits.*) George, now that you've gone as far as this, why don't you try to get a little pleasure out of life?
APLEY: Pleasure, Roger? (*Sits.*)
ROGER: Yes, why don't you come up to the poker game at the club this afternoon, George? Friday—a lot of the old crowd are playing.
APLEY: This afternoon? There's a meeting of the Boston Waifs.
ROGER: Well?

APLEY: They'd wonder where I was.
ROGER: Let them wonder!
APLEY: (*Thinks it over.*) Waifs—it's a silly name, isn't it? What do they mean—Waifs?
ROGER: You know where we play—upstairs in the club.
APLEY: (*Still not quite committed.*) Oh, yes. (*They drink.*)
ROGER: By the way, did you hear old Justice Lawton dropped dead last night, right in the club?
APLEY: He did? (*Laughs.*) Well, well!
ROGER: (*Laughs.*) That's what! A stranger got into the members' room by mistake, and the old man had a stroke. (*They laugh together.*)
WILSON: (*Appearing in doorway.*) It's a Mr. Julian Dole, sir. Are you in?
APLEY: Roger! The girl's father! (*Apley and Roger rise. Roger picks up his hat and coat, Apley picks up tray of drinks, putting his glass on it.*) Wait a minute, Wilson.
ROGER: (*Takes tray of drinks.*) It's all right. I'll go out this way. (*Exits. Apley closes doors, gestures Wilson to stop, takes flower from lapel and gives it to Wilson. Wilson puts it in his pocket.*)
WILSON: (*To the as yet unseen guest.*) Will you come in, sir?—Mr. Dole.

(*Mr. Julian H. Dole appears in the doorway. He is a man of about Apley's age, but his whole air affords a sharp contrast to Apley. Mr. Dole might be described as a high-powered business executive in the better sense. He is obviously used to dealing with people and used to being listened to.*)

APLEY: (*All affability.*) This is a very great pleasure, Mr. Dole.

(*Mr. Dole crosses to Apley; they shake hands.*)

DOLE: Mr. Apley.
APLEY: Wilson, will you take Mr. Dole's hat and coat?
DOLE: (*Very friendly.*) Hope you don't mind my coming in like this, Mr. Apley, this hour of the morning.
APLEY: Not at all, Mr. Dole. I'm delighted. (*Dole hands coat to Wilson.*) Won't you sit down . . . Wilson, will you run down to the cellar and bring up a bottle of that old Madeira—(*Wilson starts out.*)—not the Civil War, the Mexican War.
DOLE: Now, don't do that for me.
APLEY: Yes, yes. We shall want to drink a toast, I'm sure. (*Gestures Dole to sit; he does so. Wilson exits.*) This is very kind of you to call, Mr. Dole. I must tell my wife you're here. (*Moves toward door.*)
DOLE: Well—I'd like to meet Mrs. Apley. (*Apley stops.*) But sometimes if the men have a little talk first—
APLEY: Of course. Perhaps you're right, for a beginning. (*Apley picks up cushion, covers Freud with it, goes to desk for cigars.*) Will you have a cigar?
DOLE: Thank you very much—
APLEY: My father's own selection. Father's cigar maker still makes them. In a little

alley near Young's Hotel. (*Dole lights his cigar, Apley takes cigar box back to desk, then lights his own cigar.*)

DOLE: (*Looking curiously around the room.*) That's a nice pair of old paintings, Mr. Apley.

APLEY: (*Indicating paintings.*) Oh, yes. My great-grandfather and grandmother.

DOLE: Gilbert Stuarts, aren't they?

APLEY: (*Sitting.*) So you can tell a Stuart? Do you own any, Mr. Dole?

DOLE: No. Frankly, I don't like Stuart very much. (*He says this courteously, diffidently.*)

APLEY: Oh! You don't?

DOLE: I think I prefer Copley. He didn't pretend; he painted what he saw.

APLEY: Personally, I never cared much for his realism. My sister has the Copleys.

DOLE: (*Recalling.*) Yes, I remember—saw them in a loan exhibit. The Apley Copley's. Sure! Old woman with a hooked nose. (*Dole gestures nose.*)

APLEY: Yes, the Apley nose.

DOLE: (*Genuinely apologetic.*) I didn't mean—

APLEY: She was painted when she was ninety-five. That's why it looked so hooked. (*John comes in somewhat diffidently.*)

JOHN: Excuse me, Father. Wilson told me that Mr. Dole was here. . . . Good morning, sir.

DOLE: (*Rising.*) Good morning, my boy.

APLEY: This is my son, Mr. Dole.

DOLE: (*Very friendly.*) So I gather. Yes, I've seen John.

JOHN: I suppose Myrtle told you—that is, I probably should have spoken to you first, but—it happened too suddenly.

DOLE: That's all right, my boy—I wonder if the young man could go into the room and close the door for a moment. (*Back to John again.*) Do you mind? I'm talking to your father now.

JOHN: (*Looking at Apley. Taken aback.*) Of course.

APLEY: (*Gently pushing John out.*) We'll see you later, John. Mr. Dole and I are having a little talk. (*Apley closes double doors.*)

DOLE: (*Sits.*) I've noticed John hanging around the house. But then there were a lot of other boys.

APLEY: To tell you the truth, I had no idea of all this myself, till last week. And while I haven't met your charming daughter yet, I feel I know her already. And I want to tell you that we're all delighted, perfectly delighted.

DOLE: Why, thank you, Mr. Apley.

APLEY: Mr. Dole—of course I don't know what your ideas may be, yours and Mrs. Dole's, and I hope you won't mind my suggesting this—but I thought perhaps it might be better if the announcement of the engagement is made in Boston, rather than in Worcester.

DOLE: Well, isn't it customary for the bride's parents—?

APLEY: Of course. The final decision rests entirely with the bride's parents. I was just thinking of the simplest way to explain matters here, from our point of view, and I thought if you and Mrs. Dole could go so far as to take an apartment in Boston, and then if the announcement were to come from *there*, I honestly see no reason why Worcester should be brought into it at all.

DOLE: I see.
APLEY: Tell me, Mr. Dole—er—(*Hopefully.*)—you weren't born in Worcester?
DOLE: No, I wasn't. Moved there ten years ago, when I bought the die works.
APLEY: (*Seeing a ray of hope.*)Ah! Where did you come from?
DOLE: (*Flatly.*) Kansas City.
APLEY: (*Swallowing hard.*) Oh!
DOLE: (*Beginning to enjoy himself.*) I take it you've never been to Kansas City!
APLEY: (*Not wishing to discuss it.*) No—as I was saying, the advantages of your living temporarily in Boston would be—well, several.
DOLE: Such as what?
APLEY: Well, for one thing, before any definite announcement was made, it would help for us to be seen together here and there—in the nature of a preparation. For instance, I don't think it would be too difficult to get you a six months' membership at one of my clubs—we could lunch there several times a week in the main dining room, where everyone would be sure to see us.
DOLE: The main dining room.
APLEY: (*Sits.*) And then I'm not sure, but it might be possible for Mrs. Dole to be invited for several weeks to my wife's sewing circle. And naturally there are the receptions and teas and the series of small dinners. We must be careful to have everyone prepared for the engagement before it is actually announced. I think it can be done. Of course, it isn't usual, but it's possible.
DOLE: It certainly sounds interesting.
APLEY: How's that?
DOLE: (*Putting out cigar, rises.*) This is going to surprise you, Mr. Apley. I assure you I don't mean to offend you. But I don't think this would work out for my daughter!
APLEY: (*Rising.*) What is that, sir?
DOLE: The Apleys and the Doles just don't belong together—
APLEY: But that is exactly why I have suggested—
DOLE: Come now, Mr. Apley, you know it as well as I do. It's a mistake, a big mistake to mix up different people.
APLEY: Are you serious about this, Mr. Dole?
DOLE: I'm dead serious, Mr. Apley. I came here thinking this would be all right, but I've learned better. We're not the same stripe, Mr. Apley. We've got nothing in common, and John and Myrtle wouldn't have, either. I felt it the minute I came in here. The butler, the house. You. And then the way you talked. You and I can't help it. It's the way we were born. (*He stops. Apley remains silent and turns his head away.*) There's no use quarreling about something we can't help. You know I'm right—don't you?—Don't you? (*There is a long pause, Apley is slowly pulling himself together and becoming the Apley that we have known. He speaks, finally, in a tone that does not quite seem to be his own voice.*)
APLEY: (*Turning to Dole slowly.*) You have done me—a great favor, Mr. Dole. You have reminded me of something that I never should have forgotten.
DOLE: Then we're agreed?
APLEY: I am very grateful to you. I—I was not thinking on a straight line, Mr. Dole, but you have set me back upon the right track. Thank you.

DOLE: Good for you. I've enjoyed meeting you, and I mean it. Good day, Mr. Apley. (*He starts out.*)
APLEY: (*Following, stops him.*) There is just one point. (*An apprehensive glance toward closed doors.*) John is unlikely to agree with us. He and your daughter might try to do something—foolish.
DOLE: Well, I'll take care of that. Myrtle will be on the train for California before the day's over.
APLEY: Splendid.
DOLE: She has an aunt out there. She'll stay a year if necessary. Two years—
APLEY: (*Barely hearing him, looking at door.*) Yes—yes—And John shall go abroad at once.
DOLE: Well! Good-bye, Mr. Apley! I'm sorry things didn't work out differently. (*They shake hands.*)
APLEY: Good day, Mr. Dole. (*He accompanies Dole into the hall—we hear the outer door close. Then a hard-hit Apley comes slowly back into the room. He stops. Eleanor enters from stairs and then comes in.*) Eleanor! Will you come here, please?
ELEANOR: Yes, of course.
APLEY: John!
JOHN: (*Off.*) Yes, Father!
ELEANOR: Why, what's the matter, Father?
JOHN: (*Enters full of expectancy.*) Where's Mr. Dole?
APLEY: Children, I have just been taught a lesson. It was my fault that I had to learn it from a man who was not a gentleman.
JOHN: You don't mean Mr. Dole, Father?
APLEY: Mr. Dole disapproves of your marrying his daughter, John. He told me that in this very room.
JOHN: Disapproves? Well, that won't stop me! And it won't stop Myrtle, either!
APLEY: It makes you angry, doesn't it, John? It did me, at first. But Mr. Dole is right, John.
JOHN: *Right!*
APLEY: Yes, right! He said that we were not his kind, John. And we're not. He said you and Myrtle would have nothing in common, and it's true.
JOHN: I think Myrtle and I should decide that!
ELEANOR: Yes!
APLEY: It is a mistake to mix up different kinds of people—that's what he said, and he's right, John. I have been trying to believe that that is not so, but it is. We don't think the same thoughts; we don't share the same tastes; we don't live by the same loyalties.
ELEANOR: But aren't the thoughts and loyalties of all good people just about the same?
APLEY: Eleanor, I have tried my best to do what I thought would make you and John happy. It is not your fault nor mine that it can't be. This may sound harsh to you, but I want you to promise me that you will put Howard Boulder entirely out of your mind.
ELEANOR: But what is wrong with Howard Boulder, Father?
APLEY: There is nothing wrong with him. I even like him. But it would not work,

Eleanor. You would not be happy.
ELEANOR: (*Passionately.*) Father, have *you* been happy? Has the way *you* lived been so successful? Have you got so much out of life, that you can tell us what *we* ought to do? (*Wilson enters with Madeira.*)
APLEY: That has nothing to do with you, Eleanor.
WILSON: Excuse me, sir. The Madeira.
APLEY: Thank you, Wilson. Not now. (*Wilson exits. Apley has calmed himself in the interval.*) Perhaps you are right, my dear. (*Sits.*) But it's too late. Too late for all of us.
ELEANOR: (*Bursting into tears.*) It's not fair! It's not fair! (*She rushes up the stairs.*)
JOHN: Father, are you asking me not to see Myrtle again? Because I might as well tell you that I'm going to!
APLEY: I can't go on with this, John. I'm sorry. I know what you are going through. The best way for you to get over it is for you to go abroad. At once.
JOHN: You can send me away for ten years and it won't make any difference!
APLEY: There is nothing like a sea voyage at a time like this. Rome in the winter, Florence in the spring, the season in London. I might even go with you. There is nothing that makes you appreciate Boston more than getting away from it.
JOHN: I want to know what Myrtle thinks about all this!
APLEY: (*Gestures him away.*) All right, John. Go and see her. Do the best you can.
JOHN: Thank you, Father. You do know how I feel. (*Exits. Catherine comes down the stairs and into the room as John departs.*)
CATHERINE: Poor boy.
APLEY: (*Looking at Catherine.*) Yes. Poor boy.
CATHERINE: As soon as she's calmer, George, I wish you'd go up and say something kind to Eleanor. She feels so alone.
APLEY: (*Rising.*) Of course, my dear. Anything I can do.
CATHERINE: There's so little that we *can* do, isn't there?
APLEY: (*Turns toward window.*) Time takes care of most of it.
CATHERINE: (*As Apley crosses to ivy.*) George, you feel that you've done right, don't you? Suppose you could look ahead, ten years from now—
APLEY: My dear, we can only hope. (*Taking out his glasses.*) You know, I think those green aphids have pretty well disappeared from the ivy. (*He examines it at closer range.*)
CATHERINE: (*Crosses to sofa.*) I told Margaret to blow tobacco smoke on them, from one of your cigars.
APLEY: (*Crosses to above sofa.*) You mean Margaret is smoking my cigars?
CATHERINE: (*Sits, picking up sewing.*) No, no—she just burned one in a dustpan.
APLEY: Oh! Let me see—what was I going to do this afternoon? Oh, yes—(*Picks up calendar from desk.*)—the Boston Waifs—Waifs—(*He savors the word—it sounds all right to him now.*)
CATHERINE: What, George?
APLEY: Nothing, my dear. (*Sits on sofa, looking at calendar.*) My! What with one thing and another we have a busy week—The Symphony—Meeting of the Pew-Holders of King's Chapel—Association for the Propagation of Wild Flowers in Franklin Park. Annual Dinner of the Louisa May Alcott Admirers . . .

CURTAIN

EPILOGUE

SCENE: *A corner of the Berkeley Club in Boston. The furnishings are heavy, and reminiscent of those found in the gentlemen's clubs or fashionable hotels at the turn of the century. The woodwork is dark oak.*

On one wall is a bulletin board marked "Recently Deceased Members." On the other is one of those mottoes in Gothic script that used to be popular in the dens and smoking rooms of our fathers. This motto, in quaint early English, reads: "Bee at Yere Ease in This Thine Inne."

In spite of the cordial invitation the place does not look particularly easy. There are two armchairs done in red leather upholstery, with lots of buttons. Beside one of the armchairs is a cuspidor in multi-glazed Canton china, obviously a relic of an older time. There is one of those racks with newspapers on it—newspapers fastened stiffly to great wooden holders, so that reading them becomes something of a gymnastic feat.

AT RISE: *Sitting in one of the chairs is a somewhat older Roger Newcombe, for a dozen years have passed since we last beheld him. He is struggling with one of the club newspapers, and at the same time draining the last of a Scotch and soda. He raps sharply with his glass on the table—a familiar signal, apparently, since instantly a new Scotch and soda is borne in by an elderly Retainer. "Elderly" is somewhat of an understatement—he is at least eighty.*

ROGER: (*Emerging from behind his Transcript.*) Ah! Thank you, Henry. (*The drink is placed before him.*) Tell me, Henry—how long have you been in the club?

HENRY: Fifty-six years, sir.

ROGER: Fifty-six years! Ever wanted to murder anyone?

HENRY: Oh, no, sir. Only one or two of the members.

ROGER: That's right, Henry—confine it to the members. (*John comes in. A John now in his early thirties—a new John, one who gives the impression of settled middle age, of assurance of inherited position. He wears a broad mourning band on his sleeve.)*

JOHN: Oh, hello, Uncle Roger—Henry.

ROGER: Well, well! Sit down, John. *(John sits opposite Roger. Henry exits.)* Seems to me you're coming in here quite regularly now.

JOHN: You remember what Father used to say: "The only way to get used to the Berkeley Club was to keep coming to it."

ROGER: How about a drink? *(Calling.)* Henry!

JOHN: I think I will. I'm quite tired.

ROGER: *(Putting paper down.)* You don't have to explain it. *(Enter Henry.)*

JOHN: Henry, will you open my father's locker, please, and make me a Martini cocktail? The way Father taught you!

HENRY: Yes, sir.—Oh! Mrs. Apley telephoned, sir.

JOHN: Yes, Henry?

HENRY: The car cannot call for you today, sir. It is bringing the children home from their nature walk.

JOHN: Thank you, Henry.

HENRY: Oh, and Mrs. Apley also says will you stop at the pet shop, because the canary bird is ready now, sir.

JOHN: Very well, Henry.

HENRY: Thank you, sir. *(Exits.)*

ROGER: What was the matter with the canary bird?

JOHN: Its tonsils needed cutting.

ROGER: Couldn't Agnes cut them?

JOHN: Agnes has been quite busy. She's been checking over Father's Chinese bronzes, before they go to the Art Museum. Oh! I've had a long day. There was a meeting of the Boston Waifs.

ROGER: Funny how new waifs keep coming along.

JOHN: And three hours in the vaults of the State Street Trust Company. Father's estate. We're trying to change over those Municipal one-and-a-halfs to something that will pay around two percent.

ROGER: You know what your father would say to that, John. Aren't you verging a little on the radical?

JOHN: Well, times are changing. Every generation can't be exactly like the last one, can it?

ROGER: No, but it can make a damn good try—Hello! Agnes has knitted you another tie, hasn't she?

JOHN: Mmmm . . . *(Looking at it.)* Sometimes I wish she'd stop—By the way, I hope you and Aunt Amelia aren't doing anything next Wednesday. We'd like you to come for dinner. It's our tenth anniversary.

ROGER: Tenth anniversary! Well, well!

JOHN: Naturally we're keeping it very quiet. We don't want anyone to think, when we're all in mourning, that we're making an excuse to have a lot of fun.

ROGER: Just ask the family—then you won't have any fun. You know how I keep track of my wedding anniversaries, John? An extra drink each year. Took one drink on my first anniversary, two drinks on my second—I'll be married forty years in June! Yes, that's one way of getting out of Boston.

JOHN: (*Taking letter out of his pocket*.) I invited Eleanor, of course, but she and Howard always make some excuse not to leave New York. I had rather a characteristic letter from her, this morning. You know the way Eleanor goes on. "Dear John: It seems impossible that you and Agnes have been married only ten years. Doesn't it seem like more?" I don't see why she always jokes about Agnes and me.

ROGER: (*Drily*.) I can't imagine.

JOHN: And then she says: "When Howard and I came back to Boston for the funeral, I could not help thinking a good deal about the old days. I think I understand things better now—Father, Mother, you and Agnes. As Father used to say, 'There is nothing that makes you appreciate Boston more than getting away from it.' "

ROGER: Peculiar girl, isn't she?

JOHN: The funny thing is, she and Howard really seem to be so happy. I wonder if it's just a facade. Do you think they really *can* be happy, coming from such different backgrounds?

ROGER: No—o. They just *think* they're happy.

JOHN: It couldn't help but be a shock to Father, when she and Howard eloped. But he never gave the slightest sign.

ROGER: You know, I think I understood George a little better than you did. And I've got an idea that, deep down at the bottom, he was rather pleased by Eleanor's courage.

JOHN: (*Surprised*.) Do you really think he was?

ROGER: That's what I do. You know, I miss George, miss him terribly. School, and games, and girls, and Beacon Street—we went through it all together. I always went to him when anything was wrong and I always came away feeling better. I could find him any afternoon sitting right there where you're sitting.

JOHN: I wish Father and I had never quarreled. I wonder what would have happened if I had married—?

ROGER: Myrtle? You wouldn't have liked it, John—you wouldn't have liked it. (*Henry enters with the Martini*.) Well! That took quite a while, Henry.

HENRY: (*Handing tray to John, who takes the Martini*.) I'm sorry, sir. I was trying to chill the glass the way Mr. Apley liked them, and I broke one.

JOHN: There will never be anyone like Father, will there, Henry? He was the best friend we ever had.

HENRY: Yes, sir. Indeed he was, sir.

JOHN: (*Rising*.) Here's to Father. Oh, I wish you had something so you could drink too, Henry. (*Roger rises*.)

HENRY: Oh, no, sir. Thank you, sir.

ROGER: Here's to George! John, when your father took you to Paris do you remember that painting by Titian in the Louvre, "The Gentleman with a Glove"? Sargent should have painted your father that way.

JOHN: Yes, I wish he had.

ROGER: But there's one thing George never would have stood for. Not with one glove, John—not with *one* glove.

END